D0368290

Sally Gable and Carl I. Gable

PALLADIAN DAYS

Sally Gable, a church music director by training, has served on the boards of Radcliffe College, the Atlanta Symphony Orchestra, and other educational and musical organizations. Carl I. Gable, a lawyer and businessman and the author of a book on Venetian glass, has served on the boards of the Spoleto Festival USA, the Atlanta Opera, the Michael C. Carlos Museum of Emory University, and the Center for Palladian Studies in America. They divide their time between Atlanta and Villa Cornaro in Italy.

PALLADIAN
DAYS

PALLADIAN DAYS

Finding a New Life in a Venetian Country House

SALLY GABLE
and CARL I. GABLE

Anchor Books
A Division of Random House, Inc.
New York

FIRST ANCHOR BOOKS EDITION, JUNE 2006

Title-page art: Villa Cornaro—North Facade

The Library of Congress has cataloged the Knopf edition as follows:
Gable, Sally, 1939–
Palladian days : finding a new life in a Venetian country house / Sally Gable ;
with Carl I. Gable.—1st ed.
p. cm.
1. Piombino Dese (Italy)—Description and travel. 2. Piombino Dese (Italy)—
Social life and customs. 3. Gable, Sally, 1939– —Homes and haunts—Italy—
Piombino Dese. 4. Villa Cornaro (Piombino Dese, Italy).
I. Gable, Carl I. II. Title.
DG975.P5816G33 2005
945'.32—dc22   2004061596

Anchor ISBN-10: 1-4000-7873-3
Anchor ISBN-13: 978-1-4000-7873-8

Author photograph © Jean-François Jaussaud
Book design by Soonyoung Kwon

www.anchorbooks.com

Printed in the United States of America
10 9 8 7 6 5 4 3 2 1

*For Ashley,
Carl and Lisa,
Jim and Juli*

*Hoping they will
understand why we embarked on this adventure,
learn about the Veneto and the Renaissance, and
grow confident in their own ability to seize dreams.*

And so they will know where the money went.

The ancient sages commonly used to retire to [their country estates], where being oftentimes visited by their virtuous friends and relations, having houses, gardens, fountains, and suchlike pleasant places, and, above all, their virtue, they could easily attain to as much happiness as can be attained here below.

ANDREA PALLADIO,
The Four Books of Architecture

PALLADIAN
DAYS

Pizza with Palladio

"Signora Sally, tonight we're going to a celebration of pizza!"

Silvana Miolo's lilting Italian greets me as I sip my morning espresso on the south portico of Villa Cornaro. The low morning sun splashes shadows of Lombardy poplars across the lawn of the park. Swallows circle and swoop bare inches above the closely mown lawn, scooping insects from the warming air, then spiraling upward to reclaim their nests somewhere above my head. *Note to diary: Birds nesting in attic? Investigate.*

"*Una celebrazione di pizza*"? Is that what she said?

Silvana senses my puzzlement and quickly finds an alternative way to frame her news. The event, I learn upon retelling, will be a pizza party.

Silvana is a dervish of energy. Dark eyes, dramatized by thick lashes and wavy black hair, animate her face. She has been friend, Italian teacher, and villa savant since I cautiously drove the twenty miles from the Venice airport two weeks ago for my first spring at the villa. ("Remember, the lady of a villa is called a *villainess*," my husband, Carl, advised me soberly as we kissed good-bye in Atlanta.)

Carl will join me in a few weeks. I am alone for now in the sixteenth-century villa designed by the architect Andrea Palladio that we have audaciously acquired in the village of Piombino Dese, halfway to the foothills northwest of Venice. Silvana is determined that I not feel lonely; when I arrived from the airport she sent her ten-year-old son Riccardo to keep me company while I unpacked.

Silvana's improbable plans for the evening have me uneasy because of my own recent introduction to Italian, but I'm heartened to find that I needed only one repetition before understanding what is in store.

Silvana and the other Piombinesi I've met speak no English. In fact, they don't ordinarily speak Italian. Their first language is Venetan (pronounced VEHN-eh-tun), a dialect substantially different in its vocabulary and pronunciation from standard Italian and not readily intelligible to strangers. (Whenever Carl has trouble understanding something said in Italian, he tries to claim that the speaker is actually using Venetan.) Once Carl remarked to local friends over dinner that the occasion was a good opportunity for the two of us to practice our Italian for a whole evening. "Yes," Ilario agreed, surveying his family around the table, "and it's a good chance for *us* to practice *our* Italian, too!"

In succeeding years English will be taught more widely in the schools of Piombino Dese, and the young people of the town will gain confidence in using it with us, but in our early years no local people of our acquaintance speak it. No one, that is, except Ilario. Ilario Mariotto and I are the same age, but when I was leaving for college, he was boarding a ship for Australia, where he would spend four hot, exhausting years chopping sugarcane in the fields. Ilario can still speak halting English despite twenty-five years of disuse. *Note to diary: Where has my college French gone?*

Each morning I climb out of bed and assemble my limited Italian verbs and nouns into imaginary dialogues with Silvana, trying to prepare myself for her arrival. At eight o'clock she walks over from Caffè Palladio, the bar and sandwich shop that she and her husband, Giacomo, own and operate across the street from the villa. Her purpose is to open our *balcone*. *Balcone* is the Venetan—not Italian—word for shutters. The villa has forty-four immense pairs of them, most of them more than ten feet tall. In accordance with local custom, and for security as well, all of them must be closed and latched each night and opened each morning. Those on the ground floor are secured with a heavy steel bar lifted and fitted into slots on each side of the window opening. For Carl or me, it would be a thirty-minute task every morning and night. Silvana or Giacomo can do it in twenty. (Their older son Leonardo can do it in fifteen minutes, but the process is a cacophony of shutters banging, windows slamming, glass rattling, and steel clanging to wake the dead from their rest in the cemetery of the parish church a block away.) Carl and I refer to it all as the "*balcone* ceremony"; we quickly come to accept it as part of the rhythm of villa life. Even quicker, however, is Carl's decision—taken the previous October when we first arrived together as the new owners of Villa Cornaro—that the whole process should be delegated to Giacomo and Silvana in their moonlighting role as custodians of the property.

On my own now in my first spring at the villa, I soon discover the true benefit of the arrangement: Silvana's morning visits are my gateway to the world of Piombino Dese. She brings me news of the village, listens attentively to my carefully prepared yet nonetheless stumbling forays into Italian conversation, and generally presents me a role model for a *donna* in Venetan life.

Silvana never loses patience or laughs at my malapropisms. She speaks with slow precision, repeating phrases as often as necessary, rearranging them as bits of a puzzle until the meaning is apparent even to an American novice. My six months of lessons back in Atlanta with Lola Butler, an effervescent military bride from Padua, have drilled me in the basics of Italian grammar. But my brain is not prepared to process a nonstop stream of animated Italian, especially when the conversation turns to septic tanks, sewers, spigots, drains, and other topics that never arose in my dialogues with Lola but grow to fill my life in Piombino Dese.

A pizza party will be a baptism of fire.

Eight cars have arrived ahead of us when we pull into the parking lot at Pizzeria Sombrero that evening, and several others follow. I'm in the dark about the guest list for this outing, but I notice that all those climbing out of the automobiles are women. Each is immaculately dressed in tall heels and a smart suit. Many have bright scarves tossed elegantly across their shoulders with that infuriating insouciance I envy so. We enter a brightly lighted room and take seats at a single long table stretching from one end to the other. About forty women are present—at least thirty-five of them complete strangers to me—and all are in high spirits and chattering rapidly. Silvana lifts her voice to tell me, above the din, that the women in town want to welcome me to Piombino Dese with a pizza party. They are afraid I may be lonely at the villa by myself.

I am afloat in a sea of introductions and mellifluous Italian names: Lucia, Chiara, Emanuela, Pierina, Fiorella, Flora, Elena, Nadia, Enza, Maria Rosa, Luigina, Francesca. Beer is flowing. Pizzas with micro-thin crusts follow in infinite variety. Seafood pizzas arrive topped with mussels and *gamberetti*—the whole mussels, shells and all! Pizza Maria with creamy white *bufala* mozzarella and a light sweet tomato sauce. Pizza with pungent arugula. Pizza striped with *melanzane* (eggplant) and zucchini. Pizza decked with *peperoni* (not the little salami slices; these are green and red and yellow peppers from the garden). I lose count of the pizzas just as I have already lost track of the names. Perhaps I lose track of the beer as well. But most improbably, I lose my self-consciousness about speaking Italian. My grammar is no better, my vocabulary is no larger, but among friends, what do such things matter? As I wake the next morning, alone in the huge villa, in the pitch black because of the tightly closed *balcone,* my head slightly disoriented from too much beer, I smile with the realization that I have a new home among the women of Piombino Dese.

2

A Home in New Hampshire

As I settle into the pace of Piombino Dese I sometimes wonder—sitting on the south portico in the evening with a glass of pro-secco—how I ever managed with the simplicity of only one life, one circle of friends, one language. And I ponder how easily and quickly chance can divert the whole stream of one's life.

Whatever brought you to buy a Palladian villa in Italy?

It is a question Carl and I never escape. Our Atlanta friends ask, tourists and tour guides ask, occasional magazine writers and television interviewers ask, and from time to time in these quiet moments we ask ourselves. Carl has developed a simple response: "It was a full moon." I always answer with a longer version, but sometimes I think that I am only telling *how* it happened, and that I am still searching for the *why* myself.

In the spring of 1987 I decided that a well-ordered Atlanta family such as ours should have a second home in upstate New Hampshire or possibly Vermont. Although my mother was from Oklahoma and my father from Edinburgh, Scotland, I grew up in Littleton, in the White Mountains of New Hampshire, where my father was a doctor. Since Carl seemed to be weaning himself from working all seven days of the week, I felt the time was ripe for a country retreat, a place where we might, in Thoreau's phrase, "live deliberately." Two of our children were in college and the youngest was in high school. I was cheerfully making full-time work of my part-time post as music director of a small church near our home in Atlanta, the result of returning to school for a master's degree in sacred music. Ashley, Carl, and Jim applauded their mother's return to academia and found her exam-time anxiety to be a special treat. Still, my plate was not filled; I determined that a vacation house would be a lodestone to draw the family together regularly and to retain familial—or at least friendly—ties through coming decades. Like our black labrador Cleo with a new rawhide bone, I seized the idea and began gnawing away at it.

Visions sprouted in my head: a two-story clapboard cottage on Sugar Hill, or a stone house along the banks of the Gale River, its entranceway a spiderweb of climbing yellow roses. The dreams were vivid in color, scent, and sound, and particular to my native White Mountains.

A ream of National Geodetic Survey maps of northern New

Hampshire, each tightly rolled and secured with a rubber band, stood like a bouquet in a corner of our Atlanta bedroom. I'd accumulated the maps through the past ten years and, on visits to my parents, had driven over most of the roads depicted with little squiggly lines. I was often accompanied by my aging garrulous Scottish father, whose legendary love of the mountains and streams of the region translated into exhilarating storytelling with all who chose to listen and some who didn't. Perhaps we'd find just the home I'd pictured along Skookumchuck Brook running down the north slope of Cannon Mountain, or maybe a perfect bungalow on the narrow ribbon of back road twisting from Littleton to Franconia, where the Presidential Range rests like a purple velvet blanket tossed across the horizon. Or we might spot a cottage on Skinny Ridge Road west of Littleton, where high silver pastures fall away to the midnight blue mirror of Littleton Lake placidly reflecting Mount Misery.

I convinced myself that New Hampshire is easily accessible from Atlanta. A two-and-a-half-hour flight to Boston, a quick stop at the car rental counter, and then—with me driving instead of pokey Carl—just two more hours to our country retreat. Carl was noncommittal when I floated the idea—which I took to mean yes. All that remained was for me to find at a bargain price the spot that I had conjured in my mind.

That is my reason one Sunday afternoon in late April 1987, as I sit in our Atlanta living room surrounded by a sea of Brobdingnagian newspapers, for pulling out the Sunday magazine of the *New York Times*. Rather than launch immediately into the crossword puzzle, I begin to thumb the pages where ads appear for grand houses on Long Island and penthouses in Manhattan, and occasionally for summer houses in New England. I have chosen a bad week for New England summer homes, however; not a single one is listed. In the midst of my disappointment, my eye stops at an unusually unattractive ad from a Greenwich, Connecticut, realtor for a villa in the Veneto region of Italy, a villa allegedly designed by Andrea Palladio, the most influential figure in the history of western architecture.

Frankly, the whole thing seems implausible, but an interesting coincidence nonetheless. The coincidence lies in the fact that Carl and I had made plans several months earlier for a July visit to the Palladian villas in the Veneto. Our friends from London, Judith and Harold, are to meet us there.

With a "Ha!" I show the ad to Carl and tell him that if I don't find the right spot in New England, we can always settle for our own Palladian villa.

Carl reacts with a disturbing amount of interest. He pulls from our bookshelves the copy of Michelangelo Muraro's *Venetian Villas* that we purchased several years earlier, following a three-week family vacation in Florence with a quick side trip to Venice. There is Villa Cornaro staring back at us in full color. Villa Cornaro, we discover, is not just a Palladian villa; of the eighteen surviving villas designed by Palladio, it is one of the five largest, best preserved, and most influential in later architecture.

"But, Sally, it's enormous!" Judith complains two months later after the four of us have climbed from our small, un-air-conditioned rental car parked in Piazzetta Squizzato to stare, dumbstruck at first, across the street at Villa Cornaro. The villa looms above the ancient wall that surrounds it and above Via Roma as well, placid and mysterious as the Sphinx, completely detached from the petty bustle of Piombino Dese on a scorching July day.

"Enormous," Judith repeats, to emphasize her point. "Beautiful, yes, but very, *very* big." Her Israeli accent flavors her words and adds to their authority.

"Mammoth, Carl! You'd need roller skates to get from one end to the other!" Harold's grin suggests that he would be happy to don the skates.

It's a palace, I say to myself. Carl keeps his thoughts to himself also.

The gate to the villa is ajar, so we enter to see an elderly couple awaiting us on the north portico. Epifanio Marulli, a gray-haired gentleman with surprisingly bright blue eyes, was custodian of the villa long before Dick Rush, the current owner, arrived on the scene eighteen years earlier, and he has remained as Dick's custodian as well. Epifanio's wife, Elena, is with him. From a distance they are dwarfed by the thick, twenty-one-foot-tall Ionic columns rising to support the thinner Corinthian columns of the floor above. They smile shyly, no doubt wondering, as I am, how they will communicate with these strangers who speak no Italian. Harold confided earlier in the morning that he has a little "tourist Italian," as he calls it, left from vacations his family took when he was a teenager, but Carl and I have taken little comfort in it. "That should be very helpful," Carl kidded him, "as long as you don't get confused and ask the custodian for a gondola ride or an antipasto by mistake."

Carl and Sally at the gate of
Villa Cornaro

In fact, Harold has been modest once again, as is his nature. He quickly establishes halting but serviceable communications with the Marullis, to everyone's relief.

Our ascent up the villa's gradual steps brings us to a fourteen-foot-deep porch, which in turn leads us to gigantic old wooden doors and then an entrance hall. To our left and right stretch long rooms clad in giant frescos, all glowing in the bright noon sun. Ahead lies the grand salon, an enormous white cube lighted by a wall of windows facing south. The ceiling is held aloft by four massive Ionic columns solemnly observed by six elegant, larger-than-life statues of Venetian figures set into niches around the room.

My first and overwhelming impression is the immensity of the spaces—not just the floor space of the rooms, but their volume, the vast space over our heads before the ceiling caps us more than twenty-four feet above the floor in the central *salone* and almost as high elsewhere. This, I think, is not a place where mortals live. I

The grand salon—lower *piano nobile*

begin to feel disoriented, to feel that I have lost track of which room I have left or which I have entered. I should have trailed a string behind me, like Theseus in the Labyrinth, so that I will know my way out and can tell whether I have been in a certain room before.

The windows of the villa have a height and width to match the scale of the rooms. As a result, the rooms are awash with noonday light spilling in from all sides. From the south the sun bakes the terrazzo of the upstairs floor to a warmth that I can feel through the thin soles of my sandals. Antique furniture on a modest scale is placed sparingly but attractively throughout the villa—large marble tables, painted *armadi,* handsome but uninviting chairs, and one beautiful wrought-iron bed so perfect as to date and place that it could have been something that Giorgio Cornaro himself brought when he and his new bride, Elena, took possession of the villa in 1554.

Carl tells me later that for him the strongest impression came from the pastel and earth tones of the 104 frescos that blanket the walls of all the principal rooms except the central *salone* itself. Stucco frames enclose the frescos, and lively stucco putti—angelic cherubs—cluster in three dimensions above the tall doorways. The original terra-cotta and terrazzo floors that cover most of the villa extend beneath our feet the warm tones of the frescos.

Up great looping brick stairs, down tight twisted wooden ones, we stream along in the Marullis' wake. We ooh and ah reflexively at everything, mesmerized. Carl and I simply fall in love with Villa Cornaro. *Ci siamo innamorati della villa.*

3

Cup and Lip

Amore is one thing; buying a Palladian villa is another. Buying a Palladian villa is serious business under any circumstances, but especially for people with distinctly circumscribed resources such as ours. Fortunately, Carl has good experience for the task. He began his career with twenty years as a lawyer in private practice; international business was one of his specialties. Now that he has moved into the business world himself, a smaller but significant part of his work is still overseas.

We begin by flying to Washington, D.C., for a meeting with the owners, Dick and Julie Rush, and their real estate agent from Greenwich, Connecticut. The Rushes reside in Greenwich but spend time regularly in Washington, where they lived previously. We have two objectives: One is to know the couple with whom we are dealing and to let them know us, and the other is to learn more about the realities of everyday life as expatriate property owners in the Veneto. The first objective is quickly achieved. Dick, a tall, slim gentleman, and Julie, his attractive and talkative wife, are charming, yet clearly apprehensive about who might buy the villa in which they have invested eighteen years of difficult restoration.

Their genuine love for Villa Cornaro is patent. Why are they selling it? we soon ask. Because Dick, at seventy-two—ten or so years older than Julie—is trying to simplify his estate and make it easier for Julie to administer as he becomes less active. Carl and I also quickly perceive that we are way out of our league financially. One indicator: By way of illustrating his efforts to simplify his estate, Dick points out that he will soon be auctioning one of his paintings, a *Magdalene* by Titian, in a forthcoming Sotheby's sale.

Dick and Julie assure us about everything relating to villa life, although some of the assurances are less calming than they imagine. The currency-control laws that limit the ability to repatriate money invested in Italy may not apply to the sale of a villa, but in any event Italy is expected to remove the restriction within the next few years. The Red Guard is now a thing of the past in Italy; Dick has even dropped the kidnap insurance that he once carried.

"Kidnappers?" I interject.

"Don't worry about that, Sally," Carl responds. "We'll just post our balance sheet on the front gate, and they won't come near us." Dick Rush is even less amused than I am.

With only a brief pause Dick continues his list of dubious assurances. Upon closing and recording the sale of a historic structure such as the villa, he explains, there begins a sixty-day period in which the Italian government can elect to purchase the property at the same price that the buyer has paid, but the government never has any funds budgeted for this purpose, so it's not a worry.

Finally, Dick has concluded that Carl's legal background is perfect for dealing with the local authorities of Piombino Dese in case a problem "like the last one" arises in the future. Now, some might dwell on the implied compliment in Dick's remark, but Carl springs to the question that is on my lips as well: "What was the last problem?"

Thus we learn of the ancient villa's near-death experience just three years earlier. The *sindaco*—mayor—of Piombino Dese decided that the town required a new and grander soccer field, or *campo sportivo;* that the fields adjacent to the south gate of the villa—which have been farmed continuously for more than five hundred years, first as part of the villa and now as property of the half-dozen farmers who till them—were the perfect spot for it; and that, to provide a touch of grandeur, the approach to the *campo sportivo* should pass through the grounds of Villa Cornaro itself and across the *settecento* (1700s) bridge to its south gate, with the crowds of soccer fans flowing past each side of the villa as a river might divide to flow around an inconvenient boulder in the middle of its stream.

In later years, I discuss the soccer field affair with dozens of Piombino Dese residents. More than fifteen years after the event, it still looms large in the civic memory. The *sindaco,* it seems, understood Piombino Dese politics but seriously underestimated Dick Rush.

Patrician Dick Rush made common cause with the farmers, led by Ilario Mariotto, whose land would have been expropriated for the project at derisory prices; the farmers in turn attracted support from the local Communist Party. Nonetheless, Dick soon determined that he and his band of farmer and Communist allies would be unable to prevail politically against the *sindaco*. He turned to Rome for a new ally in the national Ministero di Belle Arti, which, with the agreement of the farmers concerned, issued a binding decree that the fields lying south of the villa and its former farm building may be used solely for agricultural purposes in order to preserve the historical integrity of the Palladian villa. The *sindaco* had been trumped.

Because of the decree, known as a *vincolo,* the peaceful enjoyment of the villa is assured, Dick tells us. Carl and I, of course, remain concerned about the episode and its implications for the future. Carl asks for a copy of the *vincolo* so we can review its terms ourselves.

We return home to Atlanta and within a few weeks send the Rushes a proposed contract. Perhaps our meeting tempered our enthusiasm too much. Price is never a big issue because, candidly, we think the asking price is reasonable. But we are cautious on other points. Carl wants an engineering inspection of the villa before closing, a mechanism for addressing the government's "right of first refusal," and only a modest earnest-money requirement.

One problem, Carl and I are aware, is that we don't have the cash to make the purchase! To obtain the cash, we will have to sell a lot of our stock in the public company that Carl is associated with. As Carl points out, selling the stock will result in a big capital gains tax, which is perfectly acceptable if we end up owning the villa. But if the Italian government elects to exercise its right of first refusal and buy the property away from us, we will have sold the stock and paid the tax for no purpose.

The negotiations quickly tangle in unexpected and sometimes unexplained ways. Carl concludes that Julie, who seems to have taken over the communications, may not be as resigned to selling Villa Cornaro as Dick is. For whatever reasons, the talks collapse. Carl and I are left with a somewhat empty sense of what might have been.

Yet I find that the villa has already changed me. A home in New Hampshire is too small a canvas, I've decided. A German friend in

Frankfurt, a lawyer whom we first met through Carl's work, once told me that he felt entirely alive only when he was in Manhattan. Now I realize that I have begun to feel that way about Italy.

Of course, Carl and I begin at once to plan a new vacation trip to Italy for the summer of 1988, returning to places we have seen and loved in the past, such as Lucca and Orvieto. With Carl's encouragement, in the months before our trip I consult what I now consider my real-estate bible, *The New York Times Magazine*. *Che sorpresa!* (What a surprise!) There's an ad for a restored medieval tower in Umbria near Orvieto.

Alas, when we arrive the reality proves to be but a shadow of the fantasy that our rampant imaginations have painted for us. The restoration is, to put it generously, a work in progress, with more cement being poured than it took to build Hoover Dam. The entrepreneur himself, Gianni, is a charming young man who quickly perceives that we are not to be buyers. Nonetheless, he graciously invites us back to his own home for a prosecco and a chance to meet his business partner, who is an American sculptor. Gianni assures us that his real profession is executing his partner's sculpture constructions, with real estate development only an occasional sideline. In twenty minutes he pulls his car to a stop in the parking area beside an impeccably restored thirteenth-century tower standing tall and square in the plain of Orvieto. The perfect restoration of the umber tower brings our first gasp of the afternoon.

Entering the tower, we find that the interior has been completely gutted and reconfigured in open, light, conjoined spaces of starkly modern design. Elegant and unusual contemporary furniture rests sparsely about like pieces of sculpture. Carl joins me in our second gasp. "Richard designed this," Gianni tells us, referring to his sculptor-partner. It is obvious that the tower we are now in has inspired Gianni's ungainly development efforts at the concrete bunker we have just left. Gianni leads us up narrow, gently curving steps to the ramparts of the tower, which have been transformed into a roof garden. Pots of geraniums form a necklace around the small tetragon.

Gasp No. 3: The Umbrian sky surrounds us in the infinite distance like a lavender cyclorama. The plain lies far below our feet and flows like water to the horizon, interrupted only by the great mesa of Orvieto itself. The town clutches at its high perch just a few miles to the north, close enough, it seems, for us to lean over and—with just a little stretch—shake hands with tourists standing atop its cliffs.

Gianni's sculptor-partner, a small gray-haired man, joins us. Gianni introduces him as Richard Lippold. Carl and I have agreed earlier, in a whispered exchange, that Lippold is not a name we know. After we've enjoyed a few relaxed moments with our prosecco, Gianni excuses himself to make a business call to the States. "Richard," he suggests, "while I'm doing this, why don't you show Carl and Sally the photos of your work?" With a modest shrug, Richard opens the album Gianni has placed in front of him. Carl and I prepare to gush about the sincere and awkward work that we expect to see. Gasp No. 4—the loudest, longest gasp of the day.

"That's the *Tree of Life* at Harvard!" Carl chokes out.

"An early work," Richard says.

So how were we to know that Richard Lippold is one of the most famous sculptors of the late twentieth century? We continue to turn the pages in awe. Richard talks easily about the works as we move through the album. The sculpture for the lobby of the Pan Am building, the five for the shah of Iran, the first sculpture ever commissioned by the Metropolitan Museum, the seventeen-story-high sculpture to sit outside a Seoul, Korea, office building. "Actually," Richard says, "that was designed as an eighteen-story sculpture, but the developer had a multifloor tenant lined up who didn't want the sculpture to block the view from his personal office on the eighteenth floor. So the developer begged me to let it be executed just seventeen floors tall. I try to be practical, so after some thought I finally agreed."

I can see Richard's mind thinking back over the episode as he speaks. "You know," he adds wistfully, "it really should have been eighteen stories."

On our long flight home to Atlanta a few days later, Carl and I are both pensive and even moody for most of the trip. As our plane banks to enter its final approach to Hartsfield, I reach for Carl's hand. "We've got to keep Italy in our lives, Carl."

"I wonder if Dick Rush has sold Villa Cornaro," he replies. "I think I will write him and ask." *Note to diary: Beware! Carl knows your thoughts.*

Whatever brought you to buy a Palladian villa in Italy?

I haven't answered the question at all. In realistic moments, such as when I'm wide awake in bed in the first light before dawn, I can see that.

Growth, I tell myself. I'm looking for personal growth.

What kind of answer is that? my other, more cynical self responds. You might as well say it was a full moon. I mean, it's not as if you were some underdeveloped potted plant! You have twenty-five years of friendships in Atlanta, three wonderful children out of the nest and on the wing, three church choirs eager to respond to every twitch of your upraised hand. Most people would say that's growth enough for a lifetime.

Maybe, I have to admit, "a search for growth" doesn't really explain it. As I turn in my bed, letting sleep engulf me again, a subversive new thought teases my mind.

Maybe the best word is "escape."

4

Destiny

Karma is afoot. Carl learns that Dick Rush took Villa Cornaro off the market after our earlier negotiations broke off. He arranged to donate it to his undergraduate alma mater, Dartmouth College, to use as a center for Renaissance studies. The transaction had awaited only the funding of an endowment promised by another alumnus for its maintenance and operations. But, Dick explains to Carl, the other alumnus has died before arrangements could be completed, the project has collapsed, and Dick has just put the villa back on the market, listing it for sale through Sotheby's real estate arm. Other news: The price has gone up.

Carl returns to the hunt! A new contract is drafted; clauses are hammered out. Carl retains a Venetian lawyer for advice on exchange controls, taxes, insurance issues, and the like. (Real estate conveyance itself is a matter for notaries, not lawyers, in Italy.) Gradually, most issues are resolved, generally through more risk taking on our part. Then, frustratingly, points that we thought were resolved begin to arise anew. Carl suspects that Julie Rush's fine hand may have returned to create confusion and concludes that a face-to-face meeting between himself and the Rushes is required. The Rushes are in residence at the villa, so in July 1989 Carl extends one of his regular business trips to Europe in order to visit them.

By happy coincidence, our son "young" Carl is also in Venice; he is traveling briefly through Europe after completing his summer job in Sweden. Father and son are greeted by the Rushes at the villa, treated to an elaborate lunch set in the center of the grand salon itself, and led through a meticulous tour of the villa. Carl and Dick proceed to a flurry of negotiations, punctuated by comments from Julie. Young Carl, clearly the artist among our three children, amuses himself by examining the statues, painted ceilings, chandeliers, and frescos that surround him, and by turning the pages of a newly published German book with the south facade of Villa Cornaro featured on the cover.

Miraculously, after several hours of wordsmithing, Carl and Dick sign the contract. Within a month, Villa Cornaro is ours. Of course, whether it will remain ours depends on whether the Italian government chooses to buy it away in the ensuing sixty days.

For the next two months my mind is filled with two fears: fear

The formal garden, looking north

that the government will whisk our new treasure away from us, and fear that it will not. My first fear is of losing an unexplored new life in Italy; my second is of becoming saddled with a 435-year-old white elephant pastured four thousand miles away.

Sometimes my mind retrieves the image of that first time we saw Villa Cornaro—our London friends and us parking in Piazzetta Squizzato, getting out of the car to stare across Via Roma. For us those first steps through the gate and into the boxwood garden were like those that Mary Lennox took so innocently into her own "Secret Garden." Ordinary steps, it would seem, but life-changing. Through all the visits, conferences, false starts, demands, and concessions, each step seemed tentative and revocable. Yet in retrospect, I cannot imagine the consequences of having taken a different course at any stage. From those first steps, everything moved with an inexorable force of its own.

5

Villa Cornaro ora Gable

We fly into the Treviso airport on a brilliant October morning—Carl and I and our daughter, Ashley, who is vacationing from her job as a paralegal in Washington, D.C.

Throughout the flight, my elation at beginning our great Italian adventure has wrestled with my fears. Carl has been a disappointment: I usually rely on him as my risk assessor, but he has slept contentedly all across the Atlantic and really didn't seem all that awake when we changed planes in Frankfurt. So I'm left to handle the worrying by myself.

What if we hate Italy? *Impossible.*

What if no one in town can understand our newly tutored Italian? *Possible; maybe curable with time.*

What if they understand us but don't like us? *We can work on that, too, I suppose.*

What if the expense of maintaining the villa outruns our bank account? *Unknown risk.*

What if we're kidnapped! I shake Carl awake. This is too much worry for me to be stuck with alone.

But before I can alarm Carl, our plane leaves the murky cloud cover over Germany and I watch the snowy Alps rising beneath us like a vast white-spumed sea. Then the crested waves subside and we soar out over the glistening Venetan plain.

"Buon giorno! Benarrivati!" Dick Rush, tall and thin as ever and remarkably unconcerned about his dignity, hails us excitedly as we hurry past the somnolent customs inspectors. His enthusiasm is genuine, though his Italian accent is suspect. His eagerness to emulate the renowned Italian hospitality, evident in his big grin and gesticulations, reminds me of my beloved black labrador Cleo greeting me when I've returned home. Waving his arms like a juggler, Dick chats nonstop of his pleasure in welcoming us to Italy, of

how he and Julie have prepared the villa for us with fresh touch-up paint and new wax, and of the dozens of people coming to a reception in our honor on Saturday afternoon—for we are arriving at Piombino Dese as the new owners of its Palladian villa! As a newspaper of the province headlines its brief article on the event:

Villa "Rush"
ora è "Gable"

Villa "Rush"
now is "Gable"

Dick is accompanied by Giacomo Miolo, who is driving a second car to accommodate all our luggage. It's our first meeting with Giacomo—in fact, the first time we have ever heard his name. His stocky frame and dark, handsome face contrast dramatically with Dick's tall, pale appearance. I defensively assume that Giacomo's silence, baldly highlighted by Dick's ebullience, reflects some resentment of the new American villa owners as economic imperialists. A quick memory of Dick's kidnap insurance flashes through my mind. As we gather our bags and move toward the cars for the twelve-mile trip ahead, Dick assigns me to ride with Giacomo, on grounds that Giacomo speaks only Italian (when he speaks at all, I say to myself) and that I need real-world practice for the Italian that I have been studying in Atlanta. Carl and Ashley travel with Dick.

My conversation with Giacomo begins on a high note: Giacomo says something about what a beautiful day it is, and I understand it! I begin burbling sentences that I've rehearsed in my mind about how happy we are to have become owners of Villa Cornaro, how beautiful the colors of the fields are, the things we hope to do during our current two-week stay.

But a note of mystery pervades the dialogue. To almost everything I say, Giacomo responds quietly, *"Va bayn, va bayn."* I frantically search my memory of all the Italian words with which my tutor in Atlanta has armed me, and I can find nothing similar. What is this short, pithy comment that Giacomo is flinging back at everything I say? Julie Rush unravels the mystery for me later in the day after we've arrived at the villa. Giacomo's *"va bayn"* was actually *va ben'*, a Venetan dialect corruption of the common Italian phrase *va bene*, which figuratively means "good" or "okay." *Note to diary: Buy Venetan-Italian dictionary.*

The twenty-minute ride introduces me to the forthrightness that I soon conclude is characteristic of Venetans. If there's something on their minds, they'll speak it. No squirrelly beating around the bush.

Giacomo asks how old I am. I tell him.

He asks how much we paid for the villa. I respond that my husband would not want me to say.

He asks when we are going to sell the villa to someone else, how much money we will make, and whether the buyer will be German or Japanese. I reply that we don't intend ever to sell the villa, that we hope to pass it on to our children, the way the Cornaro family passed it on from generation to generation for 250 years.

"Va bayn," he responds.

Life is opera, as every Italian knows. And if ordinary routine does not provide the requisite drama, then drama must be contrived. These are truths that Giacomo well understands. Accordingly, he is not satisfied to park the car just inside the villa's side gate, as good practice would dictate. He swooshes the car into the villa's front garden, narrowly avoiding uprooting a long row of very old and carefully manicured boxwoods, so that I can step directly from the vehicle onto the broad front steps of the villa. This is the way a true Cornaro would have arrived. With Giacomo's guidance, the new owner will receive no less.

I ascend the steps with all the emotion that Giacomo could possibly have imagined, the effect undiminished by the overloaded tourist handbag that I am carrying, so weighted that I am listing to one side.

The opera continues. In Act II Carl must carry his demure *moglie* (wife) across the threshold of their newly acquired villa. With aggressive pantomime Giacomo conveys to Carl a sense of his ceremonial obligations. In a twinkling, Carl scoops me up, handbag and all, and deposits me across the threshold and into my new life—oblivious of the fact that we don't even know the Italian word for "orthopedist" in case he throws out his notoriously quirky back.

Not at the moment, but later, I am reminded that Giorgio Cornaro, who built the villa, brought his new bride to it as soon as it was substantially completed. Would Giorgio and Elena have engaged in such frivolity if Giacomo had been there to instigate it? In those stern times I doubt that even a rich and influential Cornaro would have dared have fun in public.

6

Transition

The Rushes have timed their final departure from the villa to overlap our arrival by a few days. They want to pass along some of the lore they have acquired and ease our entry into Piombino Dese life. Dick shepherds us along Via Roma. First stop, Alimentari Battiston, the grocery store at the first door west of the villa. We're introduced to Gianni and Bianca Battiston and open a charge account; needless to say, the process does not involve the completion of any forms. The Battistons have what Americans would recognize as a corner grocery store, circa 1950, but with crowded aisles and two energized checkout lanes. The Battistons and their children, Alessandra and Franco, live over their store in the traditional manner. Yet change is in the air, Dick tells us. The Battistons' new *supermercato* is almost ready to open in a brand-new building that Gianni has built two blocks away.

We proceed down the street to open an account at the local

branch of one of the three regional banks represented in Piombino Dese. Currency controls are still in effect, so we open an "external" checking account that, we are assured, leaves us flexibility to repatriate the balance to the United States if we choose. We also open a "domestic" passbook account for the custodian of the villa to use in paying utility bills and other routine expenses. Carl is impressed by the extent of the decorative, but curiously heavy, iron grillwork that has been fitted into the facade of the bank's modernized old structure, which stands at a slight curve in Via Roma.

"They installed that after a bank robbery," Dick explains. "The robbers drove a truck into the side of the building." We look at the grillwork again. I'm not sure it could stop a truck, but the truck would know it had been in a fight.

Dick points out other useful sights as we stroll along: the post office, the *municipio* (town hall) with the office of Dick's old antagonist, the *sindaco*. Turning back toward the villa, we pass a *panificio* (bread store), an *edicola* (newsstand), a *gioielleria* (jewelry store), a *fruttivendolo* (fruit and vegetable store), a *macelleria* (butcher shop) prominently featuring meat both *bovine* and *equine*. *Note to diary: I wonder if* My Friend Flicka *has been translated into Italian.*

Most of these shops, like Alimentari Battiston, are located side by side in the former *barchessa* (bar-KESS-ah) of the villa, which faces Via Roma immediately to the villa's west. In the Venetan dialect, a *barchessa* is an all-purpose farm building, housing plows and other farm equipment, storing grain, and stabling animals. The *barchessa* of Villa Cornaro was a particularly handsome building designed by Palladio's famous follower Vincenzo Scamozzi and built about 1592 on the foundations of an earlier farm building. The structure, faced with a long rhythmic loggia of high arches finished in an ashlar pattern to resemble stone, remained intact and substantially unchanged until 1951. Then it was divided and sold off as a long row of shops, with apartments above and sometimes behind. Each new owner reworked his segment to his own taste, usually eliminating the loggia and its arches. Only the Battistons retained the original facade, at least on the ground floor—the only twenty-five feet of Renaissance heritage remaining in a tangle of bland, fungible shops. Since all signs of the structure's parentage were removed, I call it the "bastardization" of the *barchessa*.

Back at the villa, the transition does not progress as smoothly. Julie seems too upset at the prospect of final departure from the villa to provide much helpful advice. A question such as "Do you

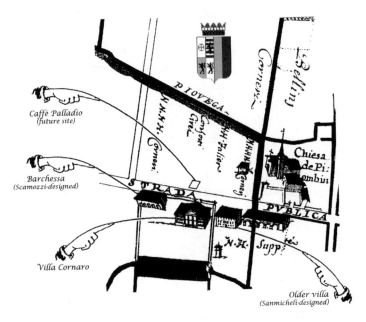

After a 1714 map of the Cornaro estates

use wax on the terra-cotta floors?" brings a response that wanders off into the long engagement of the local florist's daughter with the son of the pastry-shop owner, without ever addressing the treatment of floors.

Admiring the intercom system that provides communication from floor to floor and from end to end of the villa, I ask which room is represented by each of the ten keys on the intercom dial.

Julie says she's never been clear on that, so she just rings all the buttons each time—a system she has found perfectly satisfactory.

Dick opens the biggest issue that Carl and I must address. Epifanio Marulli, the elderly gentleman who, with his wife Elena, first showed the villa to us two years earlier, has decided to retire after all his years as custodian. Fortunately, Dick has identified for us a candidate to succeed Epifanio. Yes, it's Giacomo Miolo, my driver from the airport who proved to have such a highly developed appreciation of the dramatic gesture. I am ready to respond *"Va ben',"* but Carl and Dick agree that we should meet with Giacomo and his wife Silvana to discuss how such a relationship would work.

In fact, we have caught Giacomo and Silvana at a fortuitous moment. They own several floors of a building across Via Roma from the villa, which until recently they operated as a small hotel with a bar on the ground floor. Now, however, they're in the midst of a big gamble. They've closed the business, borrowed an enormous amount of money—Silvana later tells me how much—and are completely renovating their portion of the building. The bar is being expanded and recast as a much fancier *caffè* and sandwich shop; the floor above is being refitted as a small apartment where the Miolos and their two sons, Leonardo and Riccardo, will live in order to be close to their new business and in order to economize. They will be renting out their own substantial detached house eight blocks away.

For now, while the yearlong reconstruction is in progress, the Miolos are left with nothing to do except watch their cost overruns mount, the completion targets move out, and their bank account dwindle. They are ready for a new project—and a little income.

Yet Giacomo is a realist. Once the new *caffè* opens he can't be a hands-on custodian for us the way Epifanio was for the Rushes. But he and Silvana promise that they will find others to do what they are unable to do themselves.

We accept this offer for three reasons. First, Dick Rush, who has known them for years, recommends them; second, they seem to be a sincere, hardworking couple who are careful not to commit for more than they can deliver; and third, we have no idea where in all the world we would turn for an alternative.

7

Happy and Sad

From midweek the temperature in Piombino Dese begins to drop. We're convincingly reminded that the Veneto is on the same meridian as Montreal. What seems in August to be a charming eccentricity of the villa can become a major shortcoming in late October: Villa Cornaro has no heating system. There are fireplaces in most of the rooms, all except one of them with mantels designed by Palladio himself and executed in Verona marble, but their flues were blocked off long ago. The fireplaces were never intended to heat the villa through the winter anyway. The villas were built as summer plantation homes, with the families coming out from Venice every spring by planting time, remaining in the country until the harvest, and then returning to their palaces in Venice. So the fireplaces were only to take the chill off a spring or fall evening.

Carl and I knew we were taking a chance in making our inaugural visit in October, but we didn't want to arrive until it was certain that the Italian government would not be buying the villa away from us under its "right of first refusal." On the other hand, we couldn't bear to wait until spring for our first visit.

By Friday our activities in the villa are more and more confined to the kitchen, which the Rushes manage to heat with a bottled-gas contraption ominously called a *bombola*. (Giacomo later advises me that the name is apt; he cautions against using the two of them that are in the villa.) When Carl, Ashley, or I venture into the rest of the villa, we don our ski parkas and look more like downhillers than Italian villa owners. Dick and Julie maintain more dignity but less comfort by relying on layers of sweaters topped by jackets.

On Saturday, the day of the reception that the Rushes have

planned in order to introduce us to their friends and to say their own farewells after twenty years of associations, the weather is bone-chilling again and the sky bleak. From early morning, *fioriste* are ringing at the gate with their deliveries—enormous bouquets of lilies and roses and gladioli, each one dressed in shiny colored paper and trailing elaborate ribbon-bows. Sending flowers to a hostess in advance of an event, we learn, is an appealing Italian alternative to bringing a bottle of wine or some other small gift of appreciation. Julie reads each card with such emotion that she occasionally freezes like a statue and can neither move nor speak. Once Dick calls out, "Julie, what is it? Who's the card from?" and Julie simply cannot answer.

Dick organizes the two *bombole,* one in the dining room and the other in the grand salon. The effect is like a blowtorch set to work melting a glacier. Yet a party spirit is emerging. Flowers flood every surface. The long narrow dining table crowds three-cornered *panini,* tiny pastries, multicolored cookies, and seductive chocolates edge to edge.

For the Rushes, and probably most of the others present, the reception is a sad occasion masquerading as a happy one. Only Ashley, Carl, and I are oblivious to the glum farewell side of the affair. For us, everything is festive, albeit frigid. Dozens of Piombinesi stand about in the grand salon, huddled in their topcoats and scarves, launching barrages of Venetan dialect at each other. As we approach to introduce ourselves, they obligingly switch to Italian. I tentatively conclude that a large part of the art of speaking Italian lies in nodding with a big smile while keeping out of your eyes any glimmer of your true confusion. "Pleased to meet you." "We're so happy to be in Piombino Dese." "The villa is a marvel." I establish a pattern of Italian phrases and begin to enjoy myself as one handshake follows another. *Note to diary: Suggest tactfully to Carl that he mask his look of terror when addressed in Italian.*

Don Aldo Roma, chief parish priest, is present, stately in his white robe and earnestly friendly. Before I can respond to his first comment, three more have followed. We see Epifanio and Elena

Marulli, the now-retired custodians of the villa. We meet others who will become well known to us in future years and some whom I don't recall ever seeing again. The *sindaco* is not invited, of course, and probably would not have attended even if he had been; the memory of the soccer field war is still raw. Ernesto and Irma Formentin arrive with their daughter Nella. At Dick's request, Nella has brought her harp, and she warms her hands sufficiently to provide a short but cheery recital.

I've been looking about to spot a tall, burly Paul Bunyan who will match the image I have formed of Ilario Mariotto based on the tales I have heard—a man to brave the Australian sugarcane fields, then on his return to organize the farmers to stand foursquare with Dick in his battle with the *sindaco* over the soccer field. No such figure appears. Then I am approached by a smiling Italian man of about my age, and my size as well, a man who would have to lean to hold his place in a strong wind. Yet the hand he extends to shake mine has the resilience of solid concrete.

"I'm Ilario," he says in clear, if diffident, English. His wife Giovannina is beside him. Her strong, friendly face is framed in wavy blond hair.

"We're pleased to meet our new neighbors," she says in careful Italian.

Finally, all the food is gone, Nella has packed away her harp, and the damp chill has penetrated every bone. The crowd departs as swiftly as it arrived. My silk suit and light coat give little protection against the cold, but the prospect of so many new neighbors—all patiently prepared to help me in my new language—envelops me like a warm cocoon.

Dick and Julie Rush leave early the next morning. To our surprise, Epifanio Marulli arrives—just as though he had not retired—to load their luggage into his car as he has done for dozens of their departures in the past. We learn that Dick and Julie will be staying a few days at a hotel in Verona, where Epifanio is driving them, and then will return to the States. With little pomp, they settle in the car and Epifanio drives them slowly out the side gate and around into Via Roma. We see them pass the villa a final time and then move out of sight to the west—the fifth family to own Villa Cornaro in 435 years. Perhaps they have brought more change in the condition of the villa than any owner before them, preserving for art history one of architecture's most influential homes.

Carl and I realize that our own watch has begun.

8

A Winter for Study

Having no heating system at the villa imposes a discipline that I've appreciated from the beginning. As one benefit, we are forced to use the villa much the same way that the original Cornaro family used it. Before planting season, Giorgio Cornaro and his family would gather up their clothes, furniture, tapestries, and other household items and journey to Piombino with a small group of personal servants. They probably traveled by horse-drawn barge, leaving the lagoon at Venice to proceed up the Dese River to its intersection with the Marzènego, then up the Marzènego to the Dragonzolo, finally disembarking just fifty meters south of the villa. They would stay in the countryside through the fall harvest, supervising the storage of grain in the attic and the winemaking in the *cantina* (cellar).

So Carl, Ashley, and I return to Atlanta a week after the Rushes leave Villa Cornaro. We arrived at the villa without barge or servants, and we return to Atlanta with no grain or wine. We just carry surreal memories and a determination to spend the winter learning more about the mansion/barn that has joined our lives like a moose at a picnic. I realize that I've associated myself with a long chain of history, but it is a history I don't know, about people I never heard of, events I've never read about, and influences on the modern world that I never knew existed.

Giorgio Cornaro, Palladio's patron and the villa's first owner, died at the famous Battle of Lepanto in 1571. Lepanto? A famous battle? A later owner of the villa died in the defense of Rettimo. Where's that? Carl and I now own—arrayed in niches around the grand salon—six eight-foot-tall statues of celebrated people we have never heard of by a Renaissance sculptor whose name means nothing to us. The walls of the villa are covered with dozens of frescos depicting Bible stories I heard years ago in Sunday school and now remember only dimly. This will be a long winter.

In our search for information about the villa, we have a lead. The Rushes have told us that in the mid-1970s a government-supported organization in Vicenza—the town twenty-five miles away where Palladio lived—commissioned Douglas Lewis, a young American scholar, to write a book about Villa Cornaro. The Vicenza organization, called Centro Internazionale di Studi di Architettura Andrea Palladio (Andrea Palladio International Center for the Study of Architecture), or CISA, was then in the midst of publishing an ambitious series of books grandly entitled Corpus Palladianum, with one volume devoted to each of the structures that Palladio designed and built. The Villa Cornaro volume was delayed, however, and CISA—short of funds—ended its publication of the series after just ten volumes.

We know that the manuscript still exists. Dick Rush says he has a copy but doesn't know where he put it. He speaks a bit critically of it. It has too much information about the Cornaro family, he says, and about the prior history of the area where the villa is located, instead of concentrating exclusively on the villa itself. I begin to realize already that my own life with Villa Cornaro will be different from Dick's. For Dick, the villa is a beautiful glistening object, existing outside of time as an independent thing of beauty and sculptural purity. I am already drawn into the spirit of the villa as an object firmly rooted in its time and place, as a rational product of the bustling, optimistic, triumphant spirit of the Renaissance, and as a living structure that has supported and interacted with Piombino Dese and with the Cornaro family and later families through hundreds of years. The villa is a great cache of secrets, and I intend to pry out each one. The tenor of Dick's criticism leads me to hope that Doug Lewis is a kindred spirit.

Douglas Lewis has had the brilliant career that every genius should. The National Gallery of Art in Washington, D.C., appointed him curator of sculpture and decorative arts when he was just thirty, and he has continued to turn out meticulously researched articles and books ever since, including the definitive book on Palladio's drawings. After the collapse of CISA's Corpus Palladianum project, he abstracted the sections with his most provocative discoveries and published them in individual articles in scholarly magazines and collections in the United States, Germany, and Italy.

Carl writes to him as soon as we get back to Atlanta. Doug responds cordially with a copy of the manuscript, as well as offprints of the published articles he derived from it. The manuscript is dense to the point of being impenetrable, but Carl and I soldier away at it. We also spend time reading books and articles on Venetian history and art. By the time April arrives and I pack to leave for two months in Piombino Dese—with Carl to join me in May for the three weeks that he can get away from work—I begin to form in my mind a skeletal history of the villa, with a sense of its role in architecture and the Cornaro family's role in Venetian life.

Yet each new fact that I learn about the past makes my own future seem more complex and confusing. Perhaps more intriguing as well.

9

A Tale of a Tub

I climb into the long, skinny bathtub and stretch out full-length, my head barely above water. The villa is shuttered for the night. My two guests—friends from Atlanta—are settled in their rooms, presumably deep in their blankets to escape the cold that envelops the villa and overwhelms the inadequate electric heaters in their bedrooms and mine. I bask luxuriantly in the steamy natural perfume of the well water and watch motionless as the bar of Dove dissolves on my stomach. I am warm for the first time since my friends arrived earlier in the day, blown from the train station to our gate by a frigid April storm. My mind drifts lazily as I try to remember why it is necessary ever to leave this perfect warmth.

Suddenly all the lights of the villa go out as quietly as a candle.

The villa is shuttered tight as a tomb. Not a ray of light from even one streetlamp finds a crevice to peer through. Darkness seizes the villa.

With my mind shocked awake, I begin to review my situation: I am naked, up to my neck in water, in pitch-darkness, in a room where I have personally killed two scorpions within the past three days. My rational mind, in an effort to distract me from the temptation simply to scream in terror, tells me that the three electric heaters, bored by their pretense of producing heat, have merely turned to their favorite activity: overloading the villa's circuits. My mind is teased by two dim memories: first, that Silvana specifically told me where a candle is located in my bedroom, but that I did not pay much attention; and second, that Giacomo specifically showed me where the circuit breakers are located in a small room between the two main floors of the villa—but I didn't pay much attention to that, either. What I remember best is that, in the stairwell of tight circular wooden stairs leading to the small room, I also killed a scorpion yesterday.

Scorpions don't kill, I tell myself. *Note to diary: Learn more about scorpions.* I splash around the bathtub noisily, in the hope of prompting retreat by any scorpion within earshot, then creep out of the tub. I fumble for a towel and feel my way to the bedroom. I pat-search my bureau for the candle. Books, necklace and earrings recently removed, framed photo of Carl (why isn't he here to deal with this mess?), stack of handkerchiefs, no candle. Cross to the bedside table, like walking on ice cubes. I grasp the brass candlestick! The matches are beside it. After three tries, I ignite one of the damp matches. Light at last. I pick my way to Philip's room and Helen's room and bang on their doors in turn. Philip and Helen laugh at my predicament. Warm in their beds, they're not worried about lights; dawn will come and bring sunlight. I'm not prepared to take such a long view. Turn off your heaters, I tell them; with the load reduced, I should be able to flip the circuit breakers back on. I put on the warmest clothes I can find in the candlelight and, shivering and dodging dripping candle wax, proceed cautiously down the circular stairs toward the kitchen. The fuses and circuit breakers are in the mezzanine room that lies twenty-three steps down, between the two main floors. I find the huge array of electric switches and study each one in turn. Several have clearly flipped off. I reverse the process and am bathed instantly in light from the stairwell.

As I pick my way cautiously up the stairs, which I view as a footpath through a field cleverly booby-trapped with scorpions instead of land mines, I begin doing the arithmetic in my head: The villa is wired for 15 kilowatts of electricity, calculated to be enough for all foreseeable needs. But Helen and Philip have joined me in mid-April of what the television weathermen gleefully and repeatedly call the coldest spring Europe has seen in a hundred years. We plugged in all the villa's three electric radiators and set them on high. Still, there should have been no problem. Then I remember that my running a bath would have started the electric pump at the well that supplies water to the villa. Some lights were on, of course, and who knows what else electrical might have been at work. Anyway, it is clear that we must ration ourselves so as to have just two heaters on at the same time. Maybe we will have to draw lots to see which of the three of us will shut off his or her heater each night.

Scorpions are my first introduction to Piombino Dese wildlife. Dick Rush never told us about the scorpions. I kill fifty-five inside the villa during my first two-month visit. The first one I find lurking on a window frame in the kitchen the morning after I arrive. As I release the old serpentine iron clasp and pull open the window, this sinister black creature, like a three-inch-long lobster, moves slightly on the right-hand sill. I freeze; it freezes. Then I take off my shoe and whack the beast flat. "Welcome to the NFL," I mutter.

And I continue to whack everywhere: on the wall above my bed, on the floor under the bath mat, peering from a crack in the dining-room floor, half beneath the refrigerator, on the front portico's wall, on the grand salon's window frame. I pluck a dead one off the underside of my bed's coverlet; a live one scuttles out from under some laundry left on the floor.

We find a nest under the central table in the grand salon, disturbed when we move the furniture for a chamber-music concert. One evening, as I am cooking supper for Ilario and his family, the villa's electricity goes out and I feel my way upstairs in the dark to the circuit-breaker box. When I return to the kitchen an enormous scorpion lies sprawled next to the stove where I had just been standing a few minutes earlier. Where did it come from? One of Ashley's visiting friends expresses terror at the possibility of encountering such an animal. Of course, we assure him—with a confidence we don't feel—that we rarely see a scorpion, this is not the season for scorpions, they flee at the sight of humans, etc. After he leaves and I begin pulling the sheets from his bed, I find a three-incher tangled between the top sheet and the bedspread. I never tell him.

And I will certainly never tell him about an article I read in an Italian newspaper one morning: An Iranian family of five dies of scorpion poisoning because they drank tea brewed in a teapot where an unseen scorpion lurked. Giacomo assures me that the Italian variety is not lethal, its sting more like that of a wasp. He cautions that if we kill off all the scorpions, we will have many more of the spiders and bugs that scorpions eat. I prefer spiders. A spirited pesticide campaign brings the scorpions under control within a few years, aided by the fact that scorpions actually reproduce slowly, with just one brood a year in some types.

IO

Peace in Our Time

Carl and I have each set ourselves a mission for our first spring at Villa Cornaro. I'm determined to get the kitchen reworked with modern equipment and cabinets, and I've convinced Carl—as a man committed to eating at regular intervals—that this is in his interest as well. Carl's project is to become acquainted with the *sindaco* of Piombino Dese who bedeviled Dick Rush with the plan to build a soccer field on the farmland behind the villa. If we can establish a friendly or at least neutral relationship with the *sindaco*, Carl reasons, we improve our chances for avoiding other confrontations in the future. At a minimum we will avoid having the ill will that exists between the *sindaco* and Dick Rush automatically transferred to us. Carl's campaign ultimately produces a photo I think Dick would find amusing, taken in what we call—because of its dominant fresco—the villa's Tower of Babel room.

Carl's first step is to determine the best way to be introduced to the *sindaco*. He seeks Giacomo's advice. Giacomo suggests—to our surprise, because we don't understand Italian village life—that we should consult with Don Aldo, the parish priest, whom we met at the Rushes' welcome/farewell reception last fall. This resonates with an old (and dubious) maxim that Carl has heard somewhere, namely, that the three people most important to know in an Italian town are the *sindaco*, the priest, and the chief of the carabinieri. Giacomo raises the matter with Don Aldo and reports that we should invite Don Aldo to the villa for tea.

Within a few days Don Aldo is seated with us in the Tower of Babel room. Don Aldo is a pale man perhaps fifty-five or sixty years old. His height is little more than mine, but his carriage makes him look taller. We're already familiar with his aggressively friendly manner from our earlier introduction at the Rushes' reception. We restate our interest in achieving good relations with

the *sindaco* and leaving all controversy in the past—although Don
Aldo has already been apprised of all this by Giacomo.

"We should all meet together with the *sindaco* so this can all be
explained," Don Aldo concludes.

"We would be happy to meet at any time," Carl replies. "Whatever time is convenient."

Don Aldo rises. "Now," he says. "The *sindaco* is expecting us."
It's obvious that Don Aldo is way ahead of us on this. Carl and I
hurriedly close a few open windows on the ground floor, lock the
villa, and follow Don Aldo's quick step to the *municipio*, which is
housed in a converted eighteenth-century villa just a block away.
The *sindaco* is awaiting us in his office, as Don Aldo has promised.
I bring to the meeting an overwhelmingly negative preconception,
and nothing about the *sindaco* changes my view. He seems to be
about forty-five or fifty years old; he is muscular and full of energy,
defensive and suspicious.

We explain our purpose, although it's obvious that he has been
well briefed by Don Aldo. The *sindaco* particularly questions
whether we are long-term friends of Dick Rush or have just met in
connection with the purchase. He joins in our expressions of good-
will. Then Don Aldo surprises us a second time.

"Why don't we return to the villa and talk there?" he asks.
Clearly, Don Aldo intends to memorialize our truce with symbolic
ceremony. We all quickly agree. Back at the villa, we change our
beverage from tea to prosecco. Carl realizes that we have a unique
photo opportunity. He returns with our camera after a hurried
search, and we commence a round-robin of snapshots. At one point
I am delegated to photograph Don Aldo, the *sindaco*, and Carl in a
cheerful line like old friends. We are in the Tower of Babel room
again, but they are standing in front of a different fresco panel.
Behind them, Abraham is bowing before God; Don Aldo's head is
directly beneath Abraham's lowered face, while the *sindaco*'s is
under Abraham's derriere—a symbol Don Aldo does not foresee.

We follow our armistice with the *sindaco* by having him and his
wife for dinner, a somber affair but suitable for its purpose. Then,

when we realize that we need to retain a *commercialista* (a sort of accountant-cum-tax/business-adviser) to handle our tax filings and various other reports, we visit the *sindaco* at his office and ask him for a recommendation. In his *Autobiography*, Benjamin Franklin observes that the best way to obtain a man's approbation is to ask him for a favor, such as the loan of a book. Carl's idea is to follow Franklin's advice on the one hand, and on the other to give the *sindaco* a chance to gain favor with some ally.

In the next year, just as all the elements of Carl's program seem to be falling into place, the *sindaco* subverts our efforts by losing his bid for reelection.

II

Lessons

Like several other Palladian-villa owners, Dick Rush allowed tour groups to visit the first floor of the villa and the park. He required an appointment and charged a small admission fee. Individuals not in a tour group could visit on Saturday afternoons during the summer. Motivated by a combination of public spirit and private interest, Carl and I decide to continue the practice. On the one hand, we want to share our treasure of art and architectural history with all the world; on the other, the income will help us in a small way to maintain the villa.

Giacomo and Silvana handle the appointments and open the villa when groups arrive. My involvement is not expected. In my first spring at the villa, however, during my weeks alone, I find the groups are good company. They often provide an opportunity to speak English, for a change, even if the group is actually from Germany or France. The tours are also a way for me to expand my own store of knowledge about the villa, as well as learn what features interest tourists most.

Usually the groups are accompanied by an informed guide or

lecturer, sometimes even by a true expert on the Veneto or Palladio such as Peter Lauritzen, Bruce Boucher, or Wilma Barbieri. Often the groups themselves include knowledgeable architects or professors. Yet on some occasions they have no more guidance than that which their bus driver provides, so I become a self-instructed docent, drawing on all the research that Carl and I have been doing, on what I've learned from listening to tour guides, and from my own experiences. Even the professional guides solicit my comments on how it feels to live in a Palladian villa. Is it comfortable? How long do I live here each year? The tourists are pleased to have found a villa that is a real home, not just a museum. They stop to look curiously at the photographs of our family placed around on tables just as in our Atlanta home. They inspect the books or magazines that I've left half-read on tables and chairs. Finally one day I realize that I've begun to guide whole tours myself. Even the best guides are relaxed about it, just chiming in from time to time on points they want to emphasize. Upon reflection, I am acutely aware that I haven't mastered the nuances of Palladio, details of his influence on later Palladianism, or correspondences between Villa Cornaro and his other works. But in terms of our own magnificent villa—its individual history, its moods, its changing light, its breezes, the adjusting of its shutters to bring in fresh morning air while maintaining its indoor temperature, its unique personality— I become, over time, an expert.

As a consequence of my growing self-confidence I am less awed than prudence would dictate at meeting some of the distinguished visitors who appear from time to time, such as the directors of great museums or the well-known scholars and writers. I enjoy meeting all tourists to the villa, the well informed and the novices. I appreciate their interest in Italy, in Palladio, and in Villa Cornaro, as well as their enthusiasm and energy. Coming from dozens of countries, they are for the most part drawn by a genuine curiosity to learn more about an architect whose vision of a reborn classical architecture has helped shape the way the world looks today. I am building a great stockpile of memories.

One morning, when Silvana arrives to open the *balcone,* she tells me that an arts group from Paris will be visiting at ten o'clock. Later I see a group of smartly dressed women gathering with admirable punctuality on the sidewalk outside the front gate. Giacomo arrives from Caffè Palladio to open the gate and lead the tour guide and her party up the stone steps to the north portico, where I greet them. Even in this splendid party, my eyes are drawn to one elegantly attired woman in a memorable bright red wool knee-length coat that flares out when she moves. I can hear her outfit whispering to me, This is as good as French couture gets. *Note to diary: Why can't I ever find something like that at Loehmann's?* "Madame Chirac," the tour leader says, introducing her and the others to me. There is no possibility of my conducting a tour in French, but they all seem perfectly comfortable with English. Ten days later I receive gracious thank-you notes from four of the women—all in English. One of them purports to speak for all in extending to me an invitation to pay a reciprocal visit to the home of any of them in Paris. I presume that the offer includes the Maison de Ville, since M. Chirac is mayor of Paris, but it is clearly one of those invitations that are better appreciated than accepted. Nonetheless, I will wonder several years later, after the striking lady's husband has become president of France, whether the offer is still open.

Whatever brought you to buy a Palladian villa in Italy?

Though I hear the question continually, I don't remember ever hearing it from an Italian. An Italian might ask how much time I spend at the villa, how many servants I have to maintain it, or even how much I paid—but never *why*. If you have the opportunity to buy a Palladian villa and the resources to do so, an Italian would wonder only: Why would you *not* buy it?

The Italians are right, of course, but their view reflects an understanding of the rewards of Italian life and culture that I did not have in 1989 and would gain only with the passage of years. So I always respond to the question *why* with my story about the search for a second home in New Hampshire. In my own mind, however, the story is beginning to wear thin.

You bought the villa to escape.

That's the upsetting new notion that I work to suppress. Escape? Why would I want to escape? And from what? Carl and I have been very happy with our life in Atlanta, with our three children, our jobs and colleagues at work, our neighbors and other friends, civic duties and hobbies. Why would I want to "escape"? Yet the idea will not leave me.

I think about the things that have been most fulfilling about my early days in Piombino Dese: my ability to thrive in a new language, my exploring new friendships among Italians with life experiences so different from my own. But I think of other, less obvious points as well. I found that breaker box when I was naked, wet, in the dark, and surrounded by scorpions, I reflect with satisfaction. I've made decisions about septic tanks and water pumps in conferences with Italian plumbers and electricians. I've shown hun-

The park, looking south

dreds of intimidating visitors through my home and survived the experience.

And where was Carl? I ask smugly. Four thousand miles away, I answer—living the life I've escaped, our joint life.

His life, I add as an afterthought.

What do I mean by that? I puzzle even myself. I'm sitting on the south loggia now, watching the *rondini* (swallows) dart about searching for small flying insects in the early evening shadows just as they do in the morning. I have a glass of prosecco in hand to facilitate clear thinking. After twenty-five years of marriage, I cannot imagine life without Carl, but if "escape" is the right word, maybe what I'm escaping is Carl's life—escaping his life to find my own.

Carl's career and his business travels have imposed a sort of cicadian rhythm upon us, I realize. A week of travel to Sweden each quarter for meetings at his company's automotive-parts plant, with side trips to the plant in Germany or to see customers in France and England; a week of travel to Korea every six months to confer with the joint-venture partner in the plant there; one-day round-trippers almost every week to see customers in Detroit or visit plants in Indiana or Virginia or Minnesota.

But if "escape" was really my motivation, I cannot lay everything at Carl's doorstep. I have to examine my own late-blooming career as well. In our children's early teen years, when parenthood was at its most tedious and exasperating, I had found a blissful outlet singing in Robert Shaw's 220-voice Atlanta Symphony Orchestra Chorus. Happy college memories of singing with the Radcliffe Choral Society welled up in me, the happiest being our performance of Bach's B Minor Mass with the Boston Symphony. Robert Shaw, of course, was America's (the world's!) leading choral director, and his charismatic presence in Atlanta touched the life of every singer in the state, either directly or through his influence on voice teachers and choir directors. My life was touched as well. My heady seven years of singing and recording with his chorus led to my late master's degree in sacred music and then to my role as a church music director. I reveled in the music, in planning programs, in the camaraderie and faithful service of my choir members, but I resigned the post after five years to make possible my long stays in our new villa.

Surely that was not an "escape." It was my first real job—community volunteer work aside—since our first child, Ashley, was born. I had my own office, support from parents grateful that I was teaching their children to sing, praise from the members of the congregation who enjoyed my selections of new music or new arrangements of old favorites. Escape? I don't think so!

How honest do I have to be with myself? The *rondini* have returned to their nests, night is settling rapidly in the park, and I have finished my glass of prosecco. It is a time for candid thought: Is it possible that some of the exhilaration of my church post had worn away after five years, buffeted by occasional reminders that relationships in churches can be as political as those in any other form of association? Had I needed something beyond church music to fulfill me for a lifetime? Dark thoughts.

12

Garden and Park

Some of our early efforts at managing the villa are distinctly hit-or-miss.

Giacomo believes he will have enough time to care for the lawn and hedges himself, despite the long hours he is spending at his *caffè* now that it has reopened. We will need a new riding mower for the lawn, he explains. The walk-behind model that Epifanio Marulli used for years is too slow and decrepit. This seems reasonable enough until Giacomo launches us on a shopping expedition to find one. A dealer in Loreggia shows us a model the size of a Volkswagen Beetle.

"*Quanto costa?*" Carl asks. He has already pointed out to me that it is the Italian phrase he uses most often. His other favorite is "*Il conto, per favore.* The bill, please."

We are confused by the dealer's response. Either we misheard his answer or we are making a mistake in our mental conversion of the price from lire to dollars.

"*Lo scriva, per favore,*" Carl requests. This will all make more sense if we see it in writing.

Carl stares at the written price; I peer over his shoulder. We agree there is only one possible explanation: The mower actually *is* a Volkswagen Beetle, just an enhanced version! The price is three times what we paid for our first car when we got married. As we hurriedly leave the dealership, I decide that the Italian sun has done Carl no good at all; he is white as a sheet.

"*Nessun problema,*" Giacomo assures us. We'll find something better in Resana or, if that fails, we'll go a few miles farther to Castelfranco. We spend several more days shopping and comparing prices. Meanwhile, the grass at the villa has grown to our ankles and the weeds—a major part of the mixture—approach our knees. Carl begins to mutter speculatively about switching the park from grass to white pebbles. Finally, we find ourselves back in Loreggia, where we began. We swallow hard and write a check, grateful that the price has not gone up while we delayed.

Soon Giacomo is proudly driving the Rolls-Royce of riding mowers around the yard, seated like the rider in a dressage event, tall in the saddle, shoulders back, putting his high-stepping steed through its paces.

The romance of man and machine is not to last. By summer's end, Giacomo concludes he can no longer handle maintenance of the yard. The *caffè* is prospering; by the time the last customer has left and Giacomo has cleaned up the premises, it is past 3:00 a.m. The daylight hours are too short for him to assist Silvana with the lunchtime business, care for the villa's grounds, open the villa for tour groups, and still find time to sleep. The gardening seems to be the only dispensable item. Giacomo is firm about the need to find a new solution before the spring, when the grass will begin to grow again. Giacomo's decision is no surprise. I only wonder how he managed the yard as long as he did. Giacomo promises that he will find an alternative solution during the course of the winter.

Giacomo is Figaro, our own personal Barber of Seville with a solution for every problem. Some solutions prove more lasting than others. Upon my return to Piombino Dese in the spring, Giacomo introduces Mario, our new gardener. I protest that we don't have enough work for a full-time gardener. Giacomo explains that Mario needs full-time work, that he can do other handyman tasks, and that the cost will not much exceed the part-time options available.

Mario is a small, gnomelike man about sixty years old, a former *falegname* (carpenter) with bright blue eyes that don't see well. Sprickles of curly gray hair adorn the sides of his head, making him a perfect candidate for Santa's workshop. His family is eager for him to stop woodworking because, they say, the sawdust has given him asthma, which is exacerbated by his smoking; the fresh air in our garden will be good for his lungs—and he won't have time to smoke.

Mario begins his new career in gardening.

He likes to sit astride the mower. He rides for hours. The task metamorphoses in Mario's mind to become like painting the Golden Gate Bridge: when the job is finished, it is time to start it again. Mario doesn't like to weed, he doesn't like to prune, and he doesn't like to fertilize. He doesn't like to sweep the *cantina*, where the mower is stored. And he doesn't stop smoking. I often discover him in one of the south stairwells, gazing dreamily out a window while puffing away.

Mario doesn't much like any part of his job, except the riding. He begins arriving at about 9:00 a.m. each day; by 10:30 he is across the street at the *caffè* for a shot of grappa. Break for lunch and *riposo* at noon, return at 3:30 p.m. At the bar by 5:00 p.m. for another tipple. Each succeeding day becomes shorter in work time than the day before. After a month I break the news to Mario that instead of having a full-time gardener and no help cleaning inside the villa, I have decided to split my budget between a part-time gardener and a part-time housekeeper.

Mario takes the news cheerfully. He crosses immediately to the *caffè* for a grappa and a smoke.

We are back to square one. Giacomo is out, Mario is out. Our magnificent lawn mower sits idle in our *cantina*. The grass is growing around us. Which way should we turn? Even resourceful Giacomo seems stymied. Is that a look of desperation I see in his eye as the prospect of having to return to the saddle himself looms before him?

Of course, the answer is obvious. Whom do we call on when a tree falls in the park and must be cut up and carted away? When the long-abandoned ziggurat/cooking counter that Julie Rush left half-finished in the kitchen must be sledgehammered and removed? When a pigeon family decides to set up housekeeping in the crawl space over our bedroom? How have we overlooked the obvious answer: Ilario!

We all know that Ilario is conscientious about anything he undertakes, and he would treat the mighty mower as lovingly as he does the cows that share his home. But will he take the job on? He has his own farm that he and Giovannina must tend. Giacomo and I, in consultation with Carl by long distance, have concluded—notwithstanding my experience with Mario—that in the summer the routine yard work should actually require about one full day every two weeks. Maybe another half day a month would be needed for some extra tasks. Giacomo volunteers that during dry

Ilario Mariotto at work
at Villa Cornaro

periods he can take care of any watering the plants, hedges, and lawn might require. Obviously Ilario would not be available during the weeks of planting and harvest, when the timing of his farm-work is critical and highly sensitive to the weather, but maybe he could fit in the work during the rest of the season.

Giacomo tells me I must ask Ilario myself. Ilario feels a great allegiance to the villa, Giacomo explains, and a direct appeal from me will be hard for him to turn down.

When I bring the request to Ilario, he considers it carefully, as I knew he would. If he accepts, he will consider the task an important obligation, not something agreed to lightly. After discussion with Giovannina, Ilario accepts. With Ilario on board, we know that one problem has been definitely resolved.

13

Da Ilario

The moos bother me at first. An eruption of mooing overwhelms conversation during our antipasto course. Ilario excuses himself from the table to see what is troubling his cows. He's leaving behind a platter of homemade salami, a *caciotta* (a simple cheese) made by Giovannina, and a saucer of dull green olives that tease my taste buds.

The cows live in an adjoining apartment of the house, separated by a wall and a hallway from the dining room where we sit. Arriv-ing at the Mariotto home on our first visit, after Carl's arrival in late May, we park our car beside the corncrib, admire the ten frol-icking kittens, and find ourselves presented with a choice of side-by-side doors, as in the story of the tiger and the lady. Fortunately, Ilario and Giovannina appear in the doorway on the right to greet us, eliminating our need to choose. The door on the left, they explain, opens into the home of their eight resident cows, aligned one beside the other. At last a riddle is answered for me: If, as we are told, the corn growing in all the fields around us is to feed animals and not humans, where *are* these alleged animals? We've never seen a single cow grazing in a Venetan field. Now I understand they are all living hidden from sight, like Ilario's.

Ilario returns to the dinner table. "*Nessun problema,*" he says. "*Loro vogliono solo compagnia.* They just want a little company." The cows represent a tremendous asset for Ilario, and he always reacts immediately to any complaint he hears from them.

The table at which we're sitting—Ilario and Giovannina; their older daughter, Alessandra, and her *fidanzato* (fiancé), Stefano; their younger daughter, Valeria; and Carl and I—crowds the small sitting/dining room. A sofa clings to one wall; a large television set roosts on a tiny table in a corner.

Ilario earlier has walked me through the garden that embraces the house on the east and north. Ilario's small farm was formerly one of the fields of the villa plantation, and the villa itself peers above a row of trees in the distance. I exclaim to Ilario about the variety of his garden: fig, plum, pear, and apple trees; green beans, pole beans, tomatoes, zucchini; turban squash, onions, potatoes, all laid out in straight, manicured rows.

"This is Giovannina's garden," Ilario replies in slow, careful English. "It is very beautiful! And she planted all those flowers at the driveway—not necessary, I think; we can't eat them! But she likes the colors." A rainbow of zinnias greeted us as we drove off the little lane leading from Via Marconi to their home. A dozen sunflowers stand guard at the woodshed.

Giovannina hops up from the table and, with the girls' help, clears the antipasto dishes. She brings from the kitchen a large bowl of zucchini risotto and a small one of grated *grana*. She works to speak slowly in Italian for our challenged American ears, but sometimes she turns to address the girls in Venetan. At one point she seems to be telling Valeria to mind her manners, because Valeria sits up and takes her elbows off the table.

Although Ilario and I are the same age, our experiences have been very different. Genuine hunger was a part of everyday life in the Veneto following World War II. Ilario's older brother Mario left Piombino Dese for Australia in the late 1950s to harvest sugarcane in the province of North Queensland. Ilario followed in 1960, remaining four years before he returned to Piombino Dese. He met Giovannina the following year and they were married soon after.

Ilario looks like a very, very thin Mel Ferrer, with a narrow, angular face and high forehead. He is a gentle man who speaks softly and with great patience for us not blessed with life as Italians. He loves all life, cares lovingly for his cows, disdains chemical pesticides. His mild manner and slight build contrast sharply with Giovannina's robust energy and rapid-fire speech. She works with him in the fields, accomplishing almost as much as he.

"Why Australia?" I ask Ilario, as Giovannina clears the dishes again and brings on the *spezzatino* (stew) with polenta and a platter of succulent grilled *peperoni rossi* (sweet red peppers).

Australian recruiters traveled across southern Europe in the 1950s hunting strong, healthy men to cut sugarcane, Ilario explains. The recruiter would not even waste time in conversation with a prospective recruit until he had examined the man's hands to confirm that they were covered in calluses, a test Ilario easily passed. Examination by a dentist was next; serious dental problems would be a disqualifier also. Finally, a medical doctor verified Ilario's general good health. Ilario was ready for the Antipodes.

"Buona sera, signora Sally, signor Carlo!" Silvano Mariotto appears in the doorway, interrupting Ilario's quiet discourse. The cows have not warned us of his arrival. Silvano is Ilario's younger brother, a bit taller, not quite as thin. He nods to Carl and apologizes for his late arrival; he has finished milking his *mucche* (cows) and must leave shortly for a choir rehearsal at the church. He pours himself a glass of homemade red wine, fills his plate, and begins his supper. Silvano usually says little, though he happily joins in when we discuss early life at the villa or the postwar history of Piombino Dese.

Under my cross-examination, Ilario continues his Australian

saga. He was transported to Australia in a small ship, along with other recruits. Sailing from Venice, they rounded the Italian peninsula to Genoa, then returned south to Naples, picking up more workers at each stop. They proceeded across the Mediterranean and through the Suez Canal, paused at Port Said and Aden, then crossed the Indian Ocean to Fremantle, Melbourne, and finally Sydney. From Sydney they completed their odyssey with a plane flight to their final destination in North Queensland. There Ilario worked for six months each year in cane fields and then six months in tobacco fields. In the cane fields, three days of the week were spent cutting cane, followed by three days loading the harvest onto trucks for transport.

Hard work, Ilario admits, but he won't dwell on the hardship. "We were paid by what we cut, so we could set our own pace," he says. Ilario, I am sure, set a torrid pace.

Ilario eats so slowly! And Giovannina so fast! Before Ilario has finished his *spezzatino*, Giovannina begins slicing the pear torte I brought as dessert.

For a young man whose whole life has been consumed in cultivating a single circumscribed parcel of land, the wrench of leaving the land and boarding a ship and then a plane en route to a remote country on the opposite side of the globe must have been excruciating, the anxiety belied now by Ilario's calm in speaking of it. In fact, Ilario's father had made a move different in scale but perhaps comparable in emotional impact. Ilario's family lived and worked first in Loreggia, about four miles away from Piombino Dese. By researching in the parish records of Loreggia, Ilario has established that his family had lived there from at least as early as 1636. The family probably spent all those centuries as *mezzadri*, sharecroppers, working a single plot of ground. In 1938, however, the landowner, Mario Vianello—who also owned Villa Cornaro and its surrounding land—asked Ilario's father to remove his family to Piombino Dese to take over farming a parcel that had become available here. Ilario's father bravely accepted the offer, impelled perhaps by having too many children to survive on the parcel in Loreggia. While a farmhouse was being built for the family in Piombino Dese, they lived upstairs in the *barchessa* of the villa, approximately in the section where Marina Bighin now lives above her beauty shop. And it was there, above the stable, that Ilario was born.

"Will your grandchildren continue to farm the land?" I ask Ilario.

"Perhaps," he replies. "But they must attend university first."

14

La Cucina

What did the Rushes eat in Piombino Dese?

Not much, I conclude, peering into the large, grim room masquerading as a kitchen. A propane stove with two burners squats forlornly along the south wall, flanked by a primitive refrigerator. There's no sink or running water; that's in the adjacent laundry room. The west wall is filled by a hovering terra-cotta hood from the early 1900s. Below the hood is the masonry work for the low counter that Julie once commissioned but abandoned before completion. With the shutters closed in the evening, rays from the single bulb of the hanging central fixture struggle to light the long, narrow table directly below and are frustrated completely by the gloomy shadows that shroud the pale blue walls. Yet against the north wall, serene and magnificent, stands in unlikely contrast an eighteenth-century French armoire, its beauty and dignity undiminished by having been turned to use as a dish cupboard.

Since the propane stove would be challenged to cook a midsize hamburger patty, it is obvious that Julie and Dick looked elsewhere for nourishment. Silvana confirms to me that she and Elena Marulli frequently prepared dishes for the Rushes at their own homes and brought the meals to the villa. Julie also relied on take-out items from Alimentari Battiston next door. Julie just didn't cook.

I, on the other hand, like to cook. Visions of grand feasts of Italian cuisine color my dreams. Raising three children makes any mother a master of spaghetti; now I'm poised for grander heights. I buy every Italian cookbook I can find, feeling that my skills are increased each time I add a new volume to the shelf.

The kitchen actually illustrates the difference in the way Carl and I propose to use the villa as compared with Dick and Julie. For them the villa served primarily as a pied-à-terre for quick stops—three days to two weeks—during the course of their travels around Europe. We, on the other hand, envision a European family home with frequent visits from our three children and friends.

So the kitchen is my Project No. 1. Buying the villa itself was a stretch, but we've known all along that we would have to stretch a little farther and install a modern working kitchen to make the villa the livable home we want it to be. During the winter in Atlanta I begin by roving the aisles of Barnes & Noble. I finally settle on two books to help me focus on kitchen issues in general. I talk with friends who have redone their kitchens to get tips on any mistakes I should avoid, but this proves to be a blind alley: Either there were no mistakes, or my friends have simply learned to live with them and keep quiet. I never imagined there were so many magazines on kitchen design. I collect stacks of them. The cashier at our local pharmacy begins to point out new issues as soon as I walk through the door. I'm not surprised that there is no ready-made plan for an Italian Renaissance kitchen but, insofar as I can find, no one's ever attempted to put a modern kitchen and eating area of any sort into a large rectangular room with an eighteen-foot ceiling. Nonetheless, I begin to identify elements that appeal to me. Courtesy of Barnes & Noble again, I find a new kitchen book with cutouts of various appliances. Like a young girl with her first paper dolls, I punch out, stick down, pull up, shift around until, finally, *Eccola!* the perfect kitchen. At least I've settled on the main working elements.

Back in Piombino Dese in the spring, things go badly before they go well. The obvious starting point is Mobilificio Roncato, a mammoth furniture outlet and factory west of town toward Loreggia. Giacomo introduces us to the proprietor, Remo Roncato. The retail outlet alone seems as big as the Georgia Dome, but broken into dozens of rooms, all rigged so that the lights turn on only when someone enters the area. Behind the retail building is a factory that manufactures furniture for sale to dealers throughout the Veneto and adjacent regions. Remo has a major business, and he and his wife Maria are there from morning to night, supervising every detail from the sale of a single chair to the largest wholesale transaction.

Remo's success story is repeated over and over in the Veneto. His father was an artisan woodworker, specializing in marquetry finishes on handmade furniture. Remo joined his father in the trade, bringing the new drive and ambition—fueled by the poverty and hunger rampant in the Veneto in the early years after World War II—that seem to characterize his whole generation of Venetans. Today the single most prosperous province in all of Europe is not in Germany, as I have been conditioned to expect—it's the Veneto. But it would be hard for me to name as many as five companies that are really household names. The whole economic machine is built on thousands of commercial success stories like Remo's.

Nonetheless, Remo strikes out on my kitchen. I start to learn that I am not going to find ready-made cabinets and counters for a kitchen twenty-three feet long and eighteen feet wide. Not only is Remo's stock designed for apartments and small houses, the pieces have no symmetry. I'm convinced that if we install something asymmetrical, Palladio's ghost will rise from his grave in Vicenza and find a new home at Villa Cornaro, stalking around the kitchen every night, rattling pots, and moaning like the wind in agony from the injury to his spirit.

Of course, Remo manages to sell us two sofas before we leave his store. "The villa has over a hundred chairs," Carl grumbles, "and not one of them is comfortable to sit in."

We visit two other kitchen stores, also in vain. Giacomo comes to our rescue. He suggests we talk with Renato Rizzi about something custom-made. Renato is the architect and interior designer from Mirano who designed Giacomo's Caffè Palladio. Naturally Carl's first reaction is that we can't afford it. After discussion (Carl's) and threats (mine) we have a meeting with Renato.

"We can always say no to what he proposes," I maintain.

"I've already said no, but it didn't take," Carl responds.

Renato is somewhat awed to be working in Palladio's footsteps, but he is up to the task. Carl and I both like him immediately. He is a sticklike figure at least six foot four in height, with the air of an artist. Carl is relieved to see a calculator among his gear.

"Whatever you do here must be very big," Renato says wisely, looking around the room for the first time. He likes the clippings I show him, particularly photos for a freestanding island with a glass vitrine on the front, rising nearly four feet and screening behind it my working counters, sink, stove, microwave, and dishwasher. Carl is mollified when Renato says we should retain the kitchen table that we already have, as well as the French armoire. To our even greater surprise, he says we should also retain the large terra-cotta hood. For a new light fixture, he joins us in a trip to the attic, where he inspects an old eight-armed ceramic chandelier that Dick Rush bought in Bassano and then found no use for. "Perfect!" Renato exclaims. In fact, we end up needing just three custom items in addition to the new appliances themselves: the vitrine-cum-screen, a sink and cooking counter to fit below the terra-cotta hood, and a giant freestanding cupboard-cabinet-refrigerator unit along the south wall. He sketches them quickly. They're beautiful! Moreover, they're symmetrical! Palladio's ghost can relax.

"Use the calculator," Carl suggests politely. He wants to hear numbers. Renato works with a firm that can build the custom pieces. Within a few days he's back with final drawings and a firm price quote. Carl has always told me that the way to arrive at the true cost of a project is to double the architect's estimate. He calls it his "Architect's Rule of 2." So he's moderately surprised to hear that the quoted price from the builder is only 20 percent above the figure that he told Renato was our absolute maximum price. Then he becomes almost pleased when further bargaining reduces the quoted price by 10 percent. Renato promises that everything will be completely installed by September 1, in time for our fall return to Piombino Dese.

Meanwhile, for the remainder of our spring visit, all I have to do is learn to cook *scaloppine di vitello al marsala* on a two-burner propane stove.

"It's bigger than the Doge's Palace, Mom!"

That's Jim's first impression of the villa. Jim is our youngest child, about to start his sophomore year in college. He has never seen Villa Cornaro, even though we have bedeviled him with photographs for the year we have owned it. On a scorching August morning he and I, newly arrived from the Treviso airport, are standing in Piazzetta Squizzato, across the street from the villa. The dry summer dust that clings to the storefronts along Via Roma might seem dreary elsewhere, but here in the Veneto I decide that it's a picturesque cinnamon drape.

The new kitchen is to be installed in the coming week. Jim and I have flown over from Atlanta to witness the process and be sure that nothing goes terribly wrong. Carl and I at first feel uncertain whether the expense of a special trip is justified, even though I find a bargain plane ticket. The thought that Jim has never seen his parents' folly tips the balance. Jim has ten days open between the end of his summer job and the start of his college year, so we manage to fit in a whirlwind trip.

Giacomo has decided that a young man of college age might

need a special incentive to return often to Piombino Dese. Late in the afternoon he arrives at the villa with two very pretty young women, one a short, blond, curly-haired high school student who speaks excellent English, the other taller, with dark auburn hair. They want to practice their English, Giacomo explains transparently. I think his true agenda is to have Jim fall madly in love with a Venetan girl. Jim, the most gregarious of our children, soon wanders over to Caffè Palladio with the girls to meet other young people. His high-school Spanish helps bridge the language gap and his new friend Betty translates what he doesn't understand. In the evening he, together with Giacomo's son Leonardo and others, is off to a disco. Jim feels at home in Piombino Dese as quickly as I did.

The spirit of Palladio seems to put extra pressure on workers at the villa. There must be a sense of a historical obligation to give the villa their best. As the following week progresses, my kitchen unfolds and the parts fit together like an elegant puzzle.

The enormous, symmetrical, freestanding wall cabinet is perfectly proportioned for the room; anything less would be swallowed by the space and anything more would overwhelm it. The color—matching the walnut of the French armoire that it faces—is perfect, too. The color of that cabinet was the only point on which Carl balked at what Renato proposed. Carl thought the blond pearwood Renato suggested would look too modern. All the colors work well with the gray-black and coral tones of the granite countertops we have chosen. Culinary heaven!

In the afternoon Jim and I tootle around the countryside in our rental car. We inspect the Roman mosaic pavements in Treviso, Giotto's frescos at the Scrovegni Chapel in Padua, Palladio's often-rebuilt bridge at Bassano. We pick our way along the hairpin turns of Monte Grappa in the first range of the Alps. Of course, we take the train into Venice and revisit the Basilica, the Doge's Palace, the Accademia (ack-ah-DEH-mee-ah). I begin to think of the treasure trove of Carpaccio's huge canvases there as old friends. We board a vaporetto (motorboat-bus) to Torcello, where Venice was first settled sixteen hundred years ago, and we bathe in the Venetian sun-light reflected off the Adriatic waters to the east and the Alps to the northwest. No one has ever bested John Ruskin *(The Stones of Venice)* in describing the distant and mysterious silhouette of Venice viewed from Torcello.

> *Beyond the widening branches of the lagoon, and rising out of the bright lake in which they gather, there are a multitude of towers, dark, and scattered among square-set shapes of clustered palaces, a long and irregular line fretting the south-ern sky.*

Since we can't yet cook in our kitchen-in-progress, we have no choice but to sample restaurants of the region every evening. Carl will understand! So we're off to savor Venetan dishes at Da Barbesin, Due Mori, and Alla Torre in Castelfranco; Da Irene in Loreggia; Da Giovanni in Padua. But there's a danger in enjoying your food too much, I discover. I am so intensely devouring my *fegato alla veneziana*—calf's liver in the Venetian style, that is, with onions and parsley—outdoors at Alla Torre that I don't notice the meal that mosquitoes are making of my legs. When I crawl into bed that night, my legs look like swatches of dotted swiss.

Jim's social life is expanding like the universe in the seconds fol-lowing the big bang. With the kitchen now complete and our departure date on top of us, Jim begs to host a final dinner party at the villa for his new friends. My contribution is to cook two large pans of *lasagne* in my newly installed oven, toss a gigantic salad, and pick out dozens of *dolci* (sweets) from the *pasticceria* down the street. We set twelve places at the dining table. By 8:00 p.m. more than twenty friends have arrived. "You're an engineering student and you can't count?" I chide Jim, scrambling to find more plates. The young guests make quick work of all the *lasagne,* salad, bread, and *dolci,* and then move with equal speed through miscellaneous other things that I desperately turn up: pickles, olives, *grissini* (bread sticks), chocolates. There is lots of wine, also. Without exception the young people are friendly, well mannered, and garrulous. When the food has disappeared, they help clear the table and then wander amiably through the ground floor of the villa, admiring the frescos and architectural spaces. Finally they settle outdoors on the south portico to smoke (many of them) and talk. Jim seems to have no trouble with the language.

Jim and I wash dishes late into the night. We get to bed after 2:00 a.m. and rise at 5:00 a.m. to catch our early flight. We sleep all the way back to Atlanta.

I realize with a start that we are nearing our first anniversary of owning the villa. My mind fills with thoughts that I have pushed aside in the scurry and urgency of responding to everyday exigencies. I am reminded of the old bromide that we consume our lives with tasks of little importance but short deadlines, postponing more important matters that we convince ourselves can be done later.

Whatever brought you to buy a Palladian villa?

I am still hung up on that examination of the motives that brought me to my second life in Piombino Dese. Maybe my subconscious has been working on the problem while my conscious self has been focused on lawn mowers and kitchen appliances, because I have some new ideas now. I've gotten past the need to choose a single motivation from the grab bag of "second home" and "growth" and "escape" (and whatever else I might come up with). Now I can see that my motives are not static; all are true, just at different times and to different degrees.

I had indeed been seeking a second home for all the traditional reasons that drive city dwellers to acquire one: novelty, change of pace, relaxation, and the like. Many of our Atlanta friends seem to have preceded us in acquiring second homes on Georgia lakes or in the North Carolina mountains; some have moved farther afield to the Atlantic or Gulf coast, the western ski slopes, even Maine. My own background (and Carl's pleasure with the area) made New Hampshire a reasonable alternative.

But how much time would I have spent there in a year? One month, maybe six weeks? Probably something like that—certainly not four months. So why haven't I limited my Italian time to the same length? That, it seems, was a separate decision, but one that came so early and so easily that I never knew I was making it. Villa Cornaro is no New England lake home existing to serve my family during our holidays. Villa Cornaro is a force of nature, a vibrant personality in the lives of its owners, the farmers who till its fields, the students and researchers who study and measure its lines, the tourists excited by its spirit, the townspeople reassured by its constant presence.

My plans changed because I discovered that Villa Cornaro needs me.

15

Showtime

Since Wednesday, workers on the south steps of the villa have been banging away like frustrated drummers. They're building a huge temporary stage about four feet high overlooking the small park—about an acre—that we call our "backyard." On Thursday hundreds of folding chairs with cloth seats and backs were delivered to the side gate and other workers are setting them in rows facing the stage. The result is remarkably neat, considering how uneven the surface of the lawn has become through the years.

The electrician Giancarlo and his assistant are at work setting up and connecting spotlights and a control panel. (Giancarlo seems to have a monopoly on electrical work at the villa, based on the fact that he is the one who rewired it for Dick Rush and now no one else understands it.)

Saturday will be showtime! *Manifesti*—colorful posters—are on walls and shopwindows all through town. The event that brings so much excitement? A recital by Scuola di Danza di Castelfranco, a regional ballet school that holds its classes in Castelfranco, a much larger town and trading center lying seven miles northwest of Piombino Dese.

Now, on Friday morning, the whole troupe arrives in full dress for a brief rehearsal on the massive stage and a group photo on the villa's north steps. The dancers range from four-year-old large dolls, so left-footed I'm sure they'll find a way to trip over their own thigh-length tutus, all the way to a few late-teens whose concentration is already so intense and professional that they seem sulky and detached. There are a few males among them, but my whole attention is swallowed up by the craze of colors on the girls and young women flashing back and forth before me as they gaggle and chatter, then move from warm-ups to tentative twirling rushes across the stage.

I can sense a quiet, contented grin from my villa, that so much youth and vitality is still fascinated by its own centuries-old form and drawn to dance in its shadow.

Saturday dawns bright and sunny, perfect for the ballet that will begin at the traditional hour of nine in the evening. But Silvana wears a worried face when she arrives to open the *balcone*. Despite the splendid weather that the new morning has brought, the forecast is not good. I will not let an anonymous weatherman confound my own eyes, I tell her; my optimism is undiminished.

Piombino Dese bestrides an ancient Roman road in the Venetan plain midway between Venice on the Adriatic coast to the southeast and the Dolomite range of the Alps surging from the plain to the north and northwest. On a clear day, free of the haze and ozone that are more typical in the modern industrial era, I can stand on the north portico of the villa and see past the low line of foothills, where Asolo and the other hill towns nestle, deep into the Alps themselves, standing snow-covered all summer long. All *temporali*—storms—affecting the villa arise in the Alps and come down from the north. They have always done so. Palladio himself was well aware of the phenomenon; it led him cautiously to specify stone capitals for the columns of the villa's north porticos, even while he was experimenting with the exuberant free form of terra-cotta for the capitals of the less weathered south facade.

Shortly before lunch, Carl buzzes me on the intercom to suggest that I join him upstairs on the north portico. When I arrive, he directs my gaze northward toward the Alps. I have to agree that there is a distinct darkening in the sky along the peaks.

"There may be a storm building up, but it will never get here in time to ruin the recital," I insist.

"Maybe it will pass to the east or west," Carl says, but with less certainty. The mountain-bred storms of the Veneto are often violent, but they frequently follow a random path, so there is an element of chance in whether a particular storm sighted on the horizon will actually hit Piombino Dese.

By midafternoon the sky has darkened across the whole northern horizon, blocking all sight of the Alps, but the clouds are still far, far away. About six o'clock we hear a vague shudder from the distance that a pessimist might take to be thunder. An hour later the thunder has settled into a syncopated rhythm that cannot be denied. Flashes of light begin to cavort across the northern sky before falling to earth with a crash.

"I think it's slipping off east of us," I suggest bravely. Carl listens without comment.

The dancers and their parents begin to arrive at eight, but they show little enthusiasm for donning their costumes in the dressing rooms that have been provided in the *cantina.* Giancarlo and his assistant show much more energy in their rush to drape plastic sheets over all the electrical equipment in the backyard and secure the flaps with tape. The assistant ballet mistress, whom I discover to be an expatriate Englishwoman, and a tight knot of parents cluster on the north portico to watch the storm roiling across the sky just miles away. Its arms stretch around us to the east and west, and an early darkness envelops us.

I am not ready to surrender. "Maybe it will pass through before nine o'clock," I suggest hopefully.

Ballet students gather on the north steps
after a rehearsal

"No," the ballet mistress says. "Once the stage is wet, we won't
be able to dance on it. It wouldn't be safe for the dancers."

At precisely 8:40 the imps of hell are unleashed around us.
Sheets of rain and lightning, alternating with vast sound chambers
of thunder, strike with such fury that we are all surprised despite
having spent hours watching the storm's inexorable march across
the plain.

The storm rampages through half the night, but is followed by a
morning so brilliant it would challenge Titian himself to bring its
colors to a canvas. The sharp edges of the Alps are a glistening and
reproachful reminder of a world without smog. In our backyard the
dripping chairs and sodden stage sit sleepily under the slowly
warming sun. Gradually the heat lifts the water from the lawn and
the leaves of the trees, and the familiar rustle of wind through the
Lombardy poplars returns to wake the space.

The week passes quickly, all sunny and dry. Saturday arrives and the afternoon offers no hint of shadow in the northern sky. Giancarlo returns to strip the plastic from his spotlights. Finally the chattering dancers appear, happy now in the certainty that the show will go on. Carl and I watch in amazement as the crowd begins to pour through the front gate and flow in a swelling stream around the villa to the park. The chairs are soon filled, and still the throngs arrive. At half past nine, when the recital at last begins, there must be five hundred people gathered, a third of them standing.

The youngest children in their bright tutus are the biggest hit, but I am struck by the genuine talent of two of the teenage girls. A few years later I learn that the younger of the two, from a Piombino Dese family, has been recruited for the corps de ballet at La Scala in Milan, and that she has courageously accepted—a brave leap from the nest in family-centered Italy. (In fact, Piombino Dese must be a hotbed of terpsichorean talent: a son of a later *sindaco* now dances with the Rome ballet.)

In all, the recital is a great audience favorite, aided no doubt by the fact that so many of the spectators have relatives onstage. But there will be a long hiatus before the dancers return to Villa Cornaro. The expense of the project, as compounded by the rain delay, I am told, is more than the ballet school and its supporters can risk again without financial aid.

Several of our most vivid memories of villa life involve those same wild *temporali* that swoop in from the north at irregular intervals. I sometimes think I should name them individually, like hurricanes: Angelo, Bonifacio, Carlo, Davide, Epifanio. Our introduction to them comes early. During our first October stay at our new villa, while we are still learning the mysteries of the security systems that Giancarlo installed for Dick Rush, Carl and I settle in our upstairs bedroom at the west end of the villa for a sound sleep after a busy and happy day. The October air is chilly, but we've cocooned ourselves warmly. The *balcone* are tightly closed, of course, blocking out all light from the street and much of the sound. Suddenly, in the middle of the night, we are shocked awake by a one-two punch. First, a mighty clap of thunder explodes around the villa without warning. What can only be described as a stealth *temporale* has ambushed us! Then, as we sit rigidly upright in bed, our senses floundering for an explanation of the first crashing noise, we hear a new sound: a siren has begun to wail, loudly and nearby.

"That's the burglar alarm," Carl deduces at last. "The thunder set it off by rattling the windows." Reflexively, he leaps from bed, only to be confronted by three problems. First, he's completely underdressed for the temperature of the villa; second, the room is inky black and he can't find the light switch; and third, he has only the vaguest idea of where the burglar alarm controls are located, much less how to turn them off. By patting the wall frantically he at last locates the light switch several inches below the lowest point at which he thought it could possibly be. I gallantly find and hand him his summer bathrobe and send him shivering on his way down the circular wooden stair. We think the controls lie tucked away on a landing halfway between the ground floor and the *cantina*. Wishing him the best of luck, I immediately pop back into bed and pull up the covers.

Is it fair that Carl be sent off shivering into the night while I snuggle in bed? I ask myself. Of course it is, I respond. Who cooked dinner? Thunder hammers the villa, rain beats loudly against the *balcone*, and the burglar alarm strives to waken any neighbors whom the storm has left asleep. I now recall that the alarm system is also programmed to launch a series of three telephone calls immediately, first to the Miolos, then to the Battistons, who live next door, and finally to the local office of the carabinieri. I quickly review the possibilities. The Miolos, I am sure, will understand; I can explain it all to the Battistons in due course. But I am praying fervently that Carl finds the turnoff switch before the call is made to the carabinieri! I picture myself spending the rest of the night giving statements and filing official reports. Tension mounts. I conclude that Carl is lost, wandering around somewhere in the *cantina*. Suddenly, with all hope gone, the alarm ceases its wail, and Carl returns to bed triumphant, cold, and grumpy.

16

Gli Scquizzato

We do not meet the Scquizzatos all at once. We meet them at different times, in pairs or one at a time. The parents Memi and Francesca, a daughter, a suitor, a son, a daughter-in-law and her father and sisters, granddaughters, sisters and brothers, cousins of undefined distance. And one who looms largest in their own minds we never meet at all.

Memi is a short mass of a man. He would be called rotund if it weren't that all his bulk appears to be muscles built and tempered by a life of farmwork. Memi is an ebullient, gray-haired mesomorph, happy with life and dedicated to ensuring that everyone around him is also.

Memi is a major landowner with extensive acreage at the west edge of town, an unschooled man of assets and substance. His large henna-colored house sitting along Via Roma contains three commodious apartments: one for his son, Ottorino, Ottorino's wife, Michela, and their young daughters, Giulia and Elena; one for his bachelor brother, Livio; and one for himself, Francesca, and their daughter Wilma. Livio and Ottorino share in the farmwork.

During breaks in his farm routine, Memi bicycles slowly through Piombino Dese, ostensibly for exercise, but really for company and conversation. Occasionally he bicycles to our front gate bearing a large branch broken from one of his trees and clustered with dark crimson cherries; or he will have a bag of fresh eggs or a jar of golden peach *marmellata* that Francesca has just prepared. Memi and I have enthusiastic conversations despite the fact that I don't understand much of what he says. Memi is not troubled by petty differences between Italian and the Venetan dialect and doesn't see why anyone else would be. If it becomes clear that Carl or I will never understand some particular point he is trying to make, he moves easily to another subject, realizing that it is only the conversation that matters, not the content.

Memi always seats me beside himself at dinner, whether to give me a lesson in his Italian/Venetan amalgam or to pour me another glass of wine more easily—because I obviously enjoy his home-made wine almost as much as he does. The long dining table ends only a few feet away from Francesca's stoves, one oversize gas range and a smaller woodstove. Francesca continually jumps to her feet and turns to tend some pot, as she readies each course on a just-in-time basis that a Detroit automaker could be proud of. As the meal winds to an end, Memi becomes more and more agitated. He looks for ways to prolong the occasion. He might first amble from the room and return with cherries or peaches or some other fruit from his orchard. Later he appears with a box of chocolates that he has remembered. His resources nearing an end, he passes a bowl of hazelnuts from last season. Francesca, abetted by Wilma, comes to his aid with rounds of cheese, dessert, and coffee. Coffee without a sizable splash of grappa is just dishwater, Memi confides, as he struggles to overcome our stiff resistance to his jolting our coffee.

In appearance, Francesca contrasts dramatically with Memi. She is slim, with a light complexion. Her surprising blond hair is styl-ishly coiffed. Yet she is Memi's match in energy and hospitality. Moreover, Francesca is one of the best cooks I know, with her daughter Wilma a close contender. In all our many meals with the Scquizzatos, we've never been served the same dish twice. Almost everything Francesca cooks is produced on their farm: vegetables and fruits, chickens and eggs, pigs and goats, rabbits, guinea hens, and cows. As their granddaughters grow up, they even add three horses, not for future menus but for the girls' pleasure.

Livio is responsible for the enormous half barrels of raspberry rhododendrons and lollipop-pink hydrangeas in the flower gardens beside the house and near the street, where the family often eats al fresco on warm days when the number of guests would overflow the dining table indoors.

Several townspeople have told me the story of one memorable Sunday several years before Carl and I arrived in Piombino Dese. Francesca had prepared a lavish noontime dinner for forty or fifty relatives and friends to celebrate the First Communion of Giulia, their older granddaughter. Colorful tables sprouted in the garden among the flowerpots and rose beds, as the massive crowd passed the huge serving bowls Francesca had prepared. Following coffee and dessert, an unknown man and woman emerged from the crowd to ask for the cashier, so they could pay their bill. Inquiry disclosed that the strangers had parked their car on Via Roma, entered the garden, and sat down after spying the crowd, which they thought to be a sure sign of a great restaurant. They had been served without hesitation.

No one has told me Memi's or Francesca's reaction to the discov-

The Scquizzatos, with Sally, dining at Villa Cornaro
(l) Wilma, Memi; (r) Michela, Francesca

ery of the interlopers. I imagine that Memi's first thought would be to check whether the strangers would like a final grappa before departing.

At first, we do not meet their son Ottorino. Ottorino is a member of the town council and a political ally of the *sindaco*. Yes, the same mayor whose devious idea of placing a public sports field behind Villa Cornaro had been thwarted only by the combined efforts of Dick Rush, the local farmers, and officials in Rome. For political reasons, Ottorino several years earlier stopped joining his family when the Rushes invited them to the villa, even though his parents were the Rushes' closest friends in town. Ottorino's boycott of the villa continues even after our succession to ownership. Soon, however, Carl's peace offensive with the *sindaco* frees Ottorino to rejoin the social program. Later, when the vicissitudes of small-town politics bring the mayor defeat at the polls, who is to succeed him? Ottorino Scquizzato!

Ottorino inherits a taller version of his father's build. His wife Michela, on the other hand, is a slim, elegant whippet of a woman. Michela is always impeccably dressed, bringing to her "business-casual" outfits a chic that defies the category. Improbably, this wife of a small-town politician-farmer is a globe-trotting multinational business executive. Her fast-growing family-owned business, Tasca Abbigliamenti—a prosperous women's apparel manufacturer—may be even more improbable. It is entirely managed by five sisters, who all thrive in a brutally competitive field.

Carl and I watch Michela's skills expand as she gains experience. When we first meet, Michela's father is still active in the business he founded, but he is reducing his day-to-day involvement. Italy has a particularly male-dominated business world, and I can only speculate at his thoughts as he fathered five consecutive daughters, followed at last by a single son. In fact, he seems to have reacted much the way my own father did when faced by three daughters: He taught us to fish and hunt.

Michela, the oldest, obtains her university degree in economics and begins working in Tasca's administration. Her sister Daria is sent to fashion-design school in Italy and in New York so she can step in as the firm's chief designer. The other daughters are trained for roles in operations.

We sometimes talk with Michela about her business exploits. For Carl, this satisfies two needs: He gets to talk business, and he gets to do it in English. Michela's English is hesitant in our early years but steadily improves as her international responsibilities grow. On one early occasion, Michela proudly shows us through Tasca's sprawling manufacturing plant, situated between Asolo and Bassano. She points to the advanced new cutting tables where computer-driven cutters simultaneously produce pieces for hundreds of garments. She explains how computer programs shuffle and fit the various individual pieces of a garment to leave the least scrap, while at the same time keeping essential pieces properly aligned with the direction of the fabric. Carl is impressed by the capital investment that all the new equipment reflects.

As we return to Piombino Dese each year, we get fresh reports from Michela or, more often, her mother-in-law, Francesca, who becomes one of my closest friends. Michela's father has retired; Tasca has launched a sewing operation in Hungary; the queen of Spain has bought several Tasca dresses in Madrid; Michela has returned from China, where she is also setting up sewing operations; Tasca has opened a factory outlet in nearby Cavaso del Tomba.

Did she say factory outlet? I never pass up an outlet store; a New England gene prevents it.

"Orange? Oh, I don't think so! I could never wear orange!"

Daria merely smiles and waves the brilliant suit before my dazzled eyes the way the snake must have brandished the apple before Eve.

"You will be surprised, Signora Sally. Orange is perfect for you. You should just try it on."

Couturier wonderland! The new Tasca outlet is a treasure-house, I discover, but Michela leaves nothing to chance. Alerted by

Francesca, she is there to greet me personally when I arrive with Carl in tow. Then Michela springs her surprise: she has brought her sister Daria, the chief designer of the whole company. I feel like the Duchess of Windsor with Christian Dior hovering about.

"Purple? Daria, maybe that's a bit too strong for me," I suggest tentatively as another confection is waved before me.

Daria is holding a bright green dress highlighted with huge purple circles. The green tone tends toward the blue side of the spectrum, rather than yellow, the neckline swoops low, and the waist is encircled by a lavender cummerbund-like invention. Does she think I'm eighteen?

"All you'll need is purple shoes," Daria assures me. "Here's a handbag that will go perfectly. Just try it on, Signora Sally. These are just dresses for you to try on."

Daria plants me at an enormous mirror outside a trio of dressing rooms. The bars are draped in a myriad of styles and a rainbow of colors that she has collected from racks around the cavernous room. "Rainbow" isn't exactly the word; there are no pastels here. Everything has deep, strong hues to complement the complexion and dark hair of Italian women. Casting my eyes around, I see few black dresses and not a single white one.

Daria continues to flit about like a hummingbird, returning with the most unlikely combinations. She holds each garment up before my face and makes a lightning decision about whether to recommend it. I've never dressed and undressed so much in thirty minutes in my life, and I've never enjoyed myself so much while shopping. Even my happiest moments among the racks at Marshall's or Macy's don't compare. Daria is a magician, producing one new effect after another.

My only restraint is the specter of having to pack all my purchases in suitcases that were already full when I arrived in Italy. Reluctantly, I decide on the items I can't live without. Yes, the orange suit and the green-and-purple dress are among them. (They are my favorites.)

17

A Wedding and a Funeral

I first hear of Stefania Scquizzato several months before we arrive at Villa Cornaro as the new owners. Dick and Julie Rush want us to know that they have agreed to allow Stefania's wedding reception to be held at the villa just two weeks before we are to arrive, in the ambiguous period when we are technically owners of the villa but subject to having it bought away from us by the Italian government.

Stefania is the youngest child of Memi and Francesca Scquizzato, the sister of Ottorino and Wilma. Carl and I know nothing of the Scquizzatos at that time, of course. Stefania is a marvel, we are told—a beauty and a scholar, already with her degree from the university at Venice, just returned from an assignment as interpreter on a long, high-profile mission to China, now on the eve of her marriage to a young man whom the Rushes have met and admire. Ottorino and Wilma are clearly in the shade of their sister Stefania's bright sun.

The wedding never occurs. Carl and I never meet Stefania. She dies mysteriously in the hospital at nearby Camposampiero ten days before her wedding date and is buried in the parish cemetery in the gown she would have worn as a bride.

Stefania entered the hospital because of recurring symptoms of a virus she contracted in China. The family at first believed that the virus caused Stefania's death. In later years, a new story emerges, that she died because a hospital nurse carelessly injected air bubbles into her veins while administering an antibiotic.

As I come to know the Scquizzato family, I meet Stefania's fiancé, Mario, who haunts the Scquizzato home to share their grief. His countenance is so mournful and bereft he resembles a Saint Sebastian escaped from a sculptor's studio. After several years, his visits become less frequent. Finally, they cease altogether. He has a new *fidanzata,* Wilma says, one who does not wish to share him with a dead bride.

18

A Bright Idea

Carl is never sympathetic when I tell him I would like to go back in time and spend one day in mid-sixteenth-century Italy to see what life was like when the villa was built. He's convinced that he would turn up as a subsistence farmer, like most of his ancestors in America, so he never participates in my what-if scenarios.

I like to imagine that I am there in 1551 when Palladio first meets with the grand Venetian lord Giorgio Cornaro to discuss building a villa for him in Piombino. The Cornaros had cut a wide path in Venice ever since the city was organized some nine hundred years earlier—always rich, always involved in the top leadership, always fighting somewhere along the shore of the eastern Mediterranean to extend the Venetian empire. Giorgio's great-grandmother was a granddaughter of the emperor of Trebizond, the last remnant of the Roman Empire; his great-aunt was the queen of Cyprus. As they might say in thoroughbred breeding, you don't get better lines than that.

Did Giorgio regard Palladio with suspicion? After all, Giorgio knew perfectly well that "Palladio" wasn't even the man's real name. When he was born in Padua, his parents named him Andrea (ahn-DRAY-ah). There were a lot of Andreas around, so he was referred to as Andrea di Pietro della Gondola, that is, "Andrea, the son of Peter of the gondola." *Note to diary: Peter was a miller or a millstone maker; how does a gondola get in the picture?* Since branches of the Cornaro family were everywhere and knew everything, Giorgio was probably also aware that Andrea had made a bad start, careerwise. He began as apprentice to a stonecutter in Padua, a mainland city under Venetian control, when he was thirteen. Something went wrong, though, because he broke his contract after just three years and fled to Vicenza, a neighboring town still within Venetian territory.

Think of a man standing atop the city wall of Vicenza, watching this runaway approach from the distance, probably carrying some clothes slung over his shoulder in a sack. Would that observer ever have imagined that the arrival of the young man was one of the most important events in the history of the city, that the youth's name (or the name he was going to assume) would become synonymous with the city and ensure its fame for centuries?

I like to think that Giorgio Cornaro *did* see that future in Palladio when they met in Piombino. He knew that Palladio was still a provincial artisan, but he was a provincial who was attracting increasingly important sponsorship. About fifteen years earlier, while Andrea was still a stonecutter, his abilities caught the eye of Gian Giorgio Trissino, a provincial nobleman of Vicenza. Trissino was a wealthy dilettante architect and poet. Palladio probably came to his attention while working on a renovation that Trissino had under way at his house outside Vicenza. Trissino took Palladio to Rome several times, so Palladio became acquainted with both the ruins of Rome from classical times and the new Renaissance derivatives coming from men like Raphael and Michelangelo. It was Trissino who decided that his protégé needed a snappier name and came up with "Palladio" to suggest Pallas Athene, the Greek goddess of wisdom.

The meeting between Cornaro and Palladio in Piombino may not have been their first encounter. Trissino had spent a long sojourn in Padua in 1538–1541, maybe taking Palladio with him for part of his stay. In Padua, which was a university town, Trissino and Palladio probably spent time in the circle of Alvise Cornaro, a distant cousin of Giorgio. Alvise was a bit of a hustler, but like Trissino he was a great promoter and patron of the new Renaissance ideas in architecture. Giorgio Cornaro was living in Padua at that time, because his father was serving a term as Venice's *capitano*—military commander—for the city. So it is easy to speculate that all of them might have been introduced in Padua years earlier.

In any event, whether old friends or strangers when they meet in Piombino, Giorgio Cornaro and Palladio each need something important from the other. Palladio is trying to break into the rich circle of Venetian patrons. They have bigger pocketbooks than the provincial patrons around Vicenza who have primarily sustained him in the past, and working for them would bring a lot more prestige. Giorgio Cornaro would be a big catch.

Giorgio needs something from Palladio also. When Giorgio's father died a year earlier, in February 1550, the big family villa in Piombino—just twelve years old—was inherited by Giorgio's older brother. Giorgio inherited half of the plantation, but without anyplace on it to live. He needs a new villa urgently because he will soon marry Elena Contarini, sister of the bishop of Padua.

I can picture Palladio pacing the building site with Giorgio. Palladio has a worried look. This could be his chance to make a real mark among the Venetian grandees, but the site is impossible. On one side looms the big villa that Giorgio's brother has inherited. Michele Sanmicheli designed it. Sanmicheli was Venice's official architect for military structures—forts, gates, and the like—and one of its leading civil architects as well. If you're going to design a villa to stand just 70 feet away from one that Sanmicheli has done, you had better be very careful that yours does not look second-best.

Sanmicheli is not Palladio's only problem. On the other side of the building site stands an enormous old *barchessa*, or farm building, stretching 190 feet to the west.

Palladio swallows hard and tries to put a good face on things. "This will work perfectly. All we have to do is tear down that old *barchessa*," he says confidently.

"Impossible," Giorgio replies. "We need that for the farmwork. I can't interrupt that."

Palladio paces the site some more, shaking his head.

"Well," he says cautiously, "maybe there is another site on the plantation that we can use for the villa."

"It has to sit here," Giorgio states emphatically. "This is the only frontage on Via Castellana that I could squeeze out of my arrogant brother, and I'll be damned if I'm going to let him force me to live down some country lane!"

That's the way I imagine them talking. Maybe I saw too many movies as a child.

More pacing, more head shaking.

"In that case, we'll have to build something really tall," Palladio says pensively. "Really, really tall."

Giorgio nods as Palladio speaks, but he doesn't comment.

"And the grain will have to be stored in the attic, with the wine-making in the *cantina*," Palladio concludes.

Giorgio agrees to the concept.

I imagine I can detect a satisfied smile on Palladio's face despite his efforts to hide it. I feel like patting him on the back.

I've always wanted to build something really tall, he seems to be thinking, and I've got a dynamite idea of how to do it.

In my imagination that is how Palladio came up with Villa Cornaro's unique innovation: the projecting double portico on the villa's north facade. The double portico—that is, a porch with classical columns sitting on top of a second porch with classical columns—was his answer to the height problem. If Palladio had still been just a beginner at architecture, he might have thrown up a tall flat wall with three round-top openings cut into it for an entrance. That's what he did at Villa Godi, his first villa, twelve years earlier. But the result there looks just a bit like a fortress. The double portico at Villa Cornaro gives the whole face of the villa a warm, inviting look. It's functional, too, a sheltered space in which to sit protected from the sun or rain and either supervise the farm-work or enjoy the outdoors. Palladio used the double portico motif on both the north and south facades of the villa. He also used it on one facade at two other projects, Villa Pisani at Montagnana and

Villa Cornaro—north facade, with projecting double portico

Palazzo Antonini at Udine. In other words, it is not the double portico motif itself that is unique to Villa Cornaro.

What is unique at Villa Cornaro is a special feature that Palladio added to the double portico on the north side of the villa. He did not leave the double portico nested within the central core of the villa, which is the way he used it on the south facade and at the other two examples. Instead, he pushed the whole structure out from the villa, so that the double portico projects out into the garden. It sounds like a small change, but the effect is dramatic when you stand in the two spaces and compare them. The south portico, the one sitting within the core of the villa, feels like a room of the villa with a big picture window on one side. The projecting double por-

Villa Cornaro—south facade, with recessed double portico

tico on the north side gives a completely different feeling. When you stand on it, you feel that you're a part of the outdoors, with the garden all around you.

The projecting double portico is what has made Villa Cornaro so widely copied. The earliest surviving example in the United States is Drayton Hall, a plantation house built about 1740 outside Charleston, South Carolina, Carl's hometown. *Note to diary: Coincidence?* Some other well-known copies of the projecting double portico are at Shirley Plantation in Virginia and the Miles Brewton house, also in Charleston. The feature was probably added to these last two in the late 1700s, some years after the original structures were built.

Thomas Jefferson liked the projecting double portico. In fact, he built a projecting double portico at Monticello. Jefferson was fickle, though. Later, when he was living in Paris as American ambassador to France, he watched in fascination as the Hôtel de Salm (now the French Legion of Honor headquarters, next door to Musée d'Orsay) was built nearby, and capped by a dome inspired by another of Palladio's villas, La Rotonda. As soon as he returned to Virginia, Jefferson began tearing out the upstairs portion of Monticello, enlarging it and adding a dome to create the famous look that appears on the nickel. Jefferson's second version left no sign of his home's Villa Cornaro origins.

19

Market Day

"How will you cook those swordfish steaks?" I ask. "*Alla griglia? On the grill?*"

It's Saturday, market day in Piombino Dese. Carl and I stand at the fish counter—actually a Mercedes truck whose side panel is lifted to reveal a rolling fish market.

The genial, middle-aged stranger ahead of us orders enough swordfish for a family of fifty. He must know a lot about swordfish, I decide, and his friendly smile invites my question about cooking them. He immediately outlines for me not one but three recipes. I decide to try the top-of-the-stove one:

Place $1/_2$-inch-thick swordfish steaks in a frying pan. Pour over them a separately prepared mixture of a little vegetable oil, a little white wine, a touch of salt, two small tomatoes (chopped), and a little chopped basil. Simmer for ten minutes. *Delizioso!*

The gentleman doesn't stop with swordfish. Looking at the shipment of halibut fillets on display at the counter, he launches into a *ricetta straordinaria*—superb recipe—for them as well. He continues chattering about a rather complicated recipe for *coda di rospo* (tail of monkfish) while the fishmonger is preparing his order: a dozen swordfish steaks, half a dozen large crayfish, a kilo of bright pink shrimp.

My culinary consultant introduces himself and pulls out his business card. He lives in Piombino Dese, but we haven't met before because he travels on business much of the time in southern Italy, he explains. "Puglia, Bari, Basilicata . . ."

"Ah, Basilicata," I interject. "I've just begun reading Carlo Levi's *Cristo si è fermato a Eboli*. What a poor area!"

"Yes," he agrees, "but so very beautiful, a magnificent wilderness in Italy."

As he gathers his purchases to depart, I ask him if he is an amateur cook, since he's given me so many different recipes.

"Ah, no." He smiles. "*Non sono un cuoco, sono un mangiatore!* I'm not a cook, I'm a big eater!"

Market day is a delightful anachronism.

Piombino Dese's market day was sanctioned by a government decree in 1790 and continues to recur every Saturday. Different towns have their markets on different days. Well before Silvana arrives to open the *balcone* on Saturday morning, a garden of tents sprouts on the piazza opposite the villa and on two piazzas in the next block. Bright awnings burst forth like exuberant petals: large green-and-white stripes, sun-bleached red-and-white thinner stripes, tiny blue-and-white checks, broad orange and white swaths. Stalls erupt with pale melons, fuzzy kiwis, dull-red apples, smooth green pears, tiny green beans, tomatoes long and thin or tiny and round, eggplants a gorgeous deep shiny purple-brown waiting to be broiled in very thin slices and topped with Parmesan to make me dream of heaven. Other stands overflow with huge hanging prosciutto hams, long rosy-gray bundles of salami, all shapes and types of cheeses, some round and fat and deep yellow, others fist-size and white, the *bufala* mozzarella in wet packets concealing their delicate-textured taste, destined to combine with sweet tomatoes and freshly picked basil as a dish for deities. One movable feast of a truck roasts chickens and pork on the spot for immediate eating, enveloping the piazza in delectable aromas. Smiling Venetans vie for my business with waving arms. "*Molto buono! Molto fresco!*" they cry.

As I wander past the fish truck, a long black eel wriggles from a knot of eels squirming in a square basin set under running water. He flops over the lip of the basin and falls to the ground. Unnoticed at first, he slithers along the gutter like a convict who has gone over the wall at Alcatraz. Alas, just inches short of the drain grate that he has targeted as his escape hatch, he is apprehended by the burly fishmonger and dumped back in the basin.

Bras and panties hang from other booths; belts and shoes of all colors are spread for display. I buy two wonderful undershirts layered with cotton inside and wool outside, knowing the late autumn days of the Veneto can be savagely cold. Sheets and towels flutter like flags; there are tablecloths and kitchen tools, bolts of cloth, and huge boxes of threads—even sewing machines! Dresses, shirts, and trousers hang enticingly, handsome but often cheaply made and priced accordingly. A clever shopper can quickly assemble a new ensemble of sweater, skirt, and sandals, all from different stalls. Other vendors offer a hothouse of flowers and shrubs.

The food, the dry goods, the sewing machines—all these items are now available in local stores open every day of the week. Although some of the produce may be slightly fresher than what I buy at the Battistons' *supermercato,* much of it is not. Once, in unpacking my market purchases in the villa's kitchen, I find the tomatoes chilled from refrigeration, and the date on the container of tiny shrimp no more current than that on containers at the *supermercato.*

But the *supermercato* is all about efficiency: you enter, select, pay, leave. Missing is the grand social convocation of the weekly market, where 90 percent of the town's citizens spend several hours chatting, gossiping, parading, strutting. I am reminded of the occasional town meetings in my native New Hampshire, but the mar-

Market Day awnings fill Piazzetta Squizzato north of the villa

ket is weekly and without any agenda at all. The Piombinesi discuss their aunt's latest operation, their daughter's *fidanzato*, the cabinet members of the current government, the latest execution of a criminal in America, *burrata* mozzarella, a good recipe for swordfish. They are well dressed, well coiffed, happy to be alive—and especially happy to be living in Italy.

So the market days may continue for decades in the future, wholly without economic justification, redundant of more logical and less labor-intensive distribution systems. They exist as a social mechanism, for their charm and their tradition. For Americans, the market is an anachronism, something out of place and time. Our insistent search for the "next new thing" means we find the past irrelevant to our lives. For Italians, the market is not an anachronism. It is a warm, vital part of their lives, old-fashioned but loved for that very reason. The market connects them with their families, their fellow townspeople, and their past. The weekly ceremony brings rhythm, structure, and sense to their lives.

Perhaps the anachronism lies in America, in neighborhoods seeking to thrive without community and without the past.

20

Searching for Context

In my conversations with Dick Rush, he seems to view Villa Cornaro as an object of art existing alone in space—free from its surroundings, from its history, from the families who built it and cherished it, maintained and changed it for almost half a millennium. Dick is an art expert, which neither Carl nor I will ever be, so that may account for the difference in our feeling about the villa. We decide right away that we will never understand the villa except as a home, lodged in its history and the people who surround it now and did so in its past.

We are on the road! In our pathetically cramped, hot, underpowered, and overpriced rental car ("This model should be called the Fiat Furnace," Carl says), we're off to little towns with grand country palaces: to nearby Maser to see Villa Barbaro and to Fanzolo for Villa Emo; then farther afield for Villa Foscari (known inexplicably as "La Malcontenta") at Gambarare on the Brenta River near the lagoon of Venice; and, finally, Villa Almerico ("La Rotonda") on the outskirts of Vicenza, Palladio's adopted hometown. We are trying to arrive at our own conception of where Villa Cornaro sits in this pantheon of Palladian icons. About eighteen Palladio-designed villas still stand in the Veneto, the number depending on how you count a few whose connection with Palladio is doubtful or where changes through the centuries are so great that little of Palladio is left. We decide that Barbaro, Emo, La Malcontenta, and La Rotonda, together with Cornaro, constitute a sort of "Big Five." They are all large villas designed (except La Rotonda) for wealthy Venetian patrons; they were built substantially the way Palladio designed them; and they have not suffered fundamental changes since. So these are the ones we set off to see first. We are on the lookout for contrasts and similarities to our own villa.

Our plan almost drowns in a sea of frustration. We begin charging along the back roads of the Venetan countryside with brash assurance, soon slowing to confused bewilderment at the lack of signs on some roads and the cryptic markings on others. Finally we are reduced to the hesitant creep that is recognized worldwide as the desperate mark of the hopelessly lost. We avoid blaming each other for being lost only because there are so many other targets conveniently at hand. We begin with the roads themselves and move on to the maps we are using, the dearth of numbered routes, the Italian system of marking roads with signs that simply point randomly to nearby or distant cities ("They must teach geography in driving school," Carl grumbles), and drivers who object noisily to our stopping in the middle of an intersection to compare the directional markers with the array of towns on our map. Gradually we derive some lessons. Most useful is the realization that a large sign pointing to the right and reading, for example, "Vicenza" does not mean that the next right turn takes you to Vicenza. Only a

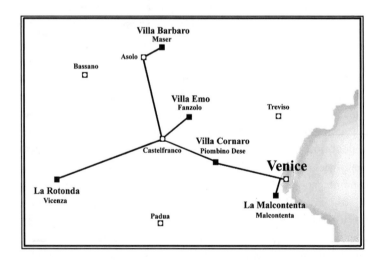

Map of five major Palladian villas
fanned across the Venetan plain west of Venice

tourist would have such a misconception, as we learned on one occasion when—Vicenza-bound—we found ourselves sitting in the midst of a rail yard surrounded by locomotives and tank cars. Such a sign actually means that somewhere in the next half mile, among the several roads to the right, is one leading to Vicenza.

"A learning experience," we assure each other, secretly happy to be in Italy on a sunny day with a pleasant mission and no fixed schedule for achieving it.

Slowly but inexorably we find all four of the villas we are seeking. The route to Villa Emo at Fanzolo seems especially circuitous, with left turns and right turns on narrow country lanes crisscrossing through miles of fields planted in corn, grain, potatoes, and beans. Only several years and a dozen visits later do we learn that there are at least two other easy, direct routes to Villa Emo. The fact that four of the five villas were built for the nobility of Venice itself—rather than for the provincial nobles of Vicenza who supported Palladio's early career—is not coincidental. (La Rotonda was built by a wealthy churchman of Vicenza, newly returned from Rome, not as a villa but as an entertainment palace in the suburban countryside.) The Venetians did not merely have bigger resources and bigger ambitions; they may have been more desperate as well. The Ottoman Turks were methodically cutting off all of Venice's contacts with the eastern Mediterranean, where the Venetian families had made their fortunes in trade and, in a few cases like the Cornaro family, in vast plantations. The Venetian families were trying to find a new harbor in which to anchor their fortunes. Plantations on the mainland—each centered on a villa—seemed like their best bet, especially because the countryside had been relatively peaceful for thirty-five years or more since Venice's disastrous War of the League of Cambrai and because of the discovery of corn in the New World. The yield from corn was six to seven times greater than the yields obtained from earlier grain crops such as millet. With so much of the families' assets newly committed to the big new plantations on the mainland, the owners found it prudent to be present on site from the planting each spring through to harvesttime, sometimes with a side trip to the Dolomites in mid-summer. That process of coming out from Venice each spring and returning in the fall is what gave rise to the *villa*—country palace—phenomenon in the sixteenth century. The prosperous Venetians wanted something of the elegance of their Venetian palaces but with less expense.

Some of the prominent Venetian architects had tried their hand at it before Palladio. One of the earliest results was Villa Giustinian at Roncade, designed in the early 1500s by Pietro Lombardo, still in the Gothic spirit with a floor plan reminiscent of the palaces in Venice. Jacopo Sansovino, Venice's leading architect in the second quarter of the 1500s, weighed in with Villa Garzoni at Pontecasale, and Michele Sanmicheli designed the first Cornaro villa at Piombino, the one that bedeviled Palladio when he began designing our own Villa Cornaro twelve years later. In other words, as Palladio moved into the thirty-year period when he would create his Big Five, he was burdened by relatively few precedents. He did not have to displace some earlier, widely accepted style for villas in order to establish his own paradigm, the look and principles that became known as Palladianism.

Villa Barbaro and Villa Emo both demonstrate one of Palladio's favorite looks. He starts with the family's residence as a tall block in the center. Then he attaches long, low *barchesse* symmetrically to the left and right. The *barchesse* are faced with repeated arches, forming a loggia. La Malcontenta was designed in this same manner, although the *barchesse* were never built. At Barbaro and Emo, Palladio added one more effect: at the far end of each *barchessa* he built a dovecote on top. The overall result is called the "five-part profile" because of the five different segments of roofline that it produces: the two dovecotes and two *barchesse* with the residential core in the middle. Palladio's symmetrical five-part profile is one of the most influential and ubiquitous designs in all of architecture. For Americans, the Capitol in Washington, D.C., is the best example. The domed center of the Capitol is analogous to the residential core at Barbaro and Maser, the Senate and the House of Representatives are the dovecotes, and the connecting segments are the *barchesse*. At the other end of the grandeur scale, almost every residential area has at least one house with a five-part profile. Usually a garage at one end stands in place of a dovecote, sometimes connected by a breezeway that recalls a *barchessa*.

La Malcontenta's most influential feature arose from its site, just as the double projecting portico did at Villa Cornaro. La Malcontenta sits on the banks of the Brenta River. The frequent floods of the Brenta required Palladio to raise the villa's *piano nobile* (principal floor) high above the floodplain. To disguise the length of the stair needed in order to reach the *piano nobile,* he placed it *beside* the projecting front portico—instead of leaving it in front—and divided the stair into two flights at right angles to each other. Because Palladio could never abide anything that was not symmetrical, he placed a matching stair on the opposite side. The result is one of the emblematic motifs of later Georgian architecture.

The principal architectural heritage of hilltop La Rotonda, of course, springs from its great dome surrounded by identical porticos on all four facades. Itself inspired by the second-century Pantheon in Rome, La Rotonda can be seen as a major source for every later building constructed with a dome over classical columns.

Why stop with a Big Five? Why not a Big Seven? Villa Poiana and Villa Badoer also have influential motifs. Maybe the only rational stopping point is a Big Eighteen.

21

Unexplored Boxes

In an early conversation, Doug Lewis mentioned that the archives of the Museo Correr in Venice hold *hundreds and hundreds* of boxes of original Cornaro family documents relating to the family's properties in Piombino Dese and elsewhere on the mainland. Those documents were the principal source for the manuscript Doug wrote about the villa twenty-five years ago.

"Did you actually read all those files?" Carl asked.

"That would take a lifetime," Doug replied.

I am haunted by the vision of those unexplored boxes. Uncovering the secrets in each of them becomes an insistent refrain in my mind. Everyday operations of the house are proceeding smoothly: the kitchen functions well, the Miolos take care of tour groups when I'm tied up or not at home, and Ilario tends the garden. The day after Carl departs for Atlanta in late May, I hop the early-morning train for Venice.

As Edgar Allan Poe suggests in "The Purloined Letter," sometimes things are best hidden in plain sight. The Museo Correr demonstrates the principle: a gem of Venice hidden in one of its most crowded spots, the Piazza di San Marco. For Carl and me the museum is a favorite destination because it showcases treasures from the long, glittering history of the Venetian Republic: enormous battle flags flown from the prows of triremes during desperate engagements with the Turks, wall-size canvases depicting storied events such as Queen Caterina Cornaro's arrival in Venice for the transfer of Cyprus to the republic in 1489, a pair of seventeenth-century shoes exactly like some drawn on the attic walls of our villa. All this is housed on the second floor of the Procuratie Nuove, the long, low building designed by Vincenzo Scamozzi that runs along the entire south side of the trapezoidal piazza, and of the adjacent building at the west end of the piazza, constructed by the French after Venice's fall to Napoléon's forces in 1797. Tourists who focus on the dramatic attractions at the east end of the piazza—the Basilica, the Campanile, the Loggetta, the Doge's Palace, the Clock Tower—easily overlook the elegant entranceway to the museum, which opens off a passageway in the Napoleonic structure.

The entrance to the museum's archives and research library is even more obscure. After many requests for directions, I find an arched passage midway along the Procuratie Nuove and cautiously stroll through it into an interior courtyard. A flight of stairs leads me to an elevator, which chugs upward to the card-catalogue room, a cramped, poorly lit space with antiquated metal cabinets. A genial middle-aged man inspects my business card, passport, and driver's license, and grants ad hoc permission to use the library; an official card will be mailed to me in Piombino Dese.

For one week I peruse the catalogue and order intriguing items from storage. I am soon convinced that—aside from Douglas Lewis or some few foreign scholars like him—only an Italian with fabulous eyesight, great intuitive abilities, and deep knowledge of Venetan and Latin and sixteenth-century Italian will succeed in gleaning the Cornaro family secrets.

The first problem is the fertility of the Cornaros. There are hundreds of entries under "Corner," the original Venetan form of the Italian name Cornaro; without a knowledge of the family tree, I'm lost in distinguishing one Giorgio ("Zorzi" in Venetan) from another. There are literally dozens of Giorgios, and equal numbers of Marcos, Giacomos, and Giovannis. Second, the card catalogue often only hints at the nature of the documents described. One typical "Cornaro" card, for instance, reads:

Fascicolo relativo alla gestione dei beni della . . . a Piombino (Treviso) 1737–1767. cart. Mss. PD C.2677/I.

To my untrained eye, this merely indicates unspecified miscellaneous documents about the administration of the estate at Piombino during the thirty years from 1737 to 1767, gathered in a carton numbered 2677.

Another "Cornaro" card reads:

Fascicolo relativo al patrimonio di . . . (acquisti, divisioni, permute, vendite, livelli, etc.) 1578–1648. cart. Mss. PD C.2611/3.

This, I infer, is a bundle of documents relating to acquisitions, territorial divisions, exchanges, sales, and leases of family property over the seventy-year period from 1578 to 1648. The brevity of these descriptions suggests that only the most cursory study of each box's contents was made; any one of the documents might hide something important about the villa during the period when its construction was finally completed. More obstacles block the way. Even if the polyglot of languages and arcane vocabulary is conquered, the early handwriting itself is often indecipherable. Moreover, many items I request cannot be found by the library assistants; they're not "lost," they simply "cannot be found." Perhaps they are misfiled, or simply buried out of sight beneath another box. Infinite patience is required as well; the time for hunting a particular cache of documents can sometimes stretch to two hours—which might end with a "cannot be found" report.

But occasionally true gold sparkles from the page. A young library assistant places before me the original account book of Villa Cornaro from 1553 to 1555—the very pages penned by Giorgio Cornaro and his estate manager during the specific years that the villa was being built. Adrenaline jolts all my limbs when I see it; I can imagine my normally straight hair drawing up in a curly halo. The first two pages seem to list the tenant farmers and employees of the estate, along with a page number for their individual accounts. Subsequent pages begin with a date, then list expenses incurred for the villa on that date, not just construction costs such as lumber and nails, but food costs for the kitchen as well. I struggle to understand the scribbles and only partially succeed:

Cassa alincontro di haver adi 14 febbraio 1554 per la venuta
del Illustrissimo [——] da Treviso [——] per la cena

per carne di vitello	*L 5*
per una raina peso [——]	*L 2 D 10*
per [——] per la tavola	*L 1 D 20*
per nolo de do cavalli per andar a Piombino	*L 2 D 8*

> *per cinque galline quattro me costa* D 40
> *e una pola costa* D 8

I conclude these are expenses incurred for a special dinner (*cena*) for a most illustrious (*Illustrissimo*) gentleman from Treviso whose name I cannot read. The expenses are for veal (*carne di vitello*), for a carp (*raina*) weighing an amount I cannot decipher, for something (flowers? wine? linen?) for the table (*tavola*), for the hiring of two horses (*cavalli*) to go to Piombino, for five hens (*galline*), four of which cost D 40 and one of which cost only D 8. *Haver* is an archaic form of the modern Italian *avere* (to have); *nolo* is a shortened version of *noleggiare* (to rent); *do* is the Venetan form of *due* (two).

There are numerous entries on other pages for Giorgio's falconers, for dinner guests, for chickens—clearly a staple of the mid-sixteenth-century diet. Covering just three years, 246 pages speak of the husbandry of the villa's first proprietor. He accounts for every type of expense, just as I try to today; my Quicken computer program would have been a big help to him—and solved the handwriting problem for me as well. Clearly I must study this early record more thoroughly, so I ask the attendant to copy it for me. He promises to do so, but regrets it will take at least a month; he'll mail the copy to me in Atlanta.

The copy arrives as promised and is now one of my treasures. But when I return to the archives on a later trip and ask to see the original, my request is returned with the notation "cannot be found." *Note to diary: I wonder if they looked around the photocopy machine?*

Since an understanding of the Cornaro genealogy seems to be an essential foundation, I move to a smaller adjoining room lined with books of genealogy and local history. Awaiting me here is Marco Barbaro's massive fifteenth-century compendium *Discendenze Patrizie*, with eighteenth-century annotations by Emmanuele Antonio Cicogna. This, I later learn, is a fountainhead of Venetian genealogy. One entire volume is devoted to multiple branches of

Cornaros, some connected and some not. The data are presented in page after page of charts, with many entries footnoted. There is a mass of information, but not in a form that is easily penetrated. I order a photocopy of this as well, confident that Carl can make sense of it all by plugging the data into the genealogy program he has on his computer. Later, we are able to match disparate Barbaro data on our computer, which provides interesting insights into marriages between different branches of the Cornaro family. While entering the data on his computer, Carl learns from Doug Lewis that there are biographies of many Cornaros in the mammoth, multivolume *Dizionario Biografico degli Italiani*—almost two hundred pages of them. Carl tracks down a copy of the *Dizionario* at Emory University in Atlanta and adds excerpts from that information as well.

All winter long Carl appears regularly at my office door with one excited report after another. "Guess how many Cornaros I have entered in the computer?" I stare dumbly. "Five hundred!" he exclaims, turning to hurry back upstairs to his task. In no time at all he's back again. "One thousand Cornaros!" he reports. The number continues to climb and Carl's enthusiasm never wanes, despite the fact that he labors as a two-fingered typist.

We end up with more than three thousand entries in our database, half of them Cornaros and the rest spouses and in-laws. The children begin to tease Carl about his adopted family, but in fact the database supplies a useful capability for identifying within the family tree most of the Cornaros that we find mentioned in books on Venetian history and art. Some of them still stymie us, of course. One in particular is a thorn in Carl's side. When the Turks were massing outside the walls of Constantinople in 1453 for their final assault on the capital of the Byzantine Empire, Emperor Constantine placed a Venetian—instead of one of his own men—in charge of the defense of each of the city's four main gates. One of those defenders-to-the-death was Fabruzzi Cornaro—but Carl cannot find a trace of him in the family genealogy.

22

A Difficult Period

"We need a booklet about the villa to sell to tourists," I report to Carl by telephone from Piombino Dese. Carl will be coming later, for the few weeks he can get away from business. In the meanwhile, we invest in daily phone calls. "I'm getting requests regularly," I tell him. "For a booklet and for postcards."

"Okay," Carl quickly responds. "Why don't you write one and we'll have it printed up."

"That's not what I had in mind," I say. Carl knows perfectly well that it is not what I had in mind. We compromise. I prepare a draft and fax it to Carl's office, using Wilma Scquizzato's fax machine. Carl produces the final version, beginning:

The name of Giorgio Cornaro (in the Venetan dialect, Zorzon Corner) is remembered in history for a reason that neither he nor his contemporaries would have expected.

The Cornaro family had provided political and military leaders to Venice for more than six hundred years. Yet Giorgio Cornaro found lasting fame not by political office (though he was descendant of a doge and was a member of the Great Council at age twenty) nor by military achievement (though he died in battle) nor by wealth (though he owned large agricultural estates on the mainland and in Crete).

Giorgio will be remembered because in 1551 he commissioned Andrea Palladio to design and build Villa Cornaro, one of the most influential structures in the history of western residential architecture.

Preparing the booklet is a useful exercise for both of us. It forces us to take stock of exactly what we do and don't know about our villa. Still relying primarily on Doug Lewis's unpublished manuscript and the published articles he derived from it, we begin to distill the aspects of the villa that are most meaningful to us.

We are intrigued, for example, that we are only the sixth family to own the villa in four and a half centuries. The Cornaro family held on to it through successive generations for 253 years. Caterino Antonio Cornaro, the last Cornaro owner of the villa and the last male descendant in his branch of the family, died in 1802, just five years after the death of the Republic of Venice at the hands of Napoléon. Other branches of the family died out through the years also, until today, I'm told, there are no Cornaros left in the Veneto. The richest and one of the most powerful families of Venice has disappeared as completely as the republic it served for more than a millennium.

Who can be found who does not know that the House of Cornaro is the greatest of the world? The House of Cornaro, is it not everywhere?

That is how an actor and orator known as Il Ruzzante (The Rustic) apostrophized the Cornaros in 1521. The two most famous women in the history of Venice are both Cornaros: Caterina Cornaro reigned as queen of Cyprus from 1468 to 1489 as a result of the family's deep involvement in that island kingdom; Elena Lucrezia Cornaro became, in 1678, the first woman in European history to earn a university degree. When evidence emerged of a coup planned by a doge of Venice in 1355, the top government leaders met at the home of a Cornaro—a future doge himself—to plan their response; when the Venetian military leader Carmagnola was executed in 1432 as a suspected traitor in the wars with Milan, a Cornaro was sent to command the Venetian forces. Giorgio Cornaro himself, who built our villa, died fighting the Ottoman Turks in the epic sea battle at Lepanto in 1571. A later owner of the villa, Caterino Domenico Cornaro, died in 1669 while commanding Venice's defense of Crete against the Turkish siege.

All that wealth, power, and fame finally vaporized, the goods of the Cornaros dispersed around the globe. Titian's portrait of Giorgio Cornaro at age twenty hangs in the Joslyn Art Museum in Omaha; Giovanni Bellini's Cornaro-commissioned *Continence of Scipio* is at the National Gallery of Art in Washington, D.C.; Andrea Mantegna's *Cult of Cybele* is at the National Gallery in London. The Pitti Palace in Florence holds Tintoretto's portrait of Alvise Cornaro. Titian's portrait of Queen Caterina Cornaro is at the Uffizi in Florence, and Gentile Bellini's at the Szépmüvészeti in Budapest. A missal, or prayer book, of one of the Cornaro cardinals—there were nine in all—was recently auctioned at Christie's in London for $4.46 million. The Grand Canal of Venice is studded with at least nine former Cornaro palaces, housing the *municipio* of Venice, police headquarters, the Venice Biennale administration, a hotel, the headquarters of a prestigious textile company, and a miscellany of other owners and tenants. And in the Cornaros' Palladian palace at Piombino Dese resides the family of a former church music director from Atlanta.

When the last Cornaro in Giorgio Cornaro's line of male descendants died in 1802, six of his cousins inherited Villa Cornaro. They sold the Piombino Dese property five years later to the Carminati-Torri family, who held it for 112 years. Then, for some reason that history does not record, Carlo Emo-Capodilista, whose brother already owned Villa Emo at Fanzolo, acquired Villa Cornaro in 1919, gaining his family the brief distinction of owning two Palladian villas at the same time. Count Emo retained Villa Cornaro for just two years, though that was time enough for him to auction its furniture at Sotheby's in New York.

Mario Vianello, a Venetian shipowner and coffee importer, succeeded the count. One of Vianello's daughters, Elena, visits us at the villa one spring day. She cheerily entertains us with stories of her childhood at the villa. Her most fearsome tale is an account of how she rode her bicycle indoors in the grand salon, careening about the original terra-cotta tiles in the shadow of Camillo Mariani's six Renaissance statues.

She visits a second time, bringing her mother, Bianca, Mario Vianello's widow, and a worn and faded photo album showing the family's days at the villa. Bianca tells us how her husband died of appendicitis in 1942 while serving as a soldier in World War II. His complaints of pain were ignored, on the theory that he was just trying to avoid combat.

Mario's brother Tito did not show Mario's business acumen in the postwar years, although even Mario might have been unable to cope with the challenges of those desperately poor times. In 1951 Tito bailed out, selling Villa Cornaro with all its fields and farm buildings to the parish church.

Why would a parish church want a Palladian estate? To run an *asilo* (kindergarten), of course!

The fields of the villa were sold off to the farm families who had cultivated them in the past. The *barchessa* on the west flank, designed by Palladio's follower Vincenzo Scamozzi and built about 1590 (on the foundations of an earlier building), was chopped up into shops with apartments above and sold to merchant families. The dirt of a small hill to the south, created to shelter the villa's icehouse, was carted to fill the lake that had stood south of the villa for at least 250 years. The seven-arch bridge was left spanning a broad, stone-lined mudhole that survives today.

To organize the villa itself as an *asilo,* the church made certain adjustments. The heating system was removed and replaced by several wood-burning stoves. Outdoor privies were erected in a row leading from the villa's west wall.

The villa's frescos and spectacular plasterwork were identified as problems. True, the Mattia Bortoloni frescos, then 234 years old, are devoted exclusively to Bible stories—Old Testament on the first floor, New Testament above—but one panel, portraying

Two farmworkers in the early twentieth century cross the
villa's seven-arch bridge on a donkey cart

Noah's flood, depicts a wholly unacceptable and potentially mind-scarring female rump. Whitewash solved that problem. The little plaster angels—putti—that spring in three dimensions above the interior doorways offered a more sinister threat. At least half of them possessed clearly discernible penises. Who can imagine the horror that such a sight might wreak upon the youngsters who would attend the *asilo,* not to mention the sensibilities of the nuns who would operate it? The penises had to go. Today the putti display only rough, curious stumps as evidence of their former masculinity. *Note to diary: Search attic for stack of discarded plaster penises.*

Was the villa's life as a kindergarten a Babylonian Captivity? Or should it be seen as a protective custody, a sheltering transition until stronger hands arrived to renew it? The best answer is probably neither.

Giacomo is alarmed when he first sees the Italian edition of the booklet that Carl and I produce for tourists. "Don Aldo will be upset," he counsels.

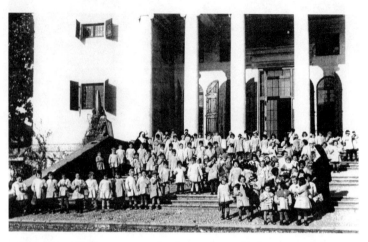

The *asilo*, or kindergarten, run by the parish at Villa Cornaro in the 1950s

After a difficult period in the 1950s and 1960s when it was used as a parochial kindergarten and then stood vacant, Villa Cornaro returned to private ownership.

That is the sentence that alarms Giacomo. Carl tries to placate him and provide a line of defense in case the criticism that Giacomo anticipates from Don Aldo actually materializes.

"It only says a 'difficult' period," Carl protests. "And the sentence refers to both the kindergarten period and the period when the villa was abandoned."

In any event, we have a closet filled with three thousand booklets in Italian and three thousand in English, so the villa's eight years as a kindergarten and twelve years as an abandoned structure will have to remain "difficult" until we can sell them.

I can think of three positive aspects of the church's ownership. First, it may have saved the villa from a worse fate. For me, the saddest villas are the ones owned by local or regional governments and used as offices or for occasional conferences. All of Palladio seems drained from them, leaving them with the air of a rundown hotel conference center. Routine maintenance is largely abandoned in favor of periodic restoration campaigns. Second, a generation of Piombino Dese residents, now in their late forties or fifties, feel an attachment to the villa because of the time they attended kindergarten here. They delight in telling me stories of their youthful hijinks at the villa. Their tales give me the willies, but I appreciate the bond they continue to feel with the villa.

Finally, by selling off the fields and *barchessa*, the church reduced the estate to a more manageable economic unit. I would delight in seeing the villa preserved to its full glorious extent of yesteryear. Deep inside, however, I realize that if the villa property had not been reduced, Carl and I could not have afforded it. Many of those who could afford it would be discouraged by the management and maintenance challenges of such a grand property. So I have decided that, though the years were "difficult," the period produced beneficial results.

On the other hand, the lake should have been left alone!

23

Change and Challenge

Our second spring at Villa Cornaro brings a big change and our first major financial challenge.

The change is personal: Carl decides to take a sabbatical from the business world. He resigns his corporate posts and joins the unemployed. For the first time we can look forward to May and June together in the Veneto, followed by two more months in September and October. For the year or so of Carl's sabbatical I will not find myself occasionally feeling lonely in the evening.

On the other hand, my progress in speaking Italian slows

abruptly. Except in our most diligent and ambitious moments, Carl and I speak English with each other at the villa. When in Piombino Dese by myself, I am totally immersed in Italian. It is a matter of speaking Italian or nothing at all. Because Carl is never alone at the villa, he hasn't had my motivation for improving his Italian, which might be described euphemistically as "less advanced."

"The technical term is 'stinks,' " Carl suggests.

When the Battistons or Scquizzatos or others organize dinner parties, or when we reciprocate, Carl gamely, though haltingly, joins in conversations about business or current events, but he has little to offer when talk turns to children or shopping. Needless to say, he is entirely silent on cooking and recipes. On balance, it leaves him a very quiet dinner partner, although he maintains a nice smile and no one seems to mind. Memi, for one, takes Carl as a personal challenge. With his usual exuberance, he leads Carl out through his extensive *orto* (fruit and vegetable garden), cheerily pointing out all his many varieties of every crop known to man. Who cares if the words he is teaching Carl are at least half Venetan instead of Italian?

As time passes, I am frustrated to see that Carl understands more and more of what is being said, but without increasing at all the amount of talking that he does. There may be an implied suggestion in the air that he would talk more if only I would talk less, but I choose not to explore it. In fact, Carl blithely buys books in Italian and marches his way through them if the index makes any reference to the Cornaro family. His Italian improves dramatically if he has a book in his hand describing Elena Lucrezia Cornaro or any other Cornaro.

So why can't he talk on the telephone?

"*Un attimo, per favore. Mia moglie parla Italiano più bene.* One moment please. My wife speaks Italian more well."

That emerges as Carl's telephone mantra, accompanied by extending the handset at arm's length in my direction. *Note to diary: I'm grateful to find one thorn to prove I'm surrounded by roses.*

·   ·   ·

"Signora Sally, do you have another bucket? Maybe a large plastic bowl?"

Rain slashes at the villa. Giacomo has dashed over from Caffè Palladio to help me close the *balcone* and protect the villa's windows.

"A bucket?" I ask. "Did something spill?"

"There's another leak in the roof, Signora Sally. *L'acqua entra come un fiume*. Water's coming in like a river," he answers. "We must place a bucket to protect the rug and the floor."

I think there is a bucket in the *cantina*, but to save time I empty a large plastic wastebasket and hand it to Giacomo. Giacomo bounds up the spiral wooden stairs, with me following as closely as I can manage. I'm anxious to see the new waterway that has opened on the second floor. A steady thread of rainwater cascades from the ceiling twenty-seven feet above our heads and splashes at our feet in the midst of a puddle that is widening rapidly across the terrazzo floor.

The emergency contained, Giacomo begins to plan ahead. "You must telephone Ilario to come tomorrow."

Ilario, I learn, has the skill and the daring to climb into the rafters over the upstairs grand salon and find the source of the leak. Sometimes he can jiggle the *tegole* (roof tiles) from the underside and cure the problem. Other times he simply leaves a bucket permanently in place in the rafters beneath the leak. There's been a problem for years, I'm told, but the appearance of new leaks has accelerated over the past winter. There seems to be another after every storm, Giacomo reports sadly.

When Carl arrives the following week I update him on what I have learned about the roof. The lines on his brow deepen visibly.

"Not a new roof!" he groans. His worry lines get even worse when I tell him that, in order to repair the latest gusher, Ilario on the following day walked out onto the sloping roof of the bedroom wing—fifty feet above the ground—to remove a pocket of accumulated dirt that seemed to have attracted its own garden of weeds and one small shrub.

"He has been doing it for several years now," Giacomo confirms. "Signor Rush had an insurance policy on Ilario's life, so there would be something for his widow in case he fell and was killed."

Carl collapses into a kitchen chair. His lawyer's mind has simply seized up at the implications of it all. I comfort him with a few meaningless phrases of encouragement and hope. His color returns as, in his typical fashion, he mentally sorts through what we must do.

"Ilario must never, *never* go onto the roof without a safety line," Carl begins, his Italian—aided by even more eloquent pantomime—rising to the occasion.

"Ilario won't wear a safety rope," Giacomo advises. "He says he knows what he's doing and is careful so he won't fall."

Carl repeats himself. No one is to go on the roof without a safety line. If Ilario won't wear one, we'll have to find someone else; if we can't find someone else, we'll just have to buy bigger buckets and more mops. Later, when we discuss the roof problem with Ilario, he agrees to follow Carl's required precaution.

Next we examine our options with the roof. Ernesto Formentin, the local *geometra*—survey engineer—whose daughter Nella played the harp at the Rushes' final reception, is familiar with the villa and has our confidence. He believes that the current roof was installed, or at least substantially renovated, in the late 1940s, just after World War II. That makes the roof about fifty years old. Over time, he tells us, there is a general buildup of dirt and decomposed leaves. Seeds of weeds and small bushes find the soil and germinate. Moss and mildew flourish as well. Their presence begins to obstruct the natural flow of rainwater, causing the water to back up like Lake Mead behind Hoover Dam. Soon the water is pouring over the uphill ends of the *tegole*. Hailstones can break tiles as well. So can fallen tree limbs, although that's less of an issue with the villa because it is taller than most surrounding trees.

After fifty years, continual problems are to be expected, Ernesto says. We might postpone installing a new roof, but it will be necessary within the next few years in any event.

Given a choice between spending money now and spending it

later, Carl and I generally opt for later. Moreover, while we are still trying to digest the cost of my magnificent new kitchen, it is especially important that we hold off on major expenses for as long as possible. We are acutely aware of the fact that Carl is not receiving a paycheck now. In this case, however, because of the safety issues, we decide to move ahead right away. Neither of us wants Ilario out on the roof—with or without a safety line.

"Right away" proves to be a more flexible concept than we imagined.

Nothing can be done without permission from the Soprintendente di Belle Arti in Venice. Villa Cornaro is a registered national monument in Italy, as well as one of about five hundred monuments on the UNESCO World Heritage list. Prior approval of the Soprintendente is required before any construction is undertaken at the villa, even a project that would seem like ordinary maintenance, such as repair or replacement of the roof. Ernesto prepares the formal application, complete with amazingly detailed drawings and specifications of the project. We've heard tales of mindless delays at the hands of the Soprintendente's office, so we prepare for a long wait.

A short while later, Ernesto surprises us with news that the Soprintendente himself wishes to pay us a visit and inspect the villa personally. The matter of a new roof is something that would never ordinarily rise to the level of receiving the Soprintendente's personal attention. The current Soprintendente, however, is rather new in his office; perhaps he has simply decided to acquaint himself with one of the prominent structures under his jurisdiction.

24

The Soprintendente

The Soprintendente is charming. He makes an immediate friend of Carl by speaking English with him. We are both impressed by his genuine interest in the smallest details of the villa, since we are obsessed with them ourselves.

He cheerfully explores the *cantina* with us, where we discuss the pros and cons of whitewashing its walls every spring to hide the blotches of mildew that build up during the winter. Dick Rush was a confirmed whitewasher, but Carl and I decided at the outset that we preferred to have a more natural look in the *cantina,* whose vaulted bays had been filled with winemaking casks until the church acquired the property in 1951. We suspended the annual whitewashing. Now the accumulated layers of whitewash are beginning to flake away and the deep red of the original brick is emerging.

"Much healthier without the whitewash," the Soprintendente assures us. "It allows the bricks to breathe."

He saves his greatest enthusiasm for the villa's graffiti. Like all of Palladio's villas, Villa Cornaro is built of brick, not stone. But the brick is covered with a pale, mellow-toned stucco or plaster *intonaco* that is scored to create the look of Istrian stone. Villa Cornaro is the only one of Palladio's villas to retain its original *intonaco,* so Palladio's original conception of the proper color for a villa has been preserved. The *intonaco* of Palladio's villas, once lost, is virtually impossible to reproduce because its appearance does not come from pigment; the *intonaco* is a mixture of sand, ground glass, and marble bits, along with who knows what else, that defies attempts to reproduce the luminous glow that it radiates in sunlight.

Preservation of the original *intonaco* at Villa Cornaro has also preserved remarkable tokens of life in the Cornaro family in the seventeenth century: the villa, especially on the more protected south facade, is covered with dozens of graffiti. Most of them record family news items.

Adi 12 marzo 1623	*On 12 March 1623*
fu fatto savio di ordini	*illustrious Signor Francesco was*
il re Sig^r Francesco	*made a Minister of the Marine*

Here's another:

Adi 13 zugno 1620   *On 13 June 1620*
naque Susanna fig^{lia} di me   *was born Susanna, the*
Andrea Corner ed era la festa di *daughter of me, Andrea*
San Antonio da Padua   *Cornaro, and it was the feast*
giorno di sabatto ad ora   *day of Saint Anthony of Padua,*
di nove   *on Saturday, at the hour of nine*

One notation is chilling even after three hundred years:

1690 9 novembre   *9 November 1690*
Io franc° Corner venni a star   *I, Francesco Cornaro, came to*
a Piombino p il sospetto   *stay at Piombino because of the*
del contagio che fu a Ven^a   *fear of plague that existed at*
e mi fermo fin del 4 Genn^{io}   *Venice, and remained until the*
sequente   *following 4 January*

Sally explains to visitors some graffiti
on the south portico

"*Incredibile!*" the Soprintendente exclaims. He bounces excitedly from one graffito to another. "Has anyone written about
this?" he asks.

"There's nothing that we know of," I reply.

We show him the earliest dated one: 1608. Not completely legible, it seems to record the election of a Cornaro son to the Grand Council.

"*Incredibile!*" he continues to exclaim at regular intervals. Together we marvel that the family was writing on the walls of its proud villa less than twenty years after the final touches were put on it. Would other Palladian villas display such memoirs of villa life if their *intonaco* had not been lost?

The second marvel is that something written outdoors in the same period that the *Mayflower* landed at Plymouth Rock has remained legible today.

"This is written in *sanguigna*," the Soprintendente concludes. His nose is practically touching the writing as he examines it. "It's an old writing medium made of a compound that includes ox-blood. That's what gives it that reddish color." We speculate that maybe there has been a chemical bonding between the writing medium and the wall surface. That might explain the survival of the graffiti.

There is more writing on the walls in the attic. Some of it records how many sacks of grain were stored in different rooms in particular years in the seventeenth century. Then there are fanciful drawings of ducks, of dragons, of the villa itself, of young dandies with plumed hats and period shoes. Another room has scribbles by soldiers billeted there in World War I. The walls of the attic are like a scrapbook of the villa's life.

Before the Soprintendente leaves, Carl springs on him a new subject. Since we first bought the villa, Carl has cast a baleful eye on two rows of six cypress trees running in parallel lines down the center of the park from the south steps of the villa. Carl objects that the trees block the view of the villa from the south and that the problem will get worse as the trees—now about twelve feet tall—continue to grow.

The Soprintendente agrees with Carl. By fall, the trees are history, uprooted by Ilario's hardy tractor.

. . .

In June we have lunch with Douglas Lewis in a busy restaurant near his office at the National Gallery of Art in Washington, D.C. Carl, with satisfaction, tells Doug what he plans with the cypresses. Doug bursts into loud laughter, tinged perhaps with a certain air of relief.

"I did the same thing!" he exclaims. "When I was writing my book about the villa, back in 1975, Dick and Julie kindly allowed me to stay at the villa. They weren't there. They said I should feel free to do whatever work I thought was in the best interest of the villa."

Doug pauses for effect. "So I had those same cypresses pulled out. They didn't belong there at all. Well, Julie was furious when she found out about it. Seems she planted them herself and loved them."

"But they are still there," I object.

"That's just it," Doug says, laughing again. "Julie replanted them! What you are taking out are her replacements."

Carl and I smile at each other. A good day's work, we are thinking.

"I'm so pleased they're gone," Doug adds.

Permission to redo the roof arrives in the fall. With trepidation, we set about finding an *impresa* (contractor) for the work.

There are three obvious candidates. First is Mario Formentin, the man on whom Dick Rush always relied for projects at the villa. Mario is the brother of Ernesto Formentin, the *geometra* who is our engineer on the project. The second possibility is Angelo Marconato, a longtime employee of Mario who broke away to set up his own firm a few years earlier. Angelo has performed two small tasks for us at the villa, but I had not realized that he did big roofing jobs as well. Then I learned that he recently finished reroofing the local church—a roof even bigger than the villa's and requiring the same old-style tiles. The third candidate is the one we know best, Franco Ferraro. Franco is the father of Lorella, the promising young ballerina who so impressed us in the recital at the villa the previous year.

Carl and I meet with each of them and discuss the work. They all agree that, because of the weather, work during the winter is not feasible. We must look to the following spring to begin.

Soon their *preventivi* (estimates) begin to arrive. The estimates vary widely; the lowest is 50 percent higher than we expected and the highest is 50 percent higher than that. One submits a very professional *preventivo* and is completely out of our price range. Another is low bidder, but we notice immediately that he has omitted one important cost item that both of the others have included. We assume that the missing item will not be overlooked when it comes time to pay, which means that the estimate, which had originally seemed attractive, was only slightly better than Angelo's, the middle bid. We worry that there might be other overlooked items in the low bid that we have failed to catch. We are also reminded that Angelo is the only one of the three with whom we have had actual experience, and that the work he did—albeit a small job— was professional and timely. We give Angelo the nod.

We arrive in Piombino Dese on May 1 the following spring expecting to see the villa cloaked in scaffolding. The only sign of activity as we pull into the yard is Ilario driving our immense lawn mower in long sweeps around the broad south lawn, now unencumbered by excess cypresses.

Where is Angelo? I phone him immediately and he appears at our door early the next morning.

"Why haven't you begun?" I ask excitedly.

"May is too rainy," Angelo replies calmly. "We will begin in June."

"The comedy begins," Carl mutters to me in English.

"When in June will you begin?" Carl asks.

Angelo pulls from his pocket a small diary and flips its pages. "Wednesday, June 3," he responds carefully.

Later Carl and I review the conversation. "At least he didn't just say 'early June,' " Carl observes.

"You're grasping at straws," I reply.

All is quiet until Tuesday, June 2. The bell at the street rings while we are sitting at breakfast. Angelo is at the front gate. He asks us to unlock the service gate to the west so he can pull his truck in. Soon he and three others are unloading large frames of scaffolding from the truck and assembling them along the north facade of the villa, where their roofing work is to begin. "Why are you a day early?" I ask. He said he would begin work on June 3, he explains. You can't begin work if you don't have your scaffolding in place.

Carl and I look at each other in some puzzlement. We seem to have found a new life-form: an entirely reliable builder.

Angelo is a man in his early fifties, with weathered skin. He has an average build and an ambling gait that suggests muscles accustomed to being sore from hard manual labor. The three young men who climb down from the truck and set to work with him would be finalists in an Angelo Marconato look-alike contest, except that they are a generation younger and half a head taller, and seem carved from steel.

"My sons," Angelo says, pointing to each of them in turn. "Stefano, Paolo, and Fabiano."

They are on the roof from morning to night, pausing only for *riposo* in the early afternoon. They appear five days a week without fail. We watch as their work moves in sectors across the broad roof.

They work to salvage as many of the old handmade *tegole* as possible, because the new replacement tiles are machine-made and have a different profile, at least on close inspection. I'm not sure that with a roof as high as the villa's, the difference is perceptible from the ground. Nonetheless, Angelo appears one morning with Ernesto Formentin to make a special request. They are concerned that the machine-made tile will be noticeable along the ridgeline. They request authority to incur the extra cost for handmade tiles to install there. Carl reluctantly agrees.

We return to Atlanta for July and August, confident that we have left the villa in conscientious hands. The following weekend, July Fourth, Ashley flies down from Washington, D.C., to welcome us home and get updated on our stay in Italy. She has just completed her first year at law school and is working for the summer at a Washington law firm. She is primed to ply us with confidence-building questions:

"Who is this Angelo?"

"If the villa collapses, do you sue here or in Italy?"

A few weeks later, alarming news arrives from Ernesto, faxed along with more of his meticulous drawings. Angelo has discovered a serious structural problem.

A previously undetected leak in the roof beside the south portico has been dumping rainwater onto two important beams. One of them, a roof beam, is rotten beyond repair. Fortunately, it can be accessed and replaced easily from above while the roof tiles are removed. The second beam is much trickier. As I try to understand the problem, I learn more than I ever thought I'd need to know about how a Palladian villa was built. Ernesto's drawings show that the second-floor columns are joined together by an enormous beam laid across the tops of their capitals. Architects call that beam an architrave. The architraves at Villa Cornaro are covered in *intonaco,* just like the rest of the exterior. Underneath the *intonaco,* however, is not brick—as in the walls of the structure—or stone, but wood. The entire architrave is a big wooden beam. Plain straw is tacked to the beam and the *intonaco* applied on top. The straw acts as a lath to provide a good bond between the beam and the stucco. I marvel that this wood, straw, and stucco sandwich has survived almost 450 years, supporting an entablature and pediment that weigh tons.

Ernesto tells us that the hidden leak Angelo found has allowed water to seep under the *intonaco* and weaken one end of the architrave. Angelo has removed the *intonaco* along the full length of the architrave to inspect the whole beam. The damage is confined to just five feet at the west end. Faxes and phone calls fly back and forth between us and Ernesto. He reassures us: Angelo will simply remove the weakened part of the beam and splice a new segment in its place. The Soprintendente's office has already approved the remedy.

My mind reels trying to imagine how all the weight above will be supported—more than seventy feet in the air—while the new beam is inserted. Carl says we should think of it like sausage making: something we don't want to know too much about.

Is Angelo qualified to do the work? we ask—perhaps an impolitic question. After all, we first met Angelo just two years earlier while he was installing kitchen tile.

"Of course," Ernesto responds. Carl and I discuss our options and decide there aren't any. We authorize Angelo to proceed, realizing that we have no idea what the work will cost, and no insurance coverage if the whole facade collapses into a heap of rubble while the repair is in progress.

Silence. Weeks pass with no further report. We warily check our fax machine each morning.

"If anything went wrong, they would have told us," Carl reassures me. His voice has no conviction. Finally, I telephone Ernesto.

"Oh, that was finished two weeks ago," he responds casually. "*Nessun problema.*" He seems surprised that I felt any anxiety about something so routine.

Ernesto has a new suggestion. While the scaffolding is in place, we should ask a restoration firm based in Padua to examine the Corinthian capitals at the top of the second-floor columns and make us a proposal for restoring them. The Corinthian capitals on the south facade of the villa are, we are reminded, atypically made of terra-cotta. Although stone would have been more durable, Palladio chose terra-cotta because it could be worked into more delicate foliage shapes at lower cost.

Carl and I agree to Ernesto's suggestion only after repeated assurances that the Padua firm will not charge for the evaluation.

September brings us back to Piombino Dese with great trepidation for our villa and our bank account. The villa, we quickly determine, is in great repair. The new roof is completed, although the scaffolding still embraces the south facade of the villa while the architrave is being re-stuccoed.

Ernesto arranges for the two principals from the Padua restoration firm to visit one morning. Together with Angelo, who joins us, we clamber up a long series of carefully secured ladders to a scaffolding deck at the level of the capitals. The second-floor porch is a distant thirty feet below us. At close range I perceive that the capitals—which seem of modest size when viewed from below—are nearly as tall as I am. The terra-cotta curlicues are more intricate and fragile than I imagined them to be from a distance.

"These capitals are like four-hundred-fifty-year-old flowerpots," Carl comments.

The restorers show us the damage to some of them and tell us how they would stabilize and repair them. They leave behind with us a detailed proposal, including convincing before-and-after photographs of similar jobs they have done in the past. Their price for the work is reasonable. In fact, there is only one argument against retaining them immediately, while the scaffolding is still in place: We can't afford it.

We've found that the unforeseen repairs will add 50 percent to the original estimated cost of the roof project. In light of the extra work required, it seems a bargain—a costly bargain.

25

Caffè Palladio

Piombino Dese families are bound in a sense of dynasty. Businesses pass down through generations within a family. Remo Roncato, the furniture manufacturer and retailer we consulted about our kitchen, began by training with his father as a woodworker. My friend Marina Bighin, who runs a beauty shop in the former *barchessa* of the villa, is the daughter of a barber. When Mario, our plumber, arrives to make repairs, he is accompanied by his tall, handsome son Stefano, who is learning the trade. Ernesto Formentin, our *geometra*, is struggling to transfer his clientele to his son Carlo. Franco Battiston, with his wife, Patrizia, is in charge of the *supermercato* when his parents Gianni and Bianca travel on their increasingly frequent holidays.

This provides a strong continuity in the community, but at a cost to the other young people, those whose parents do not own a business. No employee of the *supermercato* who is not a Battiston is so deluded as to believe that his career might lead to his heading the enterprise. No plant foreman at the Roncato factory, regardless of his aptitude or energy, will rise to become chief executive.

A young friend tells me of a contemporary who has foolishly trained at the university as a pharmacist. "It is impossible to find work as a pharmacist. Of course, the pharmacy in Piombino Dese hires only members of the family," she explains.

"Why not open a new pharmacy?" I ask.

"Impossible," she says. "Only one pharmacy license is issued in a town the size of Piombino Dese. The same is true in towns nearby." So the pharmacist-trained friend is unemployed and searching for other work.

Yet the entrepreneurial spirit flourishes. More than fifty lamp manufacturers around Piombino Dese, all small and family-owned, have sprung directly or indirectly from a single lamp factory that moved to Piombino Dese from Venice's Giudecca in the mid-1950s. Some employees left that plant to begin their own business, and the process was repeated again and again with lamp plants springing up like oversize mushrooms. Silvana's uncle Nazzareno Mason invites Carl and me to visit his small plant in Ronchi, a village within the *comune* of Piombino Dese. The factory, built beside his house, is a solid structure the size of about four basketball courts. Nazzareno handles purchasing and sales, embarking on long trips to visit his distributors and dealers in northern and eastern Europe. He has important customers in Japan as well, but in that case it is the customer who must travel to Piombino Dese. Nazzareno's wife, Danila, is in charge of shipping. Nazzareno takes us through the manufacturing area, dominated by a long, wide assembly table. Standing at one end, content to be in the midst of her family, is Nazzareno's eighty-eight-year-old mother. I am not sure she is doing much assembling, but she is cheerfully convinced that she remains a contributing member of the family enterprise. Luca, the son of Nazzareno and Danila, works across the table from his grandmother. To our surprise, Carl and I spot two familiar faces farther along the table: Ilario Mariotto's older daughter, Alessandra, and her fiancé, Stefano. I did not realize they were employed by Nazzareno.

"*Complimenti,*" Carl says to Nazzareno. Business must be very strong to be hiring workers from outside the family!

Nazzareno never attended university; he moved directly from secondary school to work in the pioneer lamp factory that moved from Venice. Now he heads his own multinational business, surrounded by a multigenerational family and a few close friends, all within seventy-five yards of his own bed.

Like Nazzareno, Giacomo Miolo grew up in a family with no business to pass along. As the youngest of nine children, eight of them sons, Giacomo would not have found a place in the family business even if there had been one; few small businesses can support eight owners. In the desperate postwar years, Giacomo's family sometimes had trouble finding enough food for their table.

"Thankfully, a stream passed in front of our house," Giacomo told me one day. "When we didn't have enough else to eat, my father would catch a fish or a few eels. God fed us and we never went hungry."

Giacomo grew up in Torreselle, a nearby village which like Ronchi is part of the *comune* of Piombino Dese. After meeting and marrying Silvana, a Piombino Dese girl, Giacomo managed to obtain a job with Gianni Battiston, who operated an eleven-room hotel and bar across Via Roma from Villa Cornaro. Giacomo and Silvana began building their own home on the bank of the Dragonzolo in a new development just a half mile upstream from the villa. Assisted by Giacomo's brothers, they built the house themselves, working on weekends. Carl speculates that Giacomo chose the site on a stream with the thought that it might feed his family if hard times return.

In a fortuitous turn of events, Gianni Battiston decided that the grocery business held more promise than running an obsolete hotel. He and Bianca built a grocery on the ground floor of the villa's former *barchessa*, beneath their own apartment. The store was little larger than a typical corner grocery of former times in the United States, but several times larger than the tiny *alimentari, fruttivendoli,* and *macellerie* from which Piombinesi, like all Italians, had been buying their packaged goods, vegetables, and meats for generations. One-stop shopping had arrived in Piombino Dese. The Battiston store, a quick success, was soon alive with shoppers—mostly women—their chatter spinning off the plaster walls like the drone of cicadas at dusk. The Battistons scurried to help customers find exactly what they wanted. And *alimentari* and *fruttivendoli* in town began to close.

Gianni offered to sell the hotel and bar to Giacomo on time. Owning one's own business is the Valhalla of every Italian family, so Giacomo and Silvana jumped at the opportunity, even though the hotel trade continued to dwindle just as Gianni had foreseen. Giacomo and Silvana managed to make a living from it and pay off their

Silvana and Giacomo Miolo at Caffè Palladio

debt, but by 1988—just as the Battistons were preparing to move to their new and enlarged *supermercato* two blocks away—they had reached a crossroads. Giacomo decided he had to expand the hotel to an economical size or close it and concentrate on the bar. Bankers resolved the issue for him. "They would not lend me the money to expand the hotel," Giacomo explains. "I think they were right."

Giacomo simply makes the best of Plan B. He will develop the grandest *caffè* in Piombino Dese. His new Caffè Palladio will be more than a dark, smoky room in which to drink and play cards. He retains Renato Rizzi, a Venetian architect-interior designer. Renato—the same Renato who later designs my kitchen at the villa—transforms the homely rectangle into a flowing pattern filled with curves. A handsome and functional bar springs from one wall in a semicircle, facing intimate circular banquettes for seating clusters of two to five customers. More tables, half hidden at the rear, lead to small terrace tables in a courtyard behind the *caffè*. Elegant, lightly stained pearwood is used throughout, trimmed with aqua stripes above the bar and banquettes and complemented by subdued rose and aqua upholstery. Light flooding from large street-side windows and from modernistic sconces dances back from a mirrored wall opposite the bar.

There are eleven *caffès*, bars, *pasticcerie*, and *gelaterie* within a radius of one kilometer from Caffè Palladio and more beyond that, all competing in at least some part of their business. At the cost of an enormous bank debt, Giacomo raises the standard by which they will be judged—much as Gianni Battiston has done with his new *supermercato*.

The renovation takes longer and costs more than Giacomo foresees, but he nonetheless reopens with a bold policy: card playing is prohibited. With a stroke, he has driven away half the clientele of his former bar, the old men of the town who gather in the afternoons and evenings for endless hands of *briscola* or *scopa*, occupying a lot of table space while spending little. Giacomo realizes that his new *caffè* must find other, freer-spending customers.

Under his new regime, Silvana opens the bar at 5:00 a.m. Her first customers are truck drivers passing through on the nearly deserted streets of early morning. By 8:00 a.m. men and women walking to their offices or to the train station have begun to queue up for an espresso and a brioche. Late morning brings mothers (and sometimes grandmothers) with babies, and a few older men in search of conversation and a morning grappa. Giacomo arrives to assist Silvana with the lunchtime crowd, when demand expands for *panini* and *tramezzini* (sandwiches). In early afternoon Leonardo, eighteen years old and already launched on the course of succeeding to the family business, relieves his parents, who return home for a long *riposo*. The afternoon is lightly trafficked, though I notice a distinct concentration of teenage girls gathering after school. The reason for this small surge is obvious to me, though Carl doesn't get it right away: Leonardo is one of the best-looking young men in the Veneto, if not all of Italy.

All of the daylight hours are only a prelude; the *caffè* awakes at night. Throngs of young people from fourteen to thirty years old stream in: girls in breathlessly tight blue jeans and midriff-baring tops, young men with day-old beards and wearing designer sunglasses perched above their foreheads, all glittering in earrings, some men with hair longer than the women, others shaved bald. Giacomo's new Caffè Palladio is the place to be. The crowd spills out onto the sidewalk, everyone gesticulating madly like floor traders at the Chicago Mercantile Exchange. Couples romantically inclined drift toward the rear terrace for quieter conversation.

Caffè Palladio is a combination social club and finishing school for teenagers and young adults. Giacomo is host and social director.

"It's the Italian equivalent of the corner of Main and Pleasant Streets in Littleton, New Hampshire, when I was growing up—only the *caffè* is warmer and better lighted," I tell Carl.

"Not at all," Carl replies. "It's the Piggy Park Drive-In in Charleston in the fifties."

Giacomo likes young people and they sense it. He doesn't permit loud and obnoxious behavior—Leonardo thinks his father is too insistent sometimes—and he keeps track of how much the young people are drinking. Occasionally he counsels on love lives and unemployment. His care is not always enough. One morning he awakes to learn that two young men who left his *caffè* at midnight in sober condition have died in an automobile accident four hours later in a town forty miles away. The carabinieri reconstruct the events and find that the men stopped for long stays at two bars in towns along the route. Giacomo's sadness is as obvious as it was on the death of his brother.

With his white-swathed head, Giacomo looks like a Sikh. A sick Sikh. His face, mottled purple, shocks us with its brilliant color against the white hospital sheets. He's okay, he murmurs quietly, just a concussion; he'll be up and around in ten days, the doctor says.

Earlier this late June evening he was tending bar at Caffè Palladio, his mind occupied by the thought that young Riccardo, now thirteen years old, is leaving with us tomorrow to spend a month in Atlanta. A village ne'er-do-well, nursing a beer, put his head down on one of the small round tables. Giacomo knew that the young man was out of work and had problems with drugs and with keeping a job. He approached, sat down, and tried to talk with the youth about employment leads. No answer. Again Giacomo tried to prompt a reaction, but got none. Giacomo at last asked him to sit up or to leave the *caffè*. As Giacomo stood and turned to walk away, the young man lurched up from the table, spun Giacomo around without warning, and landed a cracking right fist to his jaw. Giacomo fell backward and might have escaped serious harm if his head had not struck one of the round marble tables as he fell. The youth fled and someone summoned an ambulance from the hospital in Camposampiero.

Will Riccardo come with us or not? We have planned for a year now to take him on a visit to the States, his first trip outside Italy and his first plane flight. (Giacomo and Silvana hope Riccardo will practice the English he has been studying in school.) Of course Riccardo is coming! But he promises to phone his father from Atlanta once he arrives.

Riccardo is the ten-year-old child who helped me unpack that first spring of 1990; the eleven-year-old boy who produced a single golf club and solitary golf ball the next year and challenged me to a golf game in our park; the twelve-year-old kid who struggled not to cry one year later when his pet kitten escaped the *caffè* and perished beneath the wheels of a passing semi.

He coaches me in Italian when I ask him to, but is so well mannered he wouldn't dream of correcting me unless I request it.

He lends me his schoolbooks so that I can study the advanced tenses and recommends a book he thinks I'll like.

He tells me funny stories about local characters, always smiling when he admits they are *molto cattivi*—very naughty.

He's my fourth child.

The morning following Giacomo's hospitalization, Riccardo stands in our kitchen ready to depart: all five skinny feet of him, dressed in tennis shoes, navy shorts, and a new blue-and-white-striped shirt. His grin, usually four inches wide, has stretched to at least five; his black eyes glow, his black cowlick quivers with excitement.

"*Sono pronto, signora Sally. Andiamo!* I'm ready. Let's go!" We pile into the Miolos' Fiat Lancia, and Leonardo drives us to Marco Polo Airport.

An overnight stop in London is required, because in our early years in Piombino Dese it is not possible to fly from Venice to Atlanta in one day. Riccardo is wowed by the minibar and huge TV in his room, adjoining ours, but he is dismayed by the homeless and the poor begging at street intersections.

Riccardo boards our transatlantic flight the next day with the nonchalance of a jaded world traveler, pulling books and games from his backpack, examining every publication in the seat pocket. He orders a Coke and settles in.

Squirrels and the swimming pool: those are his favorite Atlanta things. A *scoiattolo*—squirrel—scampers ahead of us as the taxi turns into our driveway. Riccardo wants to chase it and I wish him luck. Then his attention is diverted to the swimming pool; a stern voice is necessary to drag him away for a late supper and bed.

Giacomo and Silvana have given Riccardo some spending money for his trip, which he immediately spends in its entirety on an amazing treasure: a Nintendo Game Boy.

Fortunately we have enrolled Riccardo in a two-week soccer day camp, which pulls him away for more exercise and companionship than the Game Boy affords. Although the camp introduces him to other boys of his age, his imperfect English and guileless, unsophisticated nature seem to hamper his efforts to establish long-term friendships. He finishes camp without any pen pals.

We want Riccardo to see more of the United States than Atlanta, so we drive him north to New Hampshire to visit my parents, a long two-day drive that provides Riccardo a sort of moving film of America. "*Troppe automobili.* Too many cars," is Riccardo's summary of the trip. But he loves the White Mountains of New Hampshire, and my mother's ginger cookies and her roast beef. And he especially loves the town park, where he clambers with other children on the monkey bars and pumps the swing so high I fear he'll sail off into the pine trees. He invites all of his new friends back to

Ashley Gable shows Riccardo Miolo the sights of Washington, D.C.

"Grammy's house." They come en masse for cookies and milk and for board games on the front porch. My mother and Riccardo are equally happy.

Riccardo telephones me after he arrives back in Italy. I had thoughtlessly given him no pocket money for the flight home; he had missed his connection in Frankfurt, so another boy had bought him a snack while they waited for a later flight to Venezia.

He is glad to be home.

26

The Fugitive Funghi

During cool September nights, special white mushrooms sprout at the foot of the Lombardy poplars that line the east and west sides of our villa's park. They lie like little handkerchiefs that capricious fairies might have dropped silently in the night. Mushrooms from a grocery are delicious; I joyfully devour them whether tiny, tall, or stringy, gray or black, raw, fried, or sautéed. On the other hand, a mushroom in the outdoors is a fungus of no more value to me than mildew in my closet. As a result, I am slow to appreciate the passions unleashed by the intermittent arrival of *pioppini* in our park.

In fact, the recurrent fungus growth at the base of our poplars proves to be a phenomenon known in wide circles of Piombinesi, the way you would know that a vein of gold runs through your neighbor's property or that your neighbor's field has a corner rich in truffles. *Pioppini,* I am to learn, are prized as an exotic and savory addition to risotto or stew.

After opening the shutters of the villa one morning, Silvana joins me in the kitchen, where I am munching my usual brioche for breakfast and picking my way through yesterday's newspaper. My morning chats with Silvana are a highlight of my day.

"Have you noticed the *funghi* that have sprung up at the poplars?" Silvana asks.

I have indeed noticed them. In fact, I have assumed that they are a new symptom of the old age and general bad health of the poplars, which are nearing the end of their normal life span.

"Will you be gathering them?" she continues.

"I view collecting mushrooms the way I view Russian roulette," I try to explain, though the vocabulary is beyond my abilities. Given a choice among nine delicious *funghi* and a single poisonous one, I am sure I would select the killer.

"In that case, may Giacomo and I gather them?" Silvana asks. She explains to me the flavorful qualities of *pioppini*.

"*Sono tuoi!* They're yours!" I quickly assure her. Late in the evening she returns to the park with Giacomo. Together they collect several large paper-bagfuls of the mushrooms.

Several weeks later a new crop of mushrooms appears, as abundant as the first. Alas, when she and Giacomo arrive in the evening to harvest them, the mushrooms have entirely vanished, every one of them. Silvana discloses the mysterious disappearance to me somewhat cautiously the next morning. She may wonder if I have changed my mind, now that I know more about the delectable crop. Perhaps I have secreted the mushrooms away myself. She avoids saying that the mushrooms have been stolen, contenting herself with the observation that they have been "taken."

"How could anyone have entered the park to get them?" I wonder aloud. "The gates are always locked."

"*Non lo so.* I do not know," Silvana replies, with the gravity that Charlie Chan would bring to a perplexing murder investigation. "But they are all gone."

In our early years at Villa Cornaro, our electrician Giancarlo is a frequent visitor as we try to understand and simplify the burglar alarm system and intercom, change the older Italian electrical outlets for others that meet the new European Union standard, and upgrade some of the indirect fluorescent lighting fixtures.

Giancarlo arrives one morning to complete another assignment. He is a small man, with a long nose, bristly mustache, recessed chin, and twinkly eyes. As usual, he brings two helpers with him, ensuring that no job will be a small undertaking. When the task is completed, I say good-bye and unlock the south door of the villa for them to leave. Within several minutes I realize I have left my keys on the central table of the grand salon and walk back to retrieve them. Through the large windows facing south, I witness a scene like a druid ritual. Giancarlo and his assistants are scurrying around the poplars, bending and weaving in quasiballetic moves, dancing rapidly from tree to tree as they scoop up the latest growth of mushrooms. Within minutes their work is accomplished. They dash to their panel truck parked beyond the west gate and speed away.

"Ah, so," I murmur.

27

Harmony and Balance

Carl claims the worst paper he ever wrote in college was the only one that he wrote earlier than the night before it was due. That has given him a nice rationale in life for completing things at the last minute, which offends my own compulsive nature. Carl is unrepentant.

"It was only the *writing* that I left for the last minute," he protests. "I *thought about* the subject for weeks."

Whatever, I say to myself, perhaps rolling my eyes so he won't think I'm completely taken in by such sophistry.

Now even Carl admits he is under the gun. He has rashly agreed to give a lecture on Palladio and his villas for the Harvard Club of Georgia. Just thinking about it in advance won't suffice. There is research to be done; there are slides to be taken, retaken, and sorted.

I think he actually enjoys the incentive it gives him to digest all we have been reading, combine it with our own experience, and develop his own Palladian synthesis. Carl and I are both book junkies. For years we have been buying every book we find on Palladio or villas of the Veneto, most books on Venice, and many on Italy. At least once a year we have to reorganize our bookcases in

Atlanta to expand the Italy section. Detective thrillers are the first to go, boxed and put in a closet. Plays we banish to shelves in the guest bedroom. Philosophy and sociology we push to shelves so high no one can read the titles, much less reach them. Only Carl knows why we don't "deaccession" some of these books that we will never read again. (Not my college lit books, of course; I may get back to those someday.)

The first authority on Palladio is the man himself. In 1570 he published *The Four Books of Architecture,* which undoubtedly is one of the most influential books ever written on the subject. *Four Books* was a sensation, translated into dozens of languages and remaining in print almost continuously for over four hundred years. The success is not just testimony to his architecture. In *Four Books* Palladio cleverly produced a true how-to guide. The book is illustrated with meticulously prepared woodcuts depicting both Palladio's own structures and classical buildings that he drew and measured in Rome. The drawings of his own work are shown in elevation and floor plan with all the key dimensions marked. Most important, whereas Michelangelo and Raphael seem to have produced beautiful Renaissance buildings instinctively, Palladio distilled a series of clear, transferable rules that less skilled architects could follow in designing their own buildings on different terrain for patrons with different needs. How much space should be left between the columns of a portico? *Two and one-quarter times the diameter of the columns is best.* How tall should an Ionic column be? *Including capital and base, nine times its diameter.* Corinthian columns? *Five and one-half times.*

Some of the modern books on Palladio are disappointing, basically just photo albums of the villas, full of angles, shadows, and sunsets, and with a preface that gives a nod to scholarship by rehashing a few truisms. Carl thinks the most useful and accessible book is Robert Tavernor's *Palladio and Palladianism,* a relatively short work still available in paperback.

The booklet that Carl and I prepared in our first year to sell to tourists refers to the "internal harmony and balance" that Palladio brought to his villas. In fact, although we can feel the calm of the villa, we don't really understand what creates it. We set about trying to learn more, turning first to *Four Books*. Palladio begins Book II by saying that in a private home the parts must "correspond to the whole and to each other." But what does that actually mean in looking at Villa Cornaro?

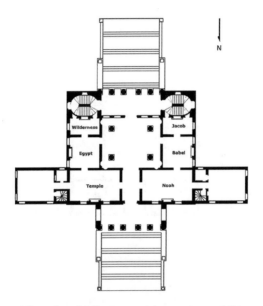

Floor plan of Villa Cornaro's lower *piano nobile,*
with frescoed rooms identified by the principal theme

Obviously, the east half of the villa is reproduced in mirror image on the west. Palladio is always symmetrical. But he must have something more than symmetry in mind. Carl notes right away that the center, or core, of the villa—that is, without the east and west wings—is close to a square, which Palladio cites in *Four Books* as a preferred shape. Of course, the Tower of Babel and Egypt rooms—we refer to the frescoed rooms by the themes of their major frescos—are also square, but we can't make much of that, so we keep looking. We also see that the seven rooms of the core, together with the entrance hall, make up a rectangle with the long side equal to one and one-half times the short side—another of Palladio's preferred shapes. Concentrating on this rectangle, the core living area, we begin to make progress. We notice that the Babel and Jacob rooms together are the same size as the Noah room.

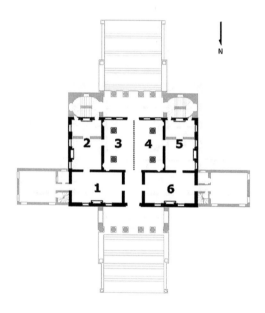

Villa Cornaro's lower *piano nobile,*
with Palladio's six repetitions of the "module" highlighted

That pulls those rooms into a pattern but still does not account for the grand salon. We start thinking of the Noah room as a module for the villa design. This leads to our breakthrough: the grand salon, we realize, is equivalent to two of the modules (that is, two Noah rooms) placed side by side. What an epiphany! We feel like code breakers, because we have puzzled out a consistent pattern running through the core living area of the villa, a pattern dramatically illustrating Palladio's stated principle of having the parts of a home "correspond to the whole and to each other."

Still we are left without an explanation for the two wings standing to the east and to the west, that is, the guest bedroom and the kitchen. In fact, we learn that those two wings were probably not built in 1552–1554 with the rest of the villa. Doug Lewis has concluded that the wings were probably not finished until a second building campaign after 1588. For Carl and me, this seems to open a bizarre possibility perhaps not considered by Doug or other scholars who have written about the villa: maybe the wings were not part of Palladio's original 1551 design. *Four Books,* which depicts Villa Cornaro complete with wings, was not published until nineteen years later—plenty of time for Palladio to add the wings to his drawing in order to show his readers how the villa *could have* looked if it were not built on such a narrow site. Interesting thought, but how would we explain the fact that the wings are actually there, just as they are shown in *Four Books?* Well, maybe Giorgio Cornaro, when he saw Palladio's new drawing, decided he liked the wings and would add them on to his villa even though it was a tight squeeze. But then Giorgio Cornaro died just one year after *Four Books* was published, leaving it to his son Girolamo to finish the project.

Maybe it is all far-fetched. In any case, it keeps Carl and me entertained for weeks, discussing the possibilities, combing through our books, and inspecting brick patterns in the stairwells for clues to what was built later.

We are still left with a big puzzle: How did Palladio decide on the dimensions of the module that he repeated throughout the villa?

At this point Carl and I learn that measuring a villa is not as easy as it sounds. First, we find that opposite walls are not always parallel. You may get one dimension if you measure along one side of a room and a different one if you measure along the other side. Second, there is the problem of deciding what unit of measurement to use. You can't use meters as Italians do today; the metric system was not developed until some two hundred years later. In *Four Books* Palladio always speaks in terms of the Vicentine foot, which was the unit of measurement in the province of Vicenza, where he lived. He even includes a woodcut illustration of a line equal in length to half a Vicentine foot. This really confounds our measurements for a while. No matter how many times we do the conversion, the actual dimensions in our villa are nowhere near round multiples of the Vicentine foot shown in *Four Books.*

Finally we sort out the problem. We have been relying on a photographic reprint of the 1738 English-language translation of *Four Books,* not a reliable source because its illustrations might vary from those in the original 1570 Italian edition. In any case, the illustrations in both editions are woodcuts, which can be somewhat elastic. With further reading we learn that every Palladian expert seems to have his own idea of a Vicentine foot, ranging from 34.7 centimeters to 35.7 centimeters. Since the villa's site was originally part of the province of Treviso, we feel we should also consider the possibility that the workers there might actually have used the Trevisan foot, not the Vicentine one, despite what Palladio wrote. A hurried transatlantic phone call to Doug Lewis produces the information that the Trevisan foot is 34.8 centimeters. Since that falls within the range of lengths we have for the Vicentine foot, we decide that is the unit we will go with. Immediately we are able to confirm that the width of the Noah room as built is 16 Trevisan feet almost on the nose, the same number that Palladio marked on the Villa Cornaro floor plan in *Four Books.*

The length of the room is more problematic. Palladio's drawing specifies it as 26.5 feet. Our own measurements show that it was built at 27.03 feet—a discrepancy of about 18.5 centimeters. The difference is important because we are trying to determine what theoretical system Palladio used to establish the ratio of width to length in the room. Vitruvius, an architect of ancient Rome whose treatise on architecture, rediscovered in the 1400s, deeply influenced Palladio and other Renaissance architects, believed that 6, 10, and 16 were "perfect" numbers and that the ratio of 6 to 10 was

The Noah room, used by the Gables for dining,
with rooms beyond aligned on an east-west axis.

commonly found in nature, including some dimensions of the
human body. In the Vitruvian system, a room whose width is 16
feet should be 26.667 feet long in order to reflect a 6:10 ratio. The
Noah room varies slightly from that ratio, both as marked by Palladio on his drawing and as built (and measured by Carl and me).
However, the marked and built dimensions are all within 12.7 centimeters (1.4 percent) of the theoretical ratio. The difference could
be explained simply as rounding or might reflect Palladio's instruction that walls be built thinner as they rise. On the other hand,
there are some other closely related mathematical ratios that might
hold the answer, such as $\sqrt{3}$, the Fibonacci series, or the golden section.

I am exhilarated to find so many mysteries still surrounding my villa after 450 years. They bring a challenge to each day, and a promise that we will never be bored in Piombino Dese.

When he leads tour groups through the villa, Carl tells them that the harmony and balance of the interior are what distinguish Palladio's own work from Palladianism. Palladianism in architecture today usually means appropriating some exterior motif, perhaps the double projecting portico of Villa Cornaro, the five-part profile of Villa Barbaro, or the oculi of Villa Poiana. Behind those copied exterior motifs hides a jumble of interior spaces. Standing in one room of a modern "Palladian" structure, you have no idea what size or shape or twist or turn awaits you beyond the next door. In a villa designed by Palladio himself, you can stand in one corner room and, without even having seen the rest of the structure, draw a complete floor plan. That is the result of Palladio's interior balance and harmony, the relationship of the parts to each other and to the whole.

"That is what you should learn from your visit to Palladio's villas," Carl tells them. "You cannot learn it any other way."

Despite Carl's agony in preparing for it, his Harvard Club speech is a big success. His approach is to back off and discuss how Palladio responded to newly emerging economic needs of his time. He points out that, although the Republic of Venice in Palladio's time continued to act like a rich and powerful nation-state with its mainland empire spread along the islands and coasts of the eastern Mediterranean, it was in fact moribund.

Three crushing events of the prior century, all within a span of about fifty years, tolled the death knell of the republic, although few recognized the peals: the fall of Constantinople to the Ottoman Turks in 1453, Columbus's discovery of America in 1492, and Vasco da Gama's pioneering of the sea route around Africa to India and the Orient in 1498. For 250 years much of Venice's wealth had come from its domination of European trade with the East. The Ottoman capture of Constantinople marked the end of the Venetian monopoly on trade in the eastern Mediterranean, while da Gama demonstrated that the Mediterranean could be bypassed completely in reaching India. Columbus brought the biggest blow of all: Trade with the New World proved much more lucrative than trade with Asia, leading to the rise of the Atlantic powers whose advanced technology in sailing ships beat out the galley ships of the Mediterranean.

By the mid-1500s the Venetians were in a fury to develop their territory on the mainland into plantations. They needed a source of wealth and agricultural produce to replace their threatened resources in the eastern Mediterranean. Most important for later architecture, the grand Venetian families needed equally grand places to live while they were in the countryside to supervise the planting and harvest seasons on their new lands. They wanted country palaces as imposing as their homes in Venice but, of course, since the country villas were only for seasonal use, they wanted something cheap.

In Carl's analysis, Palladio brought a three-part solution. First, he achieved the grandeur his Venetian patrons were seeking by adapting exterior motifs that the Romans—and the Greeks before them—had used for temples and public buildings. Second, to hold costs down, he executed his villas in brick covered with stucco to resemble marble or Istrian stone, and he used other cost-saving shortcuts such as incorporating foundations from earlier buildings or occasionally substituting terra-cotta for stone. Third, he organized his interiors with the balance and harmony that Carl and I have enjoyed exploring.

Later, Carl gives versions of the speech to several other groups in Atlanta and once even to the Newburyport Historical Society in Massachusetts. As personal Internet Web sites are introduced, Carl cajoles our son Carl—who after college turns his artist's training toward graphic design, including Web sites—into helping him assemble a site on Palladio's villas (www.boglewood.com/palladio/). The text of his Harvard Club speech is the core of the site, but he adds bells and whistles, such as a biography of Palladio, a census of the villas, and a bibliography. He also creates a time line that organizes nineteen key events of Venice's original settlement, expansion, and final decline. To everyone's surprise, the site is soon getting hundreds of visitors every day. Several college professors e-mail Carl to say they have made his Web site required reading for their students.

28

Rondini

"Oh, Signora Sally, you can't do that!" Silvana protests. Tradition is a powerful force in a Palladian villa.

We cannot replace the faux antique chairs in the Tower of Babel room with a bright tomato-red contemporary sofa, Silvana explains to me in the gentlest possible way. We must find a way to rescind the order we have just placed with the furniture store in Loreggia, she suggests.

Dick and Julie Rush furnished the villa with antique tables, chairs, sofas, *cassoni,* and *armadi,* most from the seventeenth and eighteenth centuries, though salted with a scattering of reproductions. Several pieces are as old as the villa, but only one of those—a small canopied bed—is from the Veneto. The Rushes wandered Europe and haunted the auction houses for good buys. Many pieces they shipped to the States at their departure, but other items were not worth the trouble and freight, or would not fit into their new Florida home. Dick sold them to us for a lump sum. We became owners of dozens of interesting and desperately uncomfortable chairs, numerous large tables, and several nice *armadi,* including the beautiful armoire that determined our new kitchen color scheme. There are lots of old bed frames and mattresses as well, and Julie has left enough plates and kitchenware to suffice until we can assemble our own.

Like newlyweds, Carl and I plot what we need immediately (new kitchen, new beds) and what we hope to add over time (comfortable sofas, rugs, bookcases, a new washer-dryer, good china). Afternoon sorties carry us to Bassano for a set of pretty white casual china with a raised border of lily of the valley; to Loreggia for a bright red teakettle and kitchen cups and saucers; to the De Grandis shop just down the street for gorgeous heavy pots and pans and Villeroy & Bosch wineglasses. One afternoon's excursion takes us to Castel-franco for a fax machine so that Carl can transact business while at the villa.

Our initial plan is not to change any of the furniture on the lower floor, where tourists visit, but to focus our nesting efforts upstairs, which we have to ourselves. Our plan collapses when we begin to realize that all of our leisure time downstairs is spent hud-

Renaissance wrought-iron canopied bed

dled at the kitchen table because none of the other chairs on that floor is comfortable enough to linger in. That is what leads to our tradition-shattering decision to introduce comfortable seating to the Babel room. Despite her initial misgivings, Silvana admires the sofa when it is installed, as well as the two new large brown leather chairs. Visiting tour guides and their clients are not shocked. In fact, they scarcely notice the changes because, we find, the spirit of the space is not set by the new furniture or even the several old pieces we have left; it derives as ever from Palladio's proportions and from the character and soft colors of the surrounding frescos and stuccos. The Tower of Babel room becomes our den, where we spend comfortable hours reading, visiting with guests, drinking coffee after breakfast and dinner.

Our farthest shopping destination is Milan. We find it is easily accessible via a 6:50 a.m. *treno diretto* (through train) from Castelfranco which arrives in Milan at 9:15 a.m. We wander the art deco stores there, ultimately finding a Carlo Zen suite for Carl's office above the Babel room. Its Liberty-style mahogany looks stupendous against the walls' old pale lavender-and-moss-green stenciling.

Rugs are a high priority for me, to brighten the look and soften the feel of terra-cotta and terrazzo floors. In Atlanta I make the rounds of oriental-rug shops, studying different varieties and trying to understand prices. My special favorites are those art deco rugs woven in China in the 1920s and 1930s. They sprang from the work of an Englishman named Walter Nichols who transported English wool and a fine design sense to China, creating employment for several communities. A number of imitators soon sprang up. The rugs are thick and soft, with deep background colors and art deco designs of birds and flowers. But as Wilma Scquizzato and her husband Paolo drive me around to rug stores and *mercantini*—flea markets—in the Veneto, I'm horrified at the prices, astronomically higher than anything I've seen in Georgia. I begin looking in flea markets and smaller rug shops in Atlanta and encounter some luck in finding, now and again, large Chinese deco rugs at reasonable prices. I buy five or six over a period of three years, carrying them to Lufthansa's freight service, which transports them direct to Venice. Giacomo is challenged by the process, because he has the burden of driving to Marco Polo Airport to liberate them from the customs and value-added-tax offices. He groans each time I phone him to say I've found another bargain, knowing that three or four hours of negotiation with various government officials lie ahead. He spreads the rugs in the rooms designated in my phone call: olive green in the Tower of Babel room, emerald green in the guest room downstairs, cherry red in our bedroom, umber in the east square bedroom, dark gold in the east living room, purple in the upstairs hall.

Carl makes a special project of finding us a suitable set of china. In our second spring we march into a Ginori retail shop in Padua, clutching artwork of the Cornaro family crest that Carl has asked a graphic artist friend in Atlanta to prepare. Can Ginori produce a special service with the crest in its center? "Of course," they reply without hesitation. Now we have reached the critical issue: What's the price? To our surprise, the setup charge for the special design is quite modest. Maybe our request is more routine than we thought. In the fall, our new Ginori china awaits us. Returning to the shop in Padua to pick it up, I notice that an extra plate has been produced and is displayed in the shopwindow.

Fortunately the new china brings lots of compliments at dinner parties. I need the memory of those to help me through the hand washing that each piece requires after our guests have gone home.

Sitting on the south portico as the evening sun draws the last light of the day with it over the western horizon, I see a quick shadow dart from the gray sky, skim overhead, and light in the darkened corner of a high ledge. Ilario has filled those ledges with two rows of upturned nails in order to confound pigeons. A pair of *rondini*—swallows—are blithely constructing a nest there of twigs, leaves, and grass, undaunted by the tight squeeze between nails. I should be annoyed that they have evaded our avian defenses, but I choose simply to see them as a gentle metaphor for our own happy nesting.

29

The First Lady

Elena Contarini was sixteen years old when she arrived at Villa Cornaro as a bride in the spring of 1554, ready to create her own home here. Her arrival at her new villa would have come at the end of a long day, beginning with a slow boat rowed across the lagoon from the Cornaro palace on the Grand Canal to the shore at Mestre and ending with a jouncy twenty-mile carriage ride or a barge ride. What would her reaction have been upon first seeing the huge villa, like none ever built before?

Perhaps she would have entered through the dramatic double projecting portico on the north, moving timorously through the looming wooden portal and into the enormous grand salon, its walls glistening in white. The color of the room would spring from the rich patterned *mattoni* (brick tiles) underfoot. Her new husband, at her side, might explain the purpose of the six eight-foot-tall niches spaced around the walls, imposing in the late afternoon shadows even though not yet filled. The estate manager and household servants would be waiting to greet her before she began her first tour of the fourteen-thousand-square-foot country house.

The Villa Cornaro that she saw differed in some ways from the one that awaited me when Carl first carried me across the threshold. Elena would have been greeted by crackling fires in the *caminetti* (fireplaces) in every room, warming the air and casting flickering light about the rooms to replace the last rays of the sun. In my time, of course, all the chimneys are sealed, and have been since the villa's kindergarten years. Carl is happy with that.

"I'm not about to strike a match around here," he says.

We would also worry about smoke billowing into the rooms and fogging the frescos each time some pigeon stuffs the flue with a new nest. The frescos came after Elena's time, however; she would have found the walls decorated in tapestries and oil paintings brought from the Cornaro palace in Venice.

Today, beautiful eighteenth-century parquet doors close off each room, but Elena would have found the interior doorways closed by *portiere*, decorative textiles hung from a bar suspended between two upturned iron hooks. Elena would be aghast at our furniture; the villa is tremendously overfurnished by her sixteenth-century standards, which found two chairs enough for a well-furnished room. Nor would she sympathize with my view that a residence should generally be peaceful and quiet. She would expect the villa to serve as both a residence and a commercial workplace, like the palazzi in Venice. The first *piano nobile* would be an anthill of activity. Farmworkers would be trooping about, settling accounts in the grand salon, carrying sacks of grain on their backs up the brick stairs to the attic for drying, loading grapes in season into the *cantina* for wine making. One end of the *cantina* might have housed the villa's kitchen, a floor beneath our present one. Elena, had she peered beyond, would have found the rest of the *cantina* filled with giant wine casks.

Elena's principal domain would be on the second *piano nobile* above, where she had her own bedroom and adjoining sitting room across the *andito* (hallway) from her husband's identical suite. From the south portico upstairs she could look over cultivated and carefully demarcated *campi* (farm fields) as far as she could see, some of them chocolate brown from recent plowing, others not yet tilled and still covered in green-brown stubble left from last year's harvest. One of them was the very same *campo* that Ilario farms today. She would find small *carpini* (hornbeams), recently planted, leading southward in rows to mark the east and west boundaries of the narrow but deep tract on which the mansion has been built— probably the same trees cut and sold for lumber by Tito Vianello in 1950. An *orto* lay to the west, producing fruit and vegetables for the Cornaros, their guests, and their household staff; now it is the site of the *comune*'s civic playground.

. . .

If Elena was a reflective person, perhaps she realized, even at her young age, what a rare and exotic—though highly circumscribed—life she lived. Marriage was a rarefied state for wealthy sixteenth-century Venetians, men or women. The reason is a dramatic example of the Law of Unintended Consequences. Unlike the English system of primogeniture, in which the oldest son was the principal heir of his parents, Venetian practice provided for "partible inheritance." All legitimate sons inherited the patrimony equally; daughters who married also participated, by way of their dowries (which would usually pass in turn to their children and into the family line of their husbands).

Wealthy Venetian families perceived, however, that this rule—fair and equitable on its face—would splinter even a great fortune into many minuscule ones, leaving dozens of great-grandchildren without sufficient capital to support their patrician pretensions. To avoid this result, prudent Venetians simply limited the number of their descendants. In the fifteenth century, less than two-thirds of Venetian patricians were permitted by their families to marry. In most cases, unmarried adult women did not remain at home; they spent their lives in convents. Convents required a payment from the families of novitiates, but the requirement was far less than a dowry. The convent of San Zaccaria in Venice was famous for its beautiful nuns and fabulous nights of debauchery, confirmation that it was often estate planning—not religious commitment—that led young women to become brides of Christ.

Another consequence of partible inheritance and the resulting strictures on marriage could be the sudden extinction of a famous old family name as a result of unforeseen deaths in war or by disease. The leading branch of the Giustinian family, one of Venice's most prominent, found itself in the late twelfth century without any males of an age to father children, except one son who had become a monk in the monastery of San Nicolò di Lido. The family appealed to the pope to release the monk from his vows. The son left the monastery, married the doge's daughter, and fathered six children. He then returned to the monastery, leaving his wife to rear the children. Her duties fulfilled, she entered a convent herself.

The union of Elena Contarini and Giorgio Cornaro would have been arranged by their wealthy, politically powerful families, although Giorgio probably had more direct involvement because his father was deceased. Elena, at age sixteen, had attained the average age of a Venetian bride. Giorgio, almost thirty-seven, was seven years older than the average groom. Elena would have brought with her a sizable dowry, which she would control to some degree throughout her married life.

Sometimes I wander through the villa imagining her thoughts on that first visit. Try as I may, however, I cannot project myself into her psyche. How different our lives were at age sixteen. I was a junior in boarding school, focused on exams and Saturday-night dates; she was married to a man closer in age to her father than to herself and was ensconced as the lady of a grand country estate. Did she consider herself a pawn in a cold dynastic game? Or did she relish her position and look to the future with excitement? The nuances of her world are unimaginable to me.

The couple's first son, Girolamo, named after Giorgio's father, was not born until eight years after their marriage; young Girolamo was just nine years old when Giorgio was killed at Lepanto. Girolamo's birth was followed quickly by that of a second son, Marco, who died at age eighteen. The couple's older daughter married at age sixteen with a vast dowry of eighteen thousand ducats; the second daughter became abbess of the convent of San Martino on Murano, a position that presumably reflected a financial payment. After her husband's death, Elena remained in possession of the villa at Piombino until her remarriage in 1588 to Alberto Badoer, a prominent diplomat whose family had produced seven doges of Venice.

30

Cornaro Palaces

The No. 1 vaporetto—the boat-bus that wends its slowpoke way the whole length of the Grand Canal from the grim parking decks of Piazzale Roma to the fairyland of Piazza di San Marco—is like the little girl in the nursery rhyme: When it is good, it is very, very good; when it is bad, it's horrid.

On a steamy hot afternoon in late August, as I stand inside the cabin surrounded by a few inscrutable Venetians who must be here by mistake and by hordes of sweltering, confused, and irritable tourists, all packed tighter than matches in a new matchbook, the No. 1 seems like a slow ride to hell. Amid mild curiosity as to whether a furtive hand may be in my purse, now hidden from view by the knapsack that a husky northern European youth has thrust in my face, genuine concern as to whether the boat has already passed my stop, and preliminary planning as to how I will eventually force my way through the wall of fellow passengers to disembark, my greatest concern is that all these tourists are getting the wrong impression of Venice. I want to shout, "Venice isn't like this! Come back later, around seven this evening!" Of course, I would need about fifteen languages to communicate with everyone on board, so I stand silent, gathering my energy for the campaign to reach the gangway when the boat finally bangs against the floating dock at my destination. "*Permesso, permesso,*" I mumble as I plow toward the steps, on the chance that I will be mistaken for a Venetian.

I look back at the vaporetto as it lurches away from the dock, like an awkward elephant threading its way through the clutter of gondolas, *traghetti* (ferries), water taxis, garbage boats, motorized delivery barges, and pleasure craft that scramble around it. Perhaps some of the passengers will be courageous or foolhardy enough to board again this evening, I think to myself. They should begin with a prosecco outdoors at a *caffè* on the Dorsoduro near the basilica of

Santa Maria della Salute, so they can look back across the basin of the Grand Canal toward all the storied emblems of Venice: the Basilica di San Marco and its campanile, the Palazzo Ducale, Palladio's church of San Giorgio Maggiore. The sun will sag low in the west and all the heat and chaos of the day will be dissipating. The western sky will effloresce into an infinite spectrum of reds and golds, and its reflection will stir to the surface the warm colors that the hot summer sun has chased deep into the stone and masonry of all the palaces and churches that line the Grand Canal. The commercial traffic will have abandoned the canal to the languid passage of the vaporetti and gondolas. As the sun touches the horizon, transforming Venice into a muted silhouette, they should leave their *caffè* and board the No. 1 vaporetto afresh, heading this time up the canal toward the train station and Piazzale Roma. There will be plenty of seats, but the best choice is to walk through the cabin and out the swinging doors onto the tiny stern deck. With luck, some of the four seats there will be empty and their view of the canal will be unobstructed.

Carl and I take this voyage one evening. I feel like Cleopatra inspecting the Nile shore from her pleasure barge. The proud palaces and churches of the Grand Canal glow in the pre-twilight, the flutter and lapping of the water modulating the light in ways too subtle for the conscious eye to discern but bringing the facades to dance like the dark surface that shimmers below.

In the pattern we establish of catching an early train into Venice several mornings a week, Carl and I are content at first to view the palaces of the Grand Canal as a single object, a panorama of buildings knit into one resplendent fantasy. We recognize a few individual buildings—the immense Ca' Cornaro della Ca' Grande in San Maurizio parish, for example, or the stubby, unfinished Ca' Venier dei Leoni, which lies across from it and now houses the Peggy Guggenheim Collection. Soon, however, we want to learn more about the particular palaces that were owned by the Cornaro family. We begin to pore over the index of every book on Venetian

architecture that we can find. Ultimately, we are able to track down
ten palaces on the Grand Canal that the Cornaros either built or
owned at some point in their history. Over time, the exercise allows
us to begin viewing the monuments along the canal individually
instead of collectively, and to place them at their own separate
points in time, which gives us a better appreciation of their stylistic
evolution. The process also leads us to understand better our own
villa and members of the Cornaro family who were important to its
history.

One of the Cornaro palaces, Ca' Cornaro-Piscopia, is one of the
earliest Venetian palaces still standing. Built in the early 1200s in
San Luca parish near the Rialto Bridge, it serves today (together
with an adjacent palace) as the *municipio* of Venice. One morning
we cross the Rialto Bridge and find a spot on the opposite side of
the canal that allows us to view the palace straight on. The first two
floors of the facade have the tall, narrow arches that characterize
the Veneto-Byzantine style, but the two bland upper floors were
added in the sixteenth century. To re-create the look of the original
palace, Carl scans a picture of it into his computer, then deletes the
upper two floors and drops the roof down onto the two original
floors below. The result is a stunning, balanced, and remarkably
symmetrical facade comparable in splendor, though not in size, to
the Palazzo Ducale itself—a building that must have been as
admired when it was built eight hundred years ago as it is today.

Venetian architecture evolved from that early Veneto-
Byzantine style through Gothic into the Renaissance style of
Mauro Codussi, Jacopo Sansovino, and Palladio, and later into the
baroque and rococo of Baldassare Longhena, Domenico Rossi, and
others. The Gothic style in Venice was always different from that in
northern Europe. There were pointed arches aplenty, but the sand-
bars and wooden-piling foundations in the Venetian lagoon never
allowed the reach-for-the-sky monumentalism of the northern
European Gothic. Probably because of the influence of its trade
partners in the eastern Mediterranean, Venice relied for impact on
opulent exterior decoration—murals, mosaics, foliated windows,

elaborate tracery, and cutouts in myriad variations. Then, over a period of perhaps seventy-five years, all the Gothic frills and frippery that contribute so much to the Venetian sensation of exuberant luxury were abandoned.

For years architectural historians debated which palace or church introduced to Venice the classical style of the Renaissance. New candidates emerged as frequently as doctoral theses could be penned. Gradually, however, the arguments have subsided and scholars have recognized that there is no such thing as a "first" building. The change was evolutionary, the wildly asymmetrical, gingerbread facades of the Gothic palaces gradually reorganizing into the balance, clean angles, and classical columns of the Renaissance. Thus the question of selecting which structure first evidenced enough harmony and enough classical elements to be deemed "Renaissance" becomes a matter of taste.

"The architecture raised at Venice during this period is among the worst and basest ever built by the hands of men." That was John Ruskin's assessment of the new style, expressed in his classic 1853 work *The Stones of Venice*. The dominance of Renaissance style in western architecture for five hundred years may be taken as a rejection of Ruskin's conclusion, but Ruskin was never troubled by the contrary opinion of others.

Ruskin would have had little favorable to say of the Cornaro family, since they were responsible for at least two structures that are cited as contenders for the title of first Renaissance building in Venice. The earlier and more curious Ca' del Duca, House of the Duke, has puzzled generations of tourists passing by on the No. 1 vaporetto. Near the Accademia Bridge two nondescript buildings of the 1600s (or maybe later) rise from a single massive foundation of rusticated Istrian stone. The buildings are noticeable because at one corner they obviously incorporate fragments of an earlier and more stylish building: two walls of rusticated stone, with a freestanding column at the corner where the walls meet. The foundation and the two walls are all that remain of a massive palazzo that

Marco Cornaro and his brother Andrea commissioned the stone-mason and architect Bartolomeo Bon to construct for them in 1456. If the palazzo had been finished, it would have been the largest in Venice. Unfortunately, in the following year the brothers became embroiled in a massive political scandal. Andrea was accused of bribing the heads of the Council of Forty in his election to the Zonta del Pregadi (Senate) and was banished from Venice. Marco Cornaro halted construction of the palazzo and, four years later, sold the building—scarcely begun—to Duke Francesco Sforza, the ruler of Milan, an ally of Venice at the time. A political rupture between Venice and Milan prevented Sforza from erecting his own planned palace on the Cornaro foundation. In time, other owners built the present structures, frugally incorporating not only the Cornaro foundation but the column and wall fragments as well.

The rustication of the stonework and the scale of the freestanding corner column show that the huge palace, if completed, would have marked a gigantic stride forward from the Gothic to the Renaissance in Venetian architecture. Its architect, Bartolomeo Bon, was highly respected in his own time, but perhaps if Ca' del Duca had been completed he would be regarded by posterity as his nation's first great Renaissance architect instead of its last great Gothic one.

Andrea Cornaro never returned from his banishment; he died in Cyprus in 1473, sixteen years later. During that brief period he and Marco engineered one of the most remarkable personal coups in Venetian history. From his family's immense sugar plantation on Cyprus, Andrea bankrolled the island's king, James II Lusignan, in his civil war with the forces of his half-sister Carlotta. Following the war, the Cornaro brothers extracted from James an agreement that he would marry Marco's daughter Caterina. Upon the king's death in 1473, Caterina became ruling queen of Cyprus, adding an entire country to her family's treasures.

Mauro Codussi, not Bartolomeo Bon, is usually considered Venice's first important Renaissance architect. When Pietro Lando married Bianca Cornaro, a younger sister of Queen Caterina, it was to Codussi that he turned for the design of a new palazzo on the Grand Canal. The palazzo, constructed about 1485 and now usually referred to as Ca' Corner-Spinelli, passed to one of Bianca's Cornaro nephews in 1542. Critics acclaim the palace as the first one built in Venice with a wide array of classical elements and a tightly organized facade.

In about 1542, the family asked Jacopo Sansovino to design its most prominent palazzo on the Grand Canal, Ca' Cornaro della Ca' Grande in San Maurizio parish. Sansovino, a Florentine trained in Rome, had been appointed *proto* (chief architect) of the Procurators of San Marco in 1529. He immediately set about a series of commissions that transformed Piazza di San Marco to its present state

Caterina Cornaro, queen of Cyprus, by
Camillo Mariani (c. 1590). Grand salon,
lower *piano nobile*

of perfection. The Mint, the Marciana Library, and the Loggetta at the foot of the Campanile are all his. Giorgio Vasari, the pioneer art historian of the sixteenth century, proclaimed the palazzo that Sansovino designed for the Cornaros "perhaps the finest in Italy."

Near the opposite end of the Grand Canal, in San Cassiano parish, stands the family's rococo palace, Ca' Cornaro della Regina. Despite the name, Queen Caterina never lived there; she lived, at the end of her life, in the palace that would be razed in 1723 to make way for the present structure. Domenico Rossi, architect of the palazzo at San Cassiano, found early fame by winning a competition for designing the facade of Venice's church of San Stae in 1709. Acclaim for him was not universal, however; one critic described him as "an uneducated man, but well-versed in the practical side of building, who had little or no good taste in art."

Once Carl and I start searching for Cornaro palaces, we find them everywhere and in all periods. After counting nine Cornaro palaces along the Grand Canal in the San Marco section of Venice, Carl dubs that part of the shoreline the "Cornaro Riviera."

Cornaro patronage was never limited to palaces. Carl and I soon begin following leads to Cornaro chapels as well. Guidebooks take us to the better-known ones, such as the chapel in the transept of the church of San Salvatore, where Queen Caterina is buried, and the Cornaro chapel in Santi Apostoli, the church of the Holy Apostles, where the queen's father, Marco, and her brother Giorgio are interred. The latter was designed by Mauro Codussi and is adorned with columns by Tullio Lombardo and a painting of Santa Lucia by Giambattista Tiepolo. Hugh Honour in his *Companion Guide to Venice* describes the Virgin looking down from the funeral monument of Doge Marco Cornaro in the church of Santi Giovanni e Paolo as "perhaps the finest Gothic statue in Venice." The elaborate Cornaro chapel at the church of the Frari, dating from about 1420, contains later statuary by Tullio Lombardo and Jacopo Sansovino and a luminous triptych by Bartolomeo Vivarini.

Carl and I stumble across other chapels on our own. A rainstorm leads us to seek shelter in the church of Santa Maria Mater Domini; in the left aisle we spot the Cornaro family crest set into the floor of a chapel. Investigating, we learn that Jacopo Sansovino designed the chapel for the family. In the same accidental fashion we come across the chapel in the right transept of the church of San Nicola da Tolentino commissioned by Doge Giovanni Cornaro II as his burial place. His funeral monument is embellished with busts of eleven Cornaro doges and cardinals; the altar features a painting of four saints by Palma il Giovane.

The Grand Canal's "Cornaro Riviera"

We come to realize that even though the extent of Andrea Palladio's future fame could not be known in his lifetime, it was not chance that led the Cornaro family to commission him to design one of its grand villas; the Cornaro family always sought out the great artists and architects of each period in Venice's history. A study of the art and architecture commissioned by the family opens a window onto the long history and rich artistic fabric of La Serenissima—the Most Serene Republic.

The most satisfying result of all our Cornaro explorations is that now when we ride the No. 1 vaporetto in the late evening we can pick from the massed array of buildings certain ones that we are able to place in social and historical context. We can walk the streets of Venice comfortably without a guidebook, happy to make unplanned stops in churches for renewed acquaintance with gorgeous works that seem to be a part of our personal world.

31

A Well Resorted Tavern

George Washington entertained thirty-eight houseguests at Mount Vernon during the month of September 1786. Some of them stayed more than one night. Fifteen others stopped by for dinner (always scheduled for three in the afternoon) during the same period. George and Martha rarely dined alone in their "retirement" years at Mount Vernon, where Martha directed a household staff of twelve or more. For Washington Mount Vernon was like "a well resorted tavern, as scarcely any strangers who are going from north to south or from south to north do not spend a day or two at it."

Imagine his mixed pleasure and dismay upon receiving yet another note from a wartime admirer: "Dear General, my family and I will be passing close to Mount Vernon on Wednesday next and hope we may stop to pay our respects. . . ." First, he must write a letter of invitation; then he has to figure out where he's going to bed these people; he must alert Martha so she can set extra places at the table; and, finally, he gallops around his estate to ensure that his fields and barns are producing at optimum levels so he can afford these guests.

But he would have loved the company, the conversation, and the opportunity to show the beauty and the fecundity of his beloved Mount Vernon. I feel the same way about my villa.

"Help, Sally! What do I do?" Helen is crying into the telephone. Helen is my older sister; she never cries. I learn with relief that these are tears of frustration, not panic or pain.

"We're in Milan!" she says. "We caught the train for Venice but it went to Milan." Helen and her husband Bill arrived a week ago for their first visit to Italy. They are model houseguests, pitching into household chores without being asked. They help me make dinner, set the table, fold clothes. Helen even goes out one afternoon and weeds my geranium pots on the front steps. She's learned numerous Italian phrases in their short visit and revels in trying to decipher Italian signs. Moreover, with Carl back in Atlanta, they are wonderful company.

How did they end up aboard the wayward train?

Earlier in the week, they decided on a side trip to Florence for several days of sightseeing. Florence is an easy train ride away, with only a transfer at Mestre, the mainland part of Venice. I expected them back this evening at eight-thirty.

Helen shouts her explanation into the phone. For their return trip, she and Bill arrived early at the Florence train station, fortified with abundant magazines in Italian to puzzle their way through during their three-hour trip back to Mestre. A train had already pulled in and was standing on what they took to be the designated track, so they boarded and found seats. In due course the train departed. When the conductor arrived an hour later to punch their tickets, he exclaimed something in Italian which I reconstruct as, "*Ah, signori, avete sbagliato! Questo treno va diretto a Milano!* You've made a mistake! This train goes direct to Milan!" Several repetitions later, they understood his meaning—particularly his reference to Milano.

The alternatives are clear and I review them with Helen. They can spend the night in Milan and return tomorrow morning, or they can catch a late train back to Mestre, although the train will arrive in Mestre too late for the last connection to Piombino Dese. Helen and I think alike: Better to get the difficult part over with now and then relax tomorrow. We agree that she and Bill will board the next *diretto* to Mestre, no matter the hour, and call me when they arrive; I will drive to Mestre and pick them up. In fact, being unsure of the road to the Mestre *stazione* and understanding that a woman in that area alone at night is presumed to be there on business, I walk across Via Roma to the Caffè Palladio to beg Giacomo to make the drive with me when Helen's call arrives. Of course, I don't have to beg; Giacomo is happy to help.

Helen's call from Mestre comes at midnight; Giacomo and I meet them in front of McDonald's at the Mestre *stazione* at 12:30 a.m. Never has a face looked so relieved as Helen's when she spies our approaching car. Bill looks happy as well.

The following morning Helen sends a huge bouquet of flowers to Giacomo with a sweet note. He says it is the first time in his life he's been given flowers. (Silvana tells him once is enough.)

Andy, a college classmate of ours, arrives bearing a large Smithfield ham and a package of special Virginia long-grain rice. They are an unusual challenge to the land of prosciutto and risotto. In fact, the ham spices up our fresh eggs every morning for a week in a way that sweet, mild prosciutto never would. I serve thin slices to Italian guests for Sunday's farewell dinner to Andy, draping them over a bed of ripe, white pear slices as an antipasto. Everyone relishes its sharp taste and firm texture as a contrast to prosciutto; every shred vanishes swiftly from the table. I prepare Andy's rice in an American fashion, with chopped onions, shredded carrots, fresh parsley, a touch of soy sauce and Lowry's salt—but without the southern-style gravy that Carl's mother would have insisted on. Again the Italians consume it with interest, because its texture and taste are quite distinct from their own *riso*.

Andy, bless his soul, enthusiastically gets to work in the kitchen and, at the same time, regales us with tales of former classmates. Since Carl generally limits his kitchen work to pulling wine corks, Andy's bad example makes him ill at ease.

"Sally, this is fabulous, just fabulous!" Our Atlanta friend Joe, who was my first boss when Carl and I moved to Atlanta years ago, is standing in our dining room at the west end of the long mahogany table. He has discovered that from this single point he has an uninterrupted view in four directions. He points to the east wall, seen in the distance through the entrance hall, the east salon, and the guest bedroom; to the west wall at the end of the kitchen; to the open window of the north wall just behind him; to the south wall through the Tower of Babel and Jacob's Ladder rooms. "I can see into every room. No wonder you're not afraid to be here alone; you can see if you have any unexpected visitors!"

Well, almost. The doorways of the five rooms along the north wall align perfectly. Guests in the east bedroom can look straight through to the kitchen in the morning to see if I'm up and preparing breakfast. I love this openness, this directness.

A young woman who has just completed her dissertation at the University of Venice on the iconography of the villa's frescos and stuccos arrives to present Carl and me with a copy of her thesis and thank us for the access we gave her to study and photograph the villa. Joe is so intrigued by everything that he excitedly sits in with us for the visit, even though the conversation is entirely in Italian and he doesn't speak a word of it. Afterward, he is fascinated as Carl explains that our friend Doug Lewis disagrees with the young Italian laureate's identification of the persons depicted in two of the statues in the grand salon.

Joe and his wife Barbara wander for hours through the villa, absorbing its dimensions, its colors, its presence. They have studied Palladio's life and works before arriving in Italy, and their enthusiastic delight in the villa renews our own.

Some houseguests, unlike our friends Joe and Barbara, have no real interest in Venice's history or the history of the villa but are enamored of other facets of Italian life. We see ordinary sights freshly through their eyes.

Bill, another college classmate, and his wife, Alice, are artists; she is a New York–based sculptor and landscape designer of considerable renown. Early in their stay with us at Villa Cornaro we take them to the celebrated Tomba Brion (Brion Tomb) at San Vito near Altivole, just fifteen miles north of Piombino Dese. Carl and I talk

Venetian history as we drive, but our guests' attention is elsewhere. They busy themselves pointing out unusual trees, interesting patterns in pavements we pass, and quaintly decrepit farm buildings. They remark on the cultivation of every single square meter of land, on the abrupt rise of the Dolomites following a turn in the road.

They love the small, traditional cemetery of San Vito through which we approach the adjoining Tomba Brion. Brilliant flowers, real and synthetic, adorn almost every gravestone. On some graves small photographs, framed as part of the granite surfaces, convey a remembrance of the deceased.

The Tomba Brion was completed in 1978. It was the final and one of the most unusual works of the near-legendary twentieth-century Italian architect-designer Carlo Scarpa. The work was commissioned by the widow of an industrialist who was born in the village of San Vito and prospered in Milan. As we wander, Alice voices her professional observations about the design. Its complex scheme forms a grand L embracing the mausoleum and cemetery we've just walked through. Using broad geometric forms— squares, circles, and rectangles and one vast arc—Scarpa created a playground of chiaroscuro that sits slightly above the surrounding countryside. Perimeter walls, slanting inward, establish a meditative mind-frame of utter seclusion; visitors speak little, and only in hushed tones. The two tombs themselves, of dark granite and white marble, lie under a huge gentle arc whose ceiling is tiled in gold-green-and-blue mosaics. The tombs tilt toward each other, as if the Brions will maintain their living affection past death.

"Carl, I have just one question," Elaine says.

Carl turns to listen. He is accompanying Elaine and her husband, Tom, on the No. 1 vaporetto, chugging along the Grand Canal from the Venice train station to Piazza di San Marco. Tom is a distant relative of Carl; the visit is the first time we have seen the couple in ten years.

"Where are all the palaces I've heard about in Venice?" Elaine continues.

At a loss for words, Carl looks back at the mansions they have already passed—Ca' Pesaro, Ca' Cornaro della Regina, Ca' Foscari, Ca' Rezzonico, among dozens of other stupendous residences on the most elegant "street" in Europe. "Sometimes," he reports to me that evening, "you just know from early on that it's going to be a bad day."

Carl finally finds the words to explain to Elaine that in the Venetian Republic only the doge was permitted to call his residence a *palazzo* (palace). No matter how grand their homes might be, all the other patricians had to content themselves with a *casa* (house), usually shortened to Ca' as part of the name. Yet Carl perceives that the problem for Elaine goes beyond the name: she was expecting a row of Buckingham Palaces lined up side by side. For her a palace is not defined by style, by richness of detail or historical place; it is defined by size. With that perception comes the realization that Elaine is going to be disappointed by anything he might show her in Venice.

In retrospect I see that Elaine and Tom must have felt as frustrated by their visit to the Veneto as we were. The pleasure of the Venice experience grows in direct proportion to what the visitor brings with him. For a person with an openness to exotic, overwrought beauty, to romance, to magic ripples and shadows, to pervasive history, Venice is a sensual workout. But for a person who sees Venice as an early-day Disneyland of picture-book splendor, Venice might seem opaque and unrewarding after the novelty of streets filled with water has worn off.

32

Cornaro Meets Cornaro

"How about this, Carl?" Christoph Cornaro is in our grand salon in front of the statue of Giorgio Cornaro, who built the villa.

Christoph is contorting his body to imitate Giorgio's artful but unlikely pose. He has his left hand on his hip, with his right hand extended like the statue behind him. Christoph is frustrated because he does not have a military helmet available to place beneath his left foot. Finally, he settles for shifting his weight to his right leg and bending his left knee.

"Not a bad likeness, would you say?" Christoph says to Carl, who stands ten feet away directing Christoph's gestures and photographing him.

"You should have brought your suit of armor," Carl chides. "I'm surprised an ambassador would leave home without his armor."

"I'm on holiday," Christoph protests softly.

I'm standing behind Carl, laughing at the silliness. Christoph Cornaro, I decide, is a dead ringer for Camillo Mariani's statue of Giorgio Cornaro. Both have the same high forehead, deep-set eyes, long straight nose, and small mouth; even their earlobes are alike. Their builds are identical as well, although the sculptor has supersized Giorgio like an order at McDonald's so as to fill one of the six eight-foot-high niches that line the walls of the grand salon. Apart from the fact that Giorgio is in armor while Christoph wears the neat suit of a senior diplomat, I note only one difference between the two Cornaros who are so distant in time: Giorgio sports a full head of wavy hair and a lush beard that falls to his breastplate. Christoph is bald on top and clean-shaven.

One winter morning in Atlanta I spotted the name of Christoph Cornaro in a *New York Times* article that mentioned a concert he hosted at the Austrian embassy in New Delhi. Carl wrote to Ambassador Cornaro, explained our new connection with the Cornaro family, and inquired whether the ambassador was related to the Cornaros of Venice. Christoph sent a warm reply confirming that he is indeed a relative. Further correspondence and a few phone calls led us to invite him and his American-born wife Gail to visit us at Piombino Dese the following spring.

By the time of his visit Christoph is Austria's ambassador to the

Vatican. The appointment, intended as his last assignment before retirement, is particularly appropriate for a Cornaro; the Cornaro family supplied a total of nine cardinals between 1500 and 1789. The pope himself once referred to that history during the course of a meeting with Christoph.

Carl picks up the Cornaros at the Padua train station. They have barely climbed out of the car at Piombino Dese before Carl immerses Christoph in Cornaro genealogical material; from then on the two share hours of family sleuthing. Christoph's branch of the Cornaro family was living at Bergamo, a Venetian-controlled town northwest of Venice, when Napoléon's French army—in the course of fighting the Austrians in 1797—made a brief detour to seize Venice and its mainland territory. Curiously, later warfare and diplomatic maneuvering led France to cede Venice and the Veneto to Austria. Christoph's ancestors became Austrian citizens and prominent military leaders, one of them a field marshal of the Austrian army. The Cornaros of Venice had numerous relatives residing in Bergamo when Napoléon's army arrived, but Christoph's family is unable to establish its own precise connection, because both the public and private records of his family were destroyed before anyone made an effort to sort it out.

Gail is as congenial as Christoph. We chatter like long-lost cousins, swimming in currents of children, Italy, and expatriate life. Our evenings with the Cornaros, sitting in the Tower of Babel room, talking, listening to a CD of Schoenberg and Korngold, remind me of my childhood, although my childhood home in New Hampshire was distinctly non-Palladian and my father would have tolerated nothing as modern as Schoenberg or Korngold. Christoph and Gail tell us of their experiences in Iran, where Christoph served as Austria's ambassador while the Iranians were holding our American embassy staff hostage.

On the second day of the Cornaros' visit Carl leads us on a cross-country adventure in search of other, more obscure Cornaro villas that he has identified. Our first stop is Villa Corner-Chiminelli, built by another branch of the Cornaro family about twenty-five years after our Villa Cornaro. Villa Corner-Chiminelli lies in the small town of Sant' Andrea oltre il Muson just west of Castelfranco. Its faded street-side exterior would never be noticed by a casual passerby. A phone call ahead, however, gets us admission to the remarkable garden at the rear overlooking acres of tilled farmland. The garden is especially interesting to Carl and me because of the way its trees and overgrown shrubs are laid out in a simple crossing of two pathways at right angles. It is the same layout we've seen in a 1613 watercolor of our Villa Cornaro in the archives of the Museo Correr in Venice. The trees in the garden at Villa Corner-Chiminelli—perhaps four hundred years old—have grown huge now. Their size shrinks the garden, but they suggest the way our own park would look today if it had been left untouched from Palladio's time.

For Christoph and Gail, on the other hand, the interior of Corner-Chiminelli has more appeal than the garden. Frescos, often attributed to Paolo Veronese's brother Benedetto Caliari, light the grand salon with color, even though several frescos were stolen from the villa earlier in the century. (How do you steal a fresco? Remove a section of the wall!) Two immense clear-glass Murano chandeliers are even more impressive than the remaining frescos. The clear *cristallo* is a good indicator of eighteenth-century origins.

In Atlanta, Carl seldom lets me throw anything away, no matter how overcrowded our closets. It must be a problem common to all villa owners as well, because so many of them have gathered the detritus of past centuries into a shed grandiloquently labeled "Agriculture Museum" or "Carriage Museum." Sometimes the accumulation appears to reflect a hobby of the particular owner. At Villa Godi, the Palladio-designed villa at Lonedo, you can find a fossil museum in the *cantina*. Villa Corner-Chiminelli has another unhappy variant. Because the twentieth-century owners have been shoe manufacturers, a shed beside the villa overflows with primitive early shoemaking equipment. We lose twenty minutes nodding and expressing admiration as the custodian leads us item by item through the shed. We try various ways to express our need to depart, but none of them conveys to the custodian a sufficient sense of urgency. Finally, sated with mind-numbing knowledge of early shoemaking and struggling to recall what we learned about the villa itself, we make our way to our Fiat Furnace.

We hope there is time to show our guests still another Villa Cornaro at Romano d'Ezzelino, a small town in the shadow of Bassano del Grappa that is rapidly becoming a busy suburb of that hilltop city. Alas, we have dallied too long at the Shoe Museum. The villa at Romano d'Ezzelino, now home to a private school, is closed for the afternoon *riposo*. We peer through the gate at the reworked facade of the sixteenth-century villa. Carl reads aloud to us from our guidebook, telling us of the orangerie that was added to the earlier structure under the supervision of Palladio's follower Vincenzo Scamozzi—the same man who designed the *barchessa* of our villa.

All is not lost. About three hundred yards along the road is an *enoteca* selling locally produced wine with an attractive Villa Cornaro label. Christoph is delighted; he begins calculating how many bottles he must buy for relatives back in Vienna. Carl and I buy several bottles ourselves and drink one that night after Christoph and Gail depart. We are reminded once again that a good label does not ensure a good wine. I wonder what the Vienna Cornaros will think.

A collateral benefit of having interesting houseguests is that they often reciprocate your invitation. That is how we end up the following year as houseguests of the Austrian ambassador to the Vatican.

Gail spies us in the crowd when we arrive by train at Rome's Termini Station. She expertly wends her way through the throng with us in tow. Car and driver await us at the curb. We enter the car's cool sanctuary with a conviction that we are traveling in a style far above our heads.

Now it is Christoph's turn to be tour guide. Needless to say, the sights he has arranged for us to see outshine the two villas (one of them closed) and Shoe Museum that we organized for the Cornaros in the Veneto. The highlight is an expedition to the church of Santa Maria della Vittoria. Christoph rather than a chauffeur is at the wheel, but this is no Fiat Furnace. We settle back in air-conditioned comfort. Our objective: the church's Cornaro Chapel, commissioned in 1647 by one of the Cornaro family's cardinals and designed by Gian Lorenzo Bernini. The central figure, *The Ecstasy of Saint Teresa,* depicting an angel poised to thrust a golden arrow into Saint Teresa's heart, is often described as Bernini's greatest sculpture and is sometimes cited as the greatest sculpture of the seventeenth century. Saint Teresa described her mystic experience:

> *Beside me on the left appeared an angel in bodily form. . . . He was not tall but short, and very beautiful; and his face was so aflame that he appeared to be one of the highest ranks of angels, who seem to be all on fire. . . . In his hands I saw a great golden spear, and at the iron tip there appeared to be a point of fire. This he plunged into my heart several times so that it penetrated my entrails. When he pulled it out I felt that he took them with it, and left me utterly consumed by the great love of God. The pain was so severe that it made me utter several moans. The sweetness caused by this intense pain is so extreme that one cannot possibly wish it to cease, nor is one's soul content with anything but God. This is not a physical but a spiritual pain, though the body has some share in it—even a considerable share.*

One problem: The Cornaro Chapel is closed for a lengthy restoration project. The tall chapel is completely enclosed by scaffolds, which are themselves encased in opaque plastic sheets. This presents no obstacle for Christoph, who has arranged for the chief restorer to be present in person to give us a guided tour of the entire chapel and an explanation of the restoration project. Just in case we have questions beyond the scope of the chief restorer,

Christoph has also arranged for a representative of the Soprintendente di Belle Arti to be on hand as well.

The chief restorer leads us behind the plastic curtains and up a
narrow metal stair to the first deck of scaffolding. We pause only
for a brief glance at the skirts of Saint Teresa before moving up a
second stair. On the next level we first see several workers dabbing
at the decorative plaster molding that lines the chapel. They are
cautiously removing centuries of grease and grime one square cen-
timeter at a time. Our eyes are then drawn to the luminous glow of
Saint Teresa's agonized face rising above the scaffold deck. No one
could call it stone; it's nothing but the warmest, most delicate
breathing skin. The pain and rapture of her face are not reduced by
standing just eighteen inches away instead of peering up from the
floor of the chapel two levels below. Bernini has left for posterity an
amazing statement of his insight into religion, ecstasy, women, the
human body, and stone itself.

To my left, the angel is poised like a pagan Cupid, his arm drawn
back to thrust the golden arrow into Saint Teresa's heart. But now
the angel's hand is empty. I turn to the chief restorer to say, jok-
ingly, "The arrow's missing! I hope you have it under lock and
key." The chief restorer chuckles with me, but a few minutes later I
notice that he is no longer in our small group. Have I hurt his feelings? I wonder. We are continuing our admiring inspection when I
hear a rapid pounding as someone hurriedly mounts the metal
stairs. The chief restorer pops into view and extends his hand
toward me. I suddenly realize that what he is holding casually
before me is a golden arrow.

"That's the original arrow, isn't it?" I ask reverently.

"Take it, take it," he replies.

"Bernini's original arrow?" I ask again. Stunned to see one of
the great icons of western art held before me, I am unable to move
my hands from my sides.

"Original, yes, take it," he says again.

"He really wants you to hold it, Sally," Carl speaks up from over
my shoulder, finally overcoming my paralysis. I reach out, as cau-

tiously as I would reach for a snowflake, and take the arrow in two hands. Suddenly I'm afraid that any motion I make may somehow damage the arrow. I envision my name recorded in history beside that of the man who burned the library at Alexandria. Nonetheless, I manage to turn slowly and show it to Carl. I notice that he makes no effort to reach out and hold it himself. Gail and Christoph crowd in to peer at it as well. I'm relieved to return it to the chief restorer, but my hands tingle for hours at the thought of what they held.

Soon we make our way down. As we reach the ground I see skeletons traced in intaglio on the floor of the chapel, leering up at me. I hope I have not offended them.

33

Alone Again

Carl's "sabbatical" comes to an end after twenty months—"My time outside the walls," he calls it—and he returns to the full-time workforce. Once again I'm by myself in Piombino Dese for long stays each spring and fall, although Carl has now arranged to stretch his visits to one month each season. Carl, of course, points out that he is equally by himself in Atlanta. *Note to diary: Why are men so technical?*

In the solitude of the villa, loneliness creeps in some evenings, arriving stealthily like the barely perceptible onset of a cold—first a scratchy throat, then a sniffly nose. My mornings disappear in dialogues with workmen, townspeople, Silvana, Bianca, Ilario, and Francesca. The hours of *riposo* are my own, however; only an American would call me between one and three-thirty in the afternoon. Community returns in late afternoons and early evenings, when I shop, visit nearby towns, or prepare tea on the back porch for friends. Nine o'clock signals Giacomo's arrival to close the villa. The clanking of metal bars and rapid clopping on terra-cotta tiles diminish to a faint rhythm as he works his way through the west wing, the east wing, upstairs. Finally, with a shouted *"Buona notte, signora Sally!"* he tugs the front door shut, shoots the heavy bolt with four *ching*s of the huge key, and is gone. I am left in silence.

Television is not a feasible entertainment choice for me in Italy. The Rushes have left behind an old black-and-white TV, but I can extract nothing but grade-C western movies imported from the States, plus *Colpo grosso*. *Colpo grosso* is a sophomoric evocation of the wonders of the unadorned female form; our London friend Judith aptly named it "Boobs and Bums." Lola Butler has instructed me to watch as much Italian TV as I can bear because, she says, it will accustom me to the rapid patter of Italian speech. But even the news programs are rough slogging. The female announcers are usually sultry sirens with long blond hair and enormous lips; they speak so rapidly you think you're listening to a tobacco auctioneer. Male emcees, by contrast, are older than Adam, wear wigs, and speak so slowly you want to wind them up.

So, after Giacomo leaves, I linger in the kitchen. I've made it my audio center. On the simple CD player that Carl brought over for me, I insert one after another of the CDs I've brought from Atlanta—late Beethoven string quartets, Mozart string quintets, the Lord Nelson Mass, *Il Trovatore, Samson and Delilah*. I start lists of other CDs I need in Italy. My Mac PowerBook records it all. Mostly, though, I write letter after letter to children and friends, describing the villa, Piombino Dese, new friends, recipes, Italian politics.

The older I get, the more I remind myself of my father, from whom I take so many of my habits, some good and some outrageous. My father wrote volumes of letters to his three daughters after we each left home for boarding school at about age thirteen. Was it because he missed us? Was solitude driving him, despite my mother's presence? Were his letters notes for later memoirs? Was he trying to explain himself? Here I am writing letters as furiously as he did, without understanding what has led either of us to do it.

Some evenings I just climb into the "matrimonial bed"—so called by the Italians because its twin frames, springs, and mattresses are topped by a single set of linens—and read into the night. This quickly proves too luxurious and self-indulgent for my New England psyche. I decide that while in Italy I must read books only in Italian and only by Italian authors.

Riccardo brings me three of his Italian workbooks from school and a copy of Natalia Ginzburg's *Lessico famigliare (Family Dictionary).* This is the book I devour first and love most. Ginzburg's docile mother and irascible father remind me of my own parents, and I am pulled into her Milanese world of the 1920s and 1930s. Her clear, direct, image-filled prose is easy for me to read; her astute observations on human nature are food for my evenings and, sometimes, afternoons alone. (Reading in Italian makes afternoon reading acceptable.) In the small local bookstore I find a volume of Ginzburg's essays and read about her three years in Britain with her husband, a Jew from Turin. He taught at the university there while she cared for their three children and studied the inscrutable British character. She writes—so briefly!—of her husband's death in 1943 at the hands of the Nazis and of her subsequent struggle to establish herself as a writer in Rome so that she could support the children. I weep when I read her brief summary of those few years of marriage.

Ma era quello il tempo migliore della mia vita e solo adesso che m'è sfuggito per sempre, solo adesso lo so.

But that was the best time of my life and only now that it has fled forever, only now do I realize that.

My lists of Italian words pop up *dappertutto:* on the flyleaves of books, inside kitchen cupboards, on the mirror of my vanity upstairs. *"Il fratellastro."* What was I reading when I jotted down the word for stepbrother or half-brother? Or *"il monello"* or *"zufolare"* or *"il citrullo"*? Maybe it was Primo Levi's *Favole (Fables)*, or perhaps short stories by Dino Buzzati.

Buzzati becomes my second-favorite Italian author after I read his short story "L'assalto al grande convoglio" ("Attack on the Great Convoy"). The protagonist, Gaspare Planetta, an old bandit newly released from jail, dreams of his past conquests while enduring the decline of his health and vigor. With a young protégé he plans one final glorious assault on a convoy carrying gold. Planetta's strategizing brings me back to my father in the late years of his life, dreaming of one last, great stock-market bonanza to recoup all the tuition bills of his daughters; his grandest play netted five thousand dollars. Or one last big win at the racetrack, where he once won a thousand dollars on the daily double by betting on the numbers 3 and 8, the last two digits of my zip code as a college student. The story and its attendant clouds of memories open gates of sadness and regret.

Many of Buzzati's characters, such as Giuseppe Corte in "Sette piani" ("Seven Floors"), become permanent residents in my memory. Corte moves into a retirement home, where he and the other most able patrons live on the seventh floor. For various reasons other than personal choice, he is moved to lower and lower floors until at last he resides on the ground floor: a brilliant and chilling parable of old age. My own father, I muse, now in strong health but with wandering mind at age ninety-two, has already descended to the fourth floor, or perhaps the third.

As I accustom myself to the rhythm of these evenings alone and consider my options of reading or writing, or simply listening and pondering, I begin to sense a bright lightness of heart when I hear those last clicks of the lock as Giacomo departs. A melody forms in my mind, and before I can place the CD in the player I'm dancing around the kitchen to the scherzo in Dvořák's Seventh Symphony. My first week's sniffles of loneliness transform to a sense of blissful luxury. Never have I had such large, malleable blocks of free time. Always there have been others to cook for, wash for, plan for, carpool for, select music for, meet or consult with. Suddenly I'm alone, and I find that solitude has its own satisfactions.

34

Love and Marriage

Our son Carl and his girlfriend Lisa fly through the west sitting room on the second floor. Lisa's caramel-colored hair sails behind her like a wedding veil. Carl is our middle child, the artist among us, who drew a recognizable mouse with whiskers when he was two years old. Lisa is the most sensible and focused twenty-year-old I know; in two months she will enter her final year in college, having survived on scholarships, student loans, and two simultaneous part-time jobs. Now she's applying to law school.

This is Lisa's first trip out of the United States, her second airplane flight. She and young Carl arrived yesterday, one day before Carl, Ashley, and I flew into Marco Polo Airport ourselves. They have spent their first morning in Venice.

Their excitement has nothing to do with travel, with Villa Cornaro, or with Venice: it's obvious that this is about love.

"I proposed! I proposed! And Lisa said yes!" Carl looks blissfully amazed as the two of them brake before us. Lisa's broad grin lights the large room.

"Well, it's just in time!" says Ashley, who is standing with us. "If you hadn't proposed soon, Mom would have proposed for you!"

Now, I'm sure I would never have done that, but it is just as well that I wasn't tested. Lisa is a great catch, a wonderful complement to our son's artistic nature and time-absent view of the world.

Young Carl, we learn, had secreted a modest diamond ring in his luggage on yesterday's flight from Atlanta. This morning he transferred it to his sock before taking Lisa in for her first view of Venice. They began the day, appropriately, with a vaporetto ride down the Grand Canal—as close to a gondola ride as their budget would allow. At Piazza di San Marco he invited her to sit outdoors at Caffè Florian for a cappuccino so they could admire the busy piazza and the shimmering surfaces of the Basilica and the Doge's Palace.

Lisa refused to participate. "We can't afford this place! You told me the prices are ridiculous. Plus they charge extra when the orchestra is playing—which it is. Let's go somewhere else."

But young Carl has been in Italy enough to understand the life/opera equation. Maybe he learned it from Giacomo.

"Lisa, sit down," he insisted. "This is important!" He refused to lose the drama of the moment, even at the risk of an argument.

Lisa says she was completely surprised by the proposal. She and Carl had, separately, been thinking of marriage but had never really discussed it. Some of her surprise registers in the photo of the two of them that he took to record the moment by placing his camera, set for delayed exposure, on an adjacent table at Florian's.

Carl and I are delighted at the news. The wedding, we are told, will be in Atlanta next year, so each can complete college first. A prosecco toast is in order.

Italian weddings produce the same result as the ones in America, but the road to the altar can differ markedly. The first Italian wedding I attend is Alessandra Battiston's. She marries Amedeo DeGrandis in an alliance of two prominent businesses, the Battistons' *supermercato* and the DeGrandis hardware and gift store. Alessandra and Amedeo have known each other all their lives; perhaps they planned from birth to marry. Certainly their parents were content to see them become *fidanzati* and now to marry.

Fidanzato translates literally as "engaged," but the word encompasses a range of relationships, from little more than going steady all the way to a fixed intention to marry, with wedding date set. In Piombino Dese, I conclude, it is the rule rather than the exception to be *fidanzati* for six to ten years before being married—which may help explain why Italy has one of the world's lowest birthrates. One new friend recently told us that she was first *fidanzata* for twelve years; that relationship ended, and she remained alone for four years. Now she has been *fidanzata* for another twelve years. Had I guessed her age on the basis of appearance, I would have said she was no older than thirty-five.

The state of *fidanzamento* seems to comprise three levels. After an initial period of close involvement and experience together comes a second, more expensive level. This is when the couple begin to pool resources toward the purchase of a condo or house, buy furniture and accoutrements for the home, perhaps go in on a new car together—and, of course, save up money for the wedding reception. Parents help financially in all these enterprises, depending on their own circumstances. Finally, at the third level, a wedding date is set. The prospective bride and groom reserve the church, find a restaurant or another venue for the reception, book a band, prepare their new apartment. The bride visits dozens of bridal shops in the area—they crowd the roadside like the roses on the highway into Udine—and selects a gown for a sum that is beyond my imagination. Silvana once told me how much she paid for her wedding dress thirty years ago; my eyebrows shot so high they nearly left my face. I remember wandering into Crawford Hollidge in Boston six months before my own wedding and buying a lovely silk gown on the superreduced rack for fifty dollars. A good cleaning, a few tucks here and there, and it looked fine. I've never looked at it since my wedding, except when I pulled it out to wear at our twenty-fifth anniversary party. Silvana, on the other hand, often visits the special closet where her wedding dress is hung— just to remember the day, recall her joy, repeat her vows. I like that idea of specialness and am overjoyed when Lisa asks me to join her in selecting a wedding dress at a proper bridal shop. *Note to diary: Do I have room in Atlanta to build a special closet?*

The progress of *fidanzamento* can be accelerated to just one or two years, says a friend in Treviso, who claims that modest economic circumstances dictate a longer *fidanzamento* to ensure financial stability in the union. Her own engagement lasted just one year. (Her marriage lasted ten.) Whatever the reason, all five of the weddings I've attended in Piombino Dese have followed lengthy engagements.

Italian wedding ceremonies seem almost as long as the engagements. Even the shortest I attend lasts a full hour. I remember our friend Ray coming up to Carl after Lisa and young Carl's wedding in Atlanta, saying, "Well, Carl, that lasted twenty-three minutes, exactly one minute longer than the average wedding!"

The Italian service includes a Mass and Communion, so it is bound to have a certain length. The longest I attend lasts two hours—my only experience with a "rock" wedding. Guitars substitute for the organ. The young people's choir sings numerous love songs, all in twangy nasal voices that prompt me to suspend mentally all of my training as a choir director.

The fun begins at the reception, where the sociable Venetan character blossoms. All one hundred to two hundred guests are seated at formal tables for eight or ten. A menu beside each place indicates that several antipasti will be served, followed by three or four *primi piatti,* two or three *secondi piatti,* then *formaggio, frutta,* and *dolci.* Each course is served by a dozen waiters who, while you're eating the *tagliatelle con funghi* or the *risotto agli asparagi,* are refilling your wineglass.

Toward the conclusion of the meal, toasts and jokes begin. The toasts are rarely serious and the jokes are often risqué. When all the food has been served at Alessandra and Amedeo's wedding, guests begin calling out *"Bacio! Bacio!"* first to the bride and groom, then to their family and friends. Afterward, the chant becomes wider-ranging until every couple in the room—Carl and I included—has stood for a public kiss. The only one from whom a kiss is not demanded is Don Aldo.

At Wilma and Paolo's reception, someone unveils a gigantic hand-painted poster featuring a towering Wilma with Paolo engulfed in her full bosom. At another reception, a brief limbo contest is held by several of the couple's young friends under the bride's skirts. The most memorable prank comes as a large cardboard box is presented to Alessandra Battiston at the conclusion of her reception. She opens the box with difficulty because it is so heavily taped. Inside are three loaves of baked bread—one long, skinny loaf of French bread and two round Puglia-style loaves—all conjoined in an oversize replica of male genitals.

35

King Kong

"Owning a villa is like having King Kong for a pet," Carl says at breakfast one morning.

I look up from my *La Repubblica*, the newspaper whose inscrutable headlines puzzle me each morning. *Note to diary: In America we read the headlines in order to know what is in the story; here it is the opposite.*

"King Kong?"

"Like King Kong," he says again. "You better learn to live with him like he is, because you aren't going to change him."

We spend a lot of time learning to enjoy Villa Cornaro as it is. For instance, we learn the eccentricities of the alarm system through trial and error, discovering almost weekly some novel way to set it off accidentally. We turn it on while some obscure window is open, or we walk into a room with a motion alarm, or we forget that the whole system must be recycled after a false alarm before it can be used again.

The *balcone*, we learn, are the lungs of the villa. We open them wide in the morning to inhale the cool fresh air, then close those on the east and south sides precisely as the sun rises above the trees and the day begins to heat up. In the afternoon the eastern ones can be reopened, but those on the west must be closed.

Most pesky, the bell at the north gate, on Via Roma, rings only in the kitchen. If visitors arrive when we are not in the kitchen, they can ring the bell all day and we will never know. After their frustration has reached a high level, they may think to cross the street to Caffè Palladio and ask one of the Miolos to telephone us. The telephone also is in the kitchen, but there is an extension upstairs, outside our bedroom. If we are not in either the kitchen or the bedroom, a Miolo must leave the bar—sometimes unattended—to enter the villa with the Miolos' set of keys and ring us up on the intercom. Or hunt for us on the south portico or in the park. Even that solution won't work on Mondays, of course; the *caffè* is closed on Mondays.

After a long and ultimately fruitless wait in the kitchen for a repairman one Monday, Carl decides that we have been too accepting of the status quo.

We telephone Giancarlo, our electrician–mushroom aficionado, to come by for a conference. (Actually, *I* telephone Giancarlo; Carl is still telecom-phobic in Italian.)

"Is there some way to connect the bell at the gate into the intercom system," Carl asks, "so that when someone presses the bell it will ring at each intercom instrument?"

"*Certo,*" Giancarlo responds, with a hint that the matter is elementary. In fact, he says, we will even be able to converse via intercom with the visitor at the gate.

Carl has a second idea.

"Can you fix the system so a ring by a visitor at the gate will sound different from an intercom ring made from within the villa?" Giancarlo pauses at this, either because of the technical challenge or because of the challenge of Carl's Italian, which I have trouble following myself. The different sound can be achieved, Giancarlo assures us after some reflection.

Carl and I drink a special prosecco toast in the evening, elated at the prospect of removing one of our greatest annoyances with such minimal effort.

Our elation abates the next morning when Giancarlo arrives not with his usual two supernumeraries but with three of them. One struggles under the weight of an immense spool of insulated wire. The brigade scatters through the villa. Soon they are all busily disconnecting intercom apparatus in every room.

"Having four people will let them make quick work of it," Carl says bravely but without conviction.

By midmorning all the intercom wall plates are removed and dusty gray insulated wires are spilling from the boxes behind them. Giancarlo is outside working at the gate; his assistants are strewing lengths of wire through the rooms upstairs. Carl's look has changed to mild concern.

"I should have asked for a *preventivo*," he laments. "I think he is rewiring the whole system."

By the second day the floors of the villa are tangled in enough wire to light the Pentagon. We hunt for Giancarlo to discuss what is going on, but he is not to be found. His crew, however, continues in a flurry of activity, shouting and pulling wires in no discernible pattern.

"Giancarlo must be off at his travel agent," Carl speculates. "Planning the vacation he is going to take with the profit from this job."

The third day dawns and Giancarlo returns. We don't ask for an explanation, just an estimated time of completion.

"Today," Giancarlo assures us. "We will finish this afternoon."

By five o'clock all the wire is gone, either into the walls or back on Giancarlo's panel truck. With his assistants arrayed behind him like backup singers behind Elvis, Giancarlo demonstrates the system. Everything works perfectly. The sound from the front gate is distinctly different from the sound of intercom calls within the villa, and we can hear them both in any room.

The bill arrives a few weeks later. It's about four times what we originally expected, but only half what we had come to fear. Several months later I phone Giancarlo about fixing a broken light switch. His daughter tells me that her parents are away, vacationing in Rio.

· · ·

Carl has just ordered the largest water heater in all of Piombino Dese.

He and I and the villa's longtime plumber, Mario, are sitting on the south portico discussing a new problem. The current oil-fired water heater is old and periodically protests its age by belching clouds of black smoke. I was grocery shopping earlier in the afternoon and raced home when I glimpsed billowy gray clouds wafting from our *cantina* windows.

The villa is on fire! I thought as I tore along Via Roma. Silvana stopped me at the *cancello* (gate).

"Don't be concerned. It's just the water heater," she assured me in her calm voice.

Carl called Mario and now we are deciding—over a glass of prosecco—on a solution. There is a consensus that we should switch from fuel oil to a gas water heater, which will require bringing a gas line into the villa. The only question is the size of the heater. Carl insists on a monster that will allow us and six guests all to have baths during the hour preceding dinner.

At this moment Giacomo walks around the corner of the villa and shouts up to us. "Signori, do you see that black bag hanging from the low branch over the bridge?"

We peer at the distant branch. It is almost touching the bridge, bowed down by some mysterious weight.

"*Api,*" says Giacomo. "*Tante api.* Many bees." We hop up and follow Giacomo to see the marvel at close range.

We deduce that a queen bee, along with twenty-five thousand close friends, has fled her hive and set up housekeeping at our bridge. The bees seethe about in a massive black ball clinging to the limb.

"What should we do, Giacomo?"

"*Ah, conosco una persona che . . .*" Giacomo knows exactly whom to call to come and remove them.

Giacomo's friend arrives the following evening, wearing a natty cap and nonchalantly carrying a shoebox-shaped wooden box on his shoulder. The bees are still there. He pulls the bee-laden limb to the ground and clips it off, leaving the ball of bees humming on the grass. He sets his box beside them and opens a small door in its side. He lights a smoky torch and, with a bellows, gently blows smoke at the ball of bees. Gradually, so slowly their movement is almost imperceptible, the mass of bees begins to shift and flow into the small opening of the box. When all the bees have passed from sight, he snaps the door shut and departs. It seems magical.

The following spring he brings us a jar of delectable amber honey in appreciation for the hive of bees.

Two years later we arrive at the villa in early May to find another errant swarm has set up housekeeping in our stairwell, off the southwest brick staircase. The bees have built a beautifully intricate honeycomb between the interior glass window and the *balcone* beyond. We marvel at thousands of bees constructing a vast apartment complex, but we realize they must go, for the health of the villa.

Again the bee-man arrives with the same snappy cap and conjures the bees into his box. This time he doesn't bring us any honey.

Over time we find other ways to tweak the villa for improved functionality. For example, each of the four main doors onto the two large brick stairs is locked by a different key, and the locks cannot be opened from within the stairwell. As a result, we can't lead guests up the large brick stairs—which are much grander than the tight wooden stairs—without one of us first dashing up the wooden stairs in order to unlock the door at the top. After much delay we find a locksmith to install new locks that work with a single key from either side.

The first-floor bedroom, we discover, is unusable because the adjoining bathroom has no bath. A bidet sits in splendor in the only part of the room big enough for a tub. We trade out the bidet so the bedroom can be used by guests who are unable to climb stairs.

We solve the telephone problem by switching to wireless phones—an expensive novelty in Italy at the time—so we can carry the handset around the villa with us. An answering machine gives us backup for calls we miss.

Even the burglar alarm can be improved. We combine the separate upstairs and downstairs systems. We also remove some internal sensors that require our bedroom suite to be isolated at night from the rest of the villa.

We see all these little projects as part of an effort to liberate the inherent livability of Palladio's villa. Carl is all wet about King Kong.

36

The Ultralight

Early one evening, as we sit on the south portico for our customary prosecco, munching a wedge of *Montasio* cheese and tangy green olives, we hear a drone overhead, approaching from a distance. The sound grows to a loud racket, as if a flying lawn mower were about to land on top of us. Then, barely skimming above the tips of our tall Lombardy poplars, an ultralight flashes into view. We are so startled to find such madness in Italy that we almost miss the pilot's friendly wave of his hand as the plane banks and swings away, heading toward Loreggia.

The ultralight reappears two weeks later and again ten days after that. Each time the pilot makes a distinct gesture in our direction before continuing on his low flight across the fields to the south. We are left wondering who our devil-may-care friend can be, confident that we have never personally met him.

One day as I walk down Via Roma to the *panificio* I am hailed by a *"Signora, signora"* and turn to find a short, jovial man with a broad smile.

"You are the *signora* from the villa, yes?" he asks. I confirm that I am.

"I am Umberto Nepitali," he says with pride. "I wave at you from my airplane." We chat for a few minutes and go our ways. In future months Carl and I continue to see him in the air and occasionally on the ground. We exchange waves or a few cordial words. I come to recognize Umberto's wife as well, another garrulous mesomorph, who has round brown eyes and a round smile. She delivers mail around Piombino Dese on her blue-and-white Vespa.

Returning to Piombino Dese the following spring, I offer my usual "*Salve, Umberto! Come stai?*" as we pass each other near the *municipio*.

"Ah, Signora Sally, I feel like dying," he replies, to my alarm. "If I didn't have a sixteen-year-old son, I would kill myself."

Umberto tells me his wife was crushed under a truck while making her mail deliveries during the winter.

Later Silvana tells me that Umberto has sold his ultralight.

Carl and I stop by Luigina's *pasticceria* on our way home from the post office. Today is Monday, the Miolos' Caffè Palladio is closed, and we need the caloric rush of a cappuccino and brioche. As we are paying to leave, an attractive woman is ordering a tray of pastries to take out. She is accompanied by a beautiful little girl with huge dark eyes, pale skin, and curly dark-chocolate hair in ponytails secured by ribbons pulled up high above her ears.

"*Ah, che bella!*" I exclaim. "*Quanti anni ha?* How old is she?"

"*Diciotto mesi.* Eighteen months," the woman responds with a smile. "She's my daughter's child. I keep her every day."

"How fortunate you are to have your granddaughter so close!"

"*Si,*" she agrees. She hesitates briefly, then finally volunteers, "My daughter is not married. She is not yet nineteen—too young to be married—and must complete school first. She and her *fidanzato* will marry when they finish."

She pauses. The little girl laughs up at me, then grabs her grandmother's legs.

"My daughter cried a lot at first, my husband and I cried a lot," the grandmother continues. "But then when our daughter went to the hospital and *she* was born"—looking down at the smiling child—"we were so happy! We *are* so happy. Our daughter will finish school and then be able to marry and raise her daughter."

She gathers up her package of pastries and, her granddaughter in her arms, bids us *"Buona giornata,"* and heads for her car in the piazza opposite.

Our Venetan friends wear their emotions like clothes. Joy, grief, anguish are paraded before everyone in a way vastly different from my American experience. We Americans share our joys easily, but consider it a strength to contain our grief. We praise a widow or widower for "composure" at the funeral of a spouse. If we have conflicting feelings about the birth of a grandchild out of wedlock, we do not share them with a total stranger at a pastry shop. We would not declare thoughts of suicide to a casual acquaintance on the sidewalk.

Venetans find in the visible display of strong emotions both a demonstration of character and a therapy. Emotions are stylized; grand gesture or dramatic expression is required to convey adequately one's humanity. If a friend's mother has died recently, the friend will delineate in exact detail the depth and breadth of her sorrow, and she will expect you to inquire of her feeling of loss for several months so she can render another chorus of her grief. This ritual clearly benefits those who mourn, allowing them to talk about the deceased, to reminisce, weep, and extol the virtues of their beloved. It acknowledges an acceptance of the totality of life, the understanding that bad things happen to everyone and that you must express your loss or confusion so it can be left behind.

37

Lives

Andrea Palladio is a constant presence in my thoughts when I am at Villa Cornaro. I wonder how he would like the flowers I've just placed on the dining-room table. Would he approve of the furnishings we have? I know he'd like our kitchen! And I believe he would be profoundly satisfied to see how flexible and adaptable his creation has been through the centuries for a succession of families with different needs and lifestyles.

Carl and I rented Ingmar Bergman's *Wild Strawberries* one evening last month in Atlanta. The film was obliquely interesting but inscrutable when I first saw it years ago while still in college. I was prompted to watch it again because it came up in a conversation with our college classmate Nina and her husband Frank, who recently stayed with us at the villa. Carl and Frank were discussing Erik Erikson's pioneering work *Childhood and Society,* in which Erikson posits that a person typically passes through seven "crises" in life, including an "identity crisis" in one's late teens or early twenties and an "integrity crisis" toward the end of one's career. As an undergraduate Carl took a course Erikson taught. At the point for discussing the integrity crisis, Erikson canceled his lecture and told the class to report to the Brattle, a local theater, for a private showing of *Wild Strawberries.* Erikson said the film conveyed all the class needed to know about the integrity crisis.

The story follows an elderly retired professor of medicine through the day on which he receives a prestigious honorary doctorate from his university. He revisits in his mind key episodes in his personal and professional past and rethinks his life decisions in an effort to assess his own worthiness. With Erikson's analysis as context, the film upon re-viewing is not inscrutable at all.

I wonder if Palladio ever had an integrity crisis. He was sixty-two years old when he published his *Four Books* in 1570. Was it, I speculate with Carl, the product of an integrity crisis? Carl says no; he believes *Four Books* was part of Palladio's recurring campaign to be appointed *proto* or chief architect of Venice, a goal that always eluded him.

Any integrity crisis Palladio might have had would quickly pass if he were to see the vibrant life of his Villa Cornaro today, some 450 years after he created it. Perhaps he would come on the day the *svantaggi* visit. Once a year, on a Sunday afternoon in May, the park of the villa fills with fifty or so young adults at play, kicking soccer balls, circling about in games. A casual observer at first might not notice anything awry. Then he would wonder about so many balls veering at obtuse angles into the lake bed, errant kicks crushing the begonias that circle the fountain. At last he would spot several young women sitting immobile and blank-faced in folding chairs placed in the shade of the poplars. He would realize that more than half of the participants are mentally or physically handicapped. The others are members of a local volunteer association of young adults who gather the handicapped of the area for an outing every two weeks.

During their visit one year, as I watch the event from the south portico of the villa, Marina Bighin walks up the steps to join me. Marina is the *parrucchiera* (hairdresser) whose shop is in the former *barchessa* of the villa, with her family's apartment to the rear and above. As an occasional customer, I carry memories of Marina at work in her busy shop, chattering, laughing, translating into Italian for me when there has been some choice comment in Venetan that she thinks I should hear, her own neck-length, neon-bright auburn hair swinging all the while with her rapid movements.

Her face is somber now as she sits beside me to study the crowd at play in the park.

"My life hasn't turned out the way I thought it would," she says. Her twenty-year-old younger son Giovanni stands beside us, performing intricate repetitive motions with his large hands, as if playing an invisible oboe. Giovanni is autistic. Like most handicapped people in Italy, even the severely handicapped, he lives at home with his family.

For many years Marina's mother provided much of Giovanni's care. Since her mother's death, Marina, her husband, Roberto, and their older son, Francesco, are left to manage Giovanni on their own. Marina and Roberto cherish the hope that Giovanni's condition can be treated and that he will recover to assume an independent life. They scour the Internet for news of new treatments and, for now, are optimistic about an herbal/vitamin program from the United States.

Roberto teaches history in a nearby school; Francesco began his photographic career by winning a national competition, and now he photographs art objects for the province of Padua; Marina operates her shop with two employees. Before her mother died, Marina and Roberto would dash off to classical music concerts as far away as Vicenza and Venice, often inviting me to accompany them. They would attend and critique for me every art show in the Veneto. Roberto, a good oil portraitist himself, was a regular participant in local exhibitions. Marina's dinner parties were grand displays of cooking skills and artistic presentation.

Their lives are quieter now. One or the other of them must stay home evenings unless Francesco can take their place, and Francesco must plan his life in anticipation of assuming Giovanni's care when his parents can no longer cope with it. For now, Marina and Roberto have postponed plans to visit us in Atlanta. They must wait until Giovanni is better, they say, and can get along without them.

38

The Impresario

Four workers hammer the final nails into a thirty-foot-wide wooden stage constructed over the lower portion of the villa's south steps. Their tools bang a crazy arrhythmic melody in the midday heat. Other workers align three hundred plastic chairs in rows across our park. Tomorrow night the renowned Solisti Veneti are scheduled to play a Vivaldi concert as part of a summer series sponsored by the province of Padova.

"Un gocciolo di vino, signora?" one of the workers shouts when he sees me observing from the portico. An English shout follows: "A tipple of wine you like?"

These same workers appear once, twice, or more each year to build and then dismantle a *palco*—as they call the stage platform—and deploy the chairs. I am honored they ask me to share their wine.

Once or twice a year—sometimes three or four times—we are asked by the *comune* of Piombino Dese or the province of Padua to allow the presentation of some musical or theatrical event in the park. We always agree, subject to a few ground rules designed to protect the villa. For example, we do not allow trucks carrying electronic or stage gear to drive onto the grass, and we insist that a special electric feed be connected for the lighting instead of risking a major overload to the villa's electric circuits. For choral works the performers simply stand on the south steps of the villa, but most events require construction of a temporary *palco* to give a flat performing surface.

Weather is always a risk. There seems to be a variation of Murphy's Law at work: scheduling an outdoor performance at the villa can bring rain in the midst of the deepest drought. The "Sawdust-Pile Effect," Carl calls it. Fifty years ago an uncle of his in Mississippi owned some land that had once been the site of a sawmill. A large sawdust pile had been left behind. Carl's uncle tried to burn it but found that whenever he lit the pile, the sky would cloud over and rain would extinguish the fire. He abandoned his efforts to eliminate the sawdust, but during dry periods he would still light the pile because of the certainty that it would bring rain.

Saturday morning arrives dark and overcast. Light showers drift through the park intermittently all day until about five. Then the clouds dissipate to reveal a brilliantly striated orange-red sunset.

Claudio Scimone, the tall, elegant director of Solisti Veneti, arrives to assess his options. On the one hand, the rain is gone for good. On the other, the felt carpet on the stage is soaked and humidity hangs heavy in the air. Don Aldo has agreed that the concert can be held in the church sanctuary if necessary. Maestro Scimone, however, knows that many in the audience will have been attracted to the concert because of the setting in the villa's park.

An orchestral concert on the south portico steps

Ever the professional, he decides to proceed with the concert outdoors as planned. The attendance is SRO; the music is glorious. Scimone knows how to deal with the weather: he pauses between
movements to allow his string players to retune their instruments.

James Galway is performing in the grand salon of Villa Emo, the
Palladian villa in nearby Fanzolo di Vedelago. More than a hundred
folding chairs crowd the room. The Irish flutist, adorned with flam-
ing red tie and cummerbund, stands and sways like a happy tropi-
cal bird. Sweet notes from his silver instrument, amplified by the
terrazzo floor, suffuse the room and seduce our ears. The walls of
the room are frescoed with immense figures of pagan gods and
goddesses who leer down disdainfully from their trompe l'oeil
ledges, indignant at the invasion of their quiet evening solitude.

   Carl and I attend the concert as guests of the Asolo Music
Festival, its sponsor. The fall of the Berlin Wall has inspired the
festival management to make ambitious plans for a Russian music

program for the coming summer, including performances by the legendary Soviet pianist Sviatoslav Richter and Moscow's Shostakovich Quartet. Richter will play in the eighteenth-century Teatro Accademico at Castelfranco. The Shostakovich Quartet, if Carl and I agree, will perform in the grand salon of Villa Cornaro. Our invitation to the Galway concert is intended to convince us that an indoor concert will not damage our villa.

Galway's recital reminds me why I love chamber music more than any other musical form. The intimacy of the setting creates a union with the strangers around me as we experience the exquisite sounds together. I'm ready to sign on for the Shostakovich Quartet, but Carl is more cautious. He points out that the floor of the grand salon at Villa Emo is a replacement done in terrazzo, while our floor is the original terra-cotta tile—vastly more fragile. There is already evidence of damage to our tile in several spots, vestiges of a piano recital held there shortly before we acquired the villa.

The principal danger, of course, will come from the feet of the audience's chairs. We finally consent to the concert after agreement on two safeguards: the tile floor must be protected with not one but two layers of carpet, and the quartet itself must play from a low wooden platform designed to spread the weight over a broader area.

The following summer the festival staff show all the care they have promised. My own secret fear that the carpet will deaden the sound of the instruments proves entirely unfounded. The acoustics are perfect; without the carpet the sound might have been too bright. The grand salon and the entrance hall accommodate 165 chairs, but the crowd overflows onto the south and north porticos. The performance itself—an all-Prokofiev program—is one of the great musical experiences of my life, heightened by pride that these masterful musicians are playing in my own home. Emperor Joseph II must have felt that way when Mozart played.

I have become an impresario myself.

During a trip back to Cambridge for a meeting of the Radcliffe College board of trustees, I am approached by a representative of the Radcliffe Choral Society. The RCS is planning a European tour for next summer and is searching for some reason to extend its trip into Italy. Can I arrange a performance for the group in Piombino Dese? All they need is a place to perform—plus room and board for two days and nights for fifty people!

"Piombino doesn't even have a hotel," I start to protest. "You can't stay in people's homes, because no one speaks English."

Then I stop to think. What a great cultural event this would be for both Piombino Dese and the RCS—and a great musical experience as well! Many of my happiest moments as an undergraduate were spent singing with the RCS, so I agree to contact the *comune* of Piombino Dese and its Pro Loco, the civic group that sponsors musical events in town.

As soon as I return to Piombino Dese I search out Sergio Formentin, president of Pro Loco. Sergio is Ernesto Formentin's younger son. A foot taller than his father, Sergio has bright red hair and a cheerful, positive manner. I explain the "opportunity."

"Can we find local families to host forty-five young college women?" I ask, calculating that Carl and I can host five ourselves.

"Yes, of course," he replies after only a moment's hesitation. He speaks with a lot more confidence than I feel myself. Nonetheless, we agree to proceed: Piombino Dese will be the final stop on the RCS European tour.

I phone my friends in Piombino Dese and encourage them to open their homes; Sergio's organization contacts others. We exchange and coordinate our lists. Francesca Scquizzato commits to host four singers; Livio Formentin, Ernesto's brother, also takes four; Nazzareno Mason, Silvana's uncle, accepts two. A number of people I don't know join in as well. More quickly than I ever expected, the housing seems in place.

Sergio's Pro Loco handles publicity for the concert, though little is needed. Every family in town is hosting someone or knows someone who is. *Manifesti* appear in every shopwindow. Genuine anticipation is afoot in the town.

The day of their arrival dawns, but we are in the grip of the

Sawdust-Pile Effect. The RCS bus pulls into the piazza at the *municipio* in the midst of a steady gray downpour. The square is jammed with the cars of host families come to collect their guests. Chaos reigns as we shuffle about under umbrellas, assigning students to hosts and trying to keep track of who has been sent where. We set a rendezvous time for the following morning. The choir's director Jameson Marvin and his associate director, together with three singers, come home with Carl and me.

Over glasses of prosecco and bites of sweet Asiago cheese, we share a hope that no student will go to bed hungry because she and her host family could not communicate the word for supper. We also discuss backup strategy in case the rain continues. Don Aldo, happy to learn that the RCS tour began at the Cathedral of Notre-Dame in Paris and might end in his own parish church, has confirmed that the church sanctuary is available as an alternative site.

When the singers convene at the villa Saturday morning, ducking inside to escape the continuing rain, we give them a quick tour. We also explain how to catch a train into Venice from the station just one block away. Because they will have only a few hours available for touring Venice, I distribute "A 60-Second Guide to Venice" (included as an appendix, on page 263), which Carl has prepared for the occasion.

By midafternoon the continuing rain makes it clear that an outdoor concert will be impossible. Carl and I take Jim Marvin and his associate to the church to review the layout and acoustics. After testing the liveliness of the acoustics, Jim makes the remarkable decision to place his singers four feet from one another in a vocally heterogeneous mix, a first soprano standing next to a first alto or a second soprano, and so on.

All forty-eight singers troop into the sanctuary at 8:00 p.m. and begin warming up their voices. Goose bumps cover my arms, so ethereal and beautiful is their sound. The repertoire being primarily Renaissance a capella works, the singers' tones reverberate from the marble, granite, and brick surfaces like palpable acoustic jewels.

During the concert, each woman sings confidently and with a

sweet tone; vibrato is at a minimum, and the sound produced is a miracle of clarity, pitch, and phrasing. Into my mind pops the image of *The Ecstasy of Saint Teresa* in the Cornaro Chapel in Rome. The audience of six hundred, completely filling the church, feels the same intimation of perfection. Don Aldo does as well. He springs to his feet at the conclusion, exclaiming, "*Come angeli, voi cantate come angeli!* Like angels, you sing like angels!"

39

The Perfect Risotto

Rice vs. potatoes. The controversy has loomed larger in our marriage than any dispute over the Civil War (or, as Carl's mother explained to me, the War of Northern Aggression). When Ashley was ten years old and we were discussing her school assignment, she asked, "Daddy, why did we lose the Civil War?"

I interrupted. "What do you mean, *we* lost the Civil War?"

"Well," she clarified, pausing only briefly, "Daddy and I lost the Civil War."

Potatoes appeared nightly on our New Hampshire dinner table when I was growing up. Whether because of my parents' dietary preferences or their cities of origin—Muskogee, Oklahoma; and Edinburgh, Scotland—or because my mother believed potatoes had more nutritional value than rice, we ate potatoes: baked, mashed, hash brown, pan-roasted.

Carl, growing up in South Carolina, ate enough rice and gravy to fill Colonial Lake—Uncle Ben's rice, with thick, calorie-laden gravy. His mother, as expert at southern cooking as Francesca Scquizzato is at Italian, taught me how to make a good gravy during the Christmas holidays following our June wedding. (The temperature in Charleston hit 72° on Christmas Day, and I wondered if I'd made a mistake marrying a southerner.) Nonetheless, I rarely prepare rice and gravy, assuring Carl that the extra ten thousand calories are bad for him. The real reason I don't fix rice and gravy is that I don't *like* rice and gravy.

Risotto, more valuable than a marriage counselor, is a delicious and creative combination of a special kind of rice and almost any other ingredients you want. The ubiquitous specialty appears on most restaurant menus and in every home in northern Italy. It has become a "community" dish in my mind because its preparation requires constant stirring; if guests or family want another dish served in addition to risotto, they must join me in the kitchen and stir, keeping me company while I prepare something else. "What's your favorite Italian food?" ask many American friends. "What do you eat over there?" What we eat most often is one version or another of risotto.

I decide to embark on a quest for The Perfect Risotto, determined to pin down the best recipe in the entire Veneto and disseminate it to our U.S. friends. *Note to diary: Print risotto recipe on Christmas card?* Armed with curiosity, paper, pencil, and Italian friends possessed of great culinary skills and vast imaginations, I sally forth to learn The Truth about risotto.

But it's not that simple, I find, when I begin polling my favorite Italian cooks. So much is a matter of individual taste—that, and how your mother prepared risotto.

The essential risotto is made by sautéing a chopped onion in oil and/or butter; adding condiments, rice, and broth; then crowning the creation with butter and Parmesan cheese. But that is like saying that a Palladian villa is composed of bricks and *intonaco*, or that a Monteverdi madrigal consists of notes and staves. While each of my friends indulges personal idiosyncrasies in risotto preparation, five areas of agreement emerge from my sleuthing:

1. Use a large, heavy pot (to distribute the heat evenly) and a wooden spoon (so that you don't break the grains of rice).

2. Use carnaroli rice rather than arborio. Carnaroli is harder to find in the United States, but it remains al dente longer,

especially if you plan to have leftovers. (I have used Uncle Ben's rice several times when desperate; the result is a tasty rice dish but not risotto.)

3. Use your own homemade broth prepared from pieces of chicken and/or beef bones, plus an onion, a carrot, celery, perhaps a tomato. For a vegetable broth, omit the meat ingredients. (You can substitute a good prepared bouillon simmered several hours with an onion, a carrot, parsley, and herbs, but there will be some loss of quality.) Keep your broth simmering throughout the risotto preparation.

4. Grate your Parmesan just before you need it. *Never* use the grated cheese that comes in plastic containers from your supermarket deli. (No Italian market would even offer such a corruption.)

5. At the conclusion of your risotto, when the rice is still firm and you've added the last scoop of broth, the final two tablespoons of butter, and the grated Parmesan, let the risotto "rest" for two minutes, covered in the pot, before transferring it to a serving dish; this enhances the flavor and the creaminess.

Silvana's squash risotto is my favorite *riso* dish in all the world, perhaps because it is as beautiful as it is delicious. A rich golden-orange *risotto della zucca* is made not with zucchini but with a winter squash—Hubbard or turban—or even with pumpkin itself. Silvana *always* prepares her own broth.

SILVANA'S SQUASH RISOTTO

1 winter squash
$\frac{1}{4}$ cup finely minced yellow onion
$\frac{1}{2}$ teaspoon minced garlic

4 tablespoons extra-virgin olive oil
6 to 8 cups rich vegetable broth, heated to simmering
2 cups carnaroli rice
Salt and pepper
3 tablespoons grappa or brandy
2 tablespoons butter
$^2/_3$ cup grated Parmesan cheese
2 tablespoons chopped parsley

Peel the squash and cut it up into *pezzettini* (small pieces). Sauté the onion and garlic in the olive oil over low-medium heat until soft; add the squash cubes and $^1/_4$ cup of the vegetable broth. Simmer until the squash is soft, about 15 minutes.

Raise the heat to medium-high. Add the rice, stir well, and keep stirring until the mixture absorbs the liquid and begins to stick to the pan. Then begin adding $^1/_2$ cup of broth at a time, stirring until the liquid is absorbed. Continue the cycle for 18 to 20 minutes, until the rice is tender but not mushy, creamy but not runny. Taste for texture; add salt and pepper if needed.

Remove from the heat. Stir in the grappa, butter, Parmesan, and chopped parsley. Let sit covered for two minutes before serving. *Una meraviglia!*

Carl's favorite risotto is Wilma's *risotto agli asparagi.* Wilma says to use green asparagus, not white, when making soup or risotto, because green creates a more intense flavor.

WILMA'S ASPARAGUS RISOTTO

6 to 8 cups rich vegetable or chicken broth, heated to
    simmering
1 pound green asparagus
4 tablespoons extra-virgin olive oil
1 small yellow onion, minced

2 cups carnaroli rice
²/₃ cup dry white wine
2 tablespoons butter
Salt and pepper
²/₃ cup grated Parmesan cheese

Break off and discard the tough bottom ends from the aspara-gus, then wash the stalks well and cut them into one-inch pieces. (If the stalks are very thick or not very fresh, be sure to peel them and, in the next step, sauté a few minutes longer.)

Heat the olive oil in a heavy pot and sauté the onion over low heat. When the onion is soft, add the asparagus and con-tinue sautéing for 6 to 8 minutes.

Turn the heat to medium-high. Add the rice and mix well. Add the white wine and let the rice absorb it. Add ¹/₂ cup of the simmering broth. Stir, letting the rice absorb all the liquid until the mixture begins to stick to the bottom of the pan. Then add more broth. Repeat this sequence of adding broth and stirring continuously until the rice is the proper texture. Approximately 18 minutes after you add the rice, the risotto will be almost done. Test to be sure the rice is al dente but not too firm. Stir in a final ¹/₂ cup of broth if needed.

Remove from the heat, stir in the butter, the salt and pep-per if needed, and the Parmesan. Cover the pan and let rest for 2 minutes. *Buon appetito!*

Wilma also makes a memorable asparagus soup. Begin by sautéing raw potato cubes with the onion and asparagus, she says. When they are tender, puree the mixture, add 4 cups of rich chicken broth, simmer a few minutes, and finish by adding a little milk and butter. *Che buono!*

Marina Bighin one night served us a *primo piatto* of scrump-tious risotto created from the most unlikely pairing of vegetables: eggplant and zucchini. I like eggplant in any form whatsoever—

broiled, fried, souffléed, stuffed—but this was my first eggplant risotto. It's so delicious, I'll have to call it:

MARINA'S RISOTTO

$\frac{1}{2}$ cup finely chopped yellow onion
3 tablespoons extra-virgin olive oil
1 eggplant, peeled and cubed
1 zucchini, cubed
5 to 7 cups vegetable broth, heated to simmering
2 cups carnaroli rice
3 tablespoons good grappa or brandy
2 tablespoons butter
$\frac{2}{3}$ cup grated Parmesan cheese

Sauté the onion in the olive oil over low heat until it is soft. Add the cubed eggplant and zucchini to the sauté, along with $\frac{1}{4}$ cup of the broth.

After five minutes, raise the heat to medium-high and add the rice. Stir until the rice has absorbed the liquid. Add the grappa. Stir until all the liquid is absorbed. Then add another $\frac{1}{2}$ cup of the broth, stirring well until the mixture almost sticks to the pan. Repeat this process of adding broth and stirring for about 18 minutes, then taste for texture.

When the rice is almost ready, al dente and not too soft, remove it from the heat and add one final $\frac{1}{2}$ cup of broth, the butter, and the Parmesan. Stir well and cover. Let the risotto rest for 2 minutes, then serve. *O mamma mia!*

My first risottos were prepared only with butter, no oil, because of a risotto book I found at a remainder sale.

Silvana saw me making a butter-only risotto one day and objected, "*O, Sally, burro è troppo pesante!* Butter is too heavy." So now, with most risottos, I use good olive oil for the sautéing part, adding butter only at the end.

Several friends, Irene among them, insist on beginning a risotto with half butter, half oil. Beginners might start with this compromise mixture; later they can decide what they prefer in their own risotto.

I've included some more favorite recipes from my Piombino Dese friends in an appendix at page 253.

40

Authority

The train station in Piombino Dese is one long block from the villa. Trains leave hourly for the forty-minute ride into Venice. Once, twice, or even three times a week Carl and I become famished for the myriad flavors of the lagoon city, so we catch the 8:30 a.m. train for a morning in town. We return to Piombino Dese about 2:00 p.m. for a late lunch and a brief *riposo*.

Many of our fellow passengers on the early train are students at the University of Venice. Like most Italian universities, the University of Venice is a commuter school, drawing students from their homes throughout the eastern Veneto. Many students are already aboard when the train pulls into Piombino Dese; others board at each of the six stops into the city. They are easily recognizable by their youth, their books and large portfolios, their chatter and easy camaraderie. Some mornings we spot the children of friends in the crowd, and they break away to come and converse with us as we wait on the train platform.

One such young friend tells us that her professor, learning that she is from Piombino Dese, has expressed an interest in visiting Villa Cornaro. We encourage her to bring her professor for tea. She arrives at 4:00 p.m. on the date agreed, in the company of both her professor and his wife. The professor is a charming, ebullient gentleman. I have anticipated his visit with great interest because he is a noted authority on Roman and Renaissance art and architecture. Perhaps I can pry from him some insights into our beloved villa.

In a most engaging manner, the professor lectures to us nonstop for three hours as we walk through the villa and then sit for tea on the south portico. His discourse combines the interesting, the possible, and the improbable, all delivered with equal certainty and enthusiasm. Among the books he has written is one on the evolution of Italian gardens through the past four hundred years. He urges us to remove our small pots of begonias lining the south entrance steps and to install large pots of lemon trees in rows through the park leading to the bridge.

"Begonias," he says disparagingly, "entered Italy only in 1927. They have no place at this ancient monument." Lemon trees, he assures us, will survive Venetan winters if we move them in the fall to a sheltered spot on the southwest corner of the villa and cover them with heavy plastic. Carl and I have discussed installing lemon trees in the past, but worry that Ilario would have trouble wrestling five-hundred-pound pots to their winter shelter.

The bridge at the far side of the park, the professor informs us, originally had a "parapet," or low wall, along both sides; he delivers this pronouncement as we drink tea on the south portico. He has not walked out to the bridge to examine its edges, nor does he suggest any possibility that his statement is a hypothesis. In physically examining the bridge later, Carl and I can find no trace of lost parapets.

Our visitor assures us that the spaces between the side columns on the south portico are $1^{1}/_{2}$ times the diameter of the column bases. This, he says, is based on his study of Roman houses. I refrain from mentioning that I have measured these spaces; they are precisely $2^{1}/_{4}$ times the diameter of the column bases, just as Palladio recommends in the first of his *Four Books:*

> *The ancients . . . approved of those intercolumniations that were of two diameters and a quarter, and they reckoned this a beautiful and elegant manner of intercolumniations.*

No one knew who painted the frescos of our villa until 1950, when Nicola Ivanoff, a Russian scholar, discovered the original signed contract between the artist and his patron, Andrea Cornaro. The contract from 1716 lay among those thousands of cartons of documents in the archives of the Museo Correr in Venice that I still puzzle over. Young Mattia Bortoloni, the contract revealed, was paid four hundred ducats for painting 104 frescos and several doors throughout the villa.

Twenty-five years after Ivanoff's discovery, Douglas Lewis returned to the same trove to uncover a whole range of further findings that had eluded Italian scholars through centuries of commentary on Palladio and the villa. Doug demonstrated that Villa Cornaro was not a construction of the 1560s as previously maintained, but rather a design of 1551—and therefore perhaps Palladio's earliest major villa for a Venetian patron. The redating significantly affects the view of Palladio's artistic development.

Doug also disproved another factoid of architectural history. For centuries scholars had chortled that the pioneering art historian Giorgio Vasari was mistaken in 1568 when he wrote, in *Lives of the Painters, Sculptors, and Architects,* that "Sanmicheli also built the Casa Cornara at Piombino." Poor Vasari, they said with some glee, is confused about Palladio's villa in Piombino; he thinks it was designed by Sanmicheli. Doug found documents proving that for more than two hundred years the Sanmicheli and Palladio villas stood side by side. In fact, he located a 1707 rendering of the two villas. The Sanmicheli villa was razed in 1795.

I have learned firsthand just how arduous and tedious Doug's work was, the painstaking perusal of records written in Latin, Venetan, and Italian—all in a handwriting baffling to a modern American eye.

A famous, elderly Italian authority on Palladio visits the villa one day early in our ownership, leading a study group of about a hundred young men and women. His books and articles on Palladio are known throughout the world. Carl accompanies the group as the scholar explains, arms waving enthusiastically, head bobbing energetically, that the original villa owners would have ridden their horses up the broad, gently rising southern steps of the villa and dismounted directly onto the portico. That is simply not true, as he would have known if he had examined the stairs—or even talked with a horseman. It's clear from inspection that the present steps were reconfigured sometime in the past, so they are no longer in their original profile. Initially, as illustrated in *Four Books,* the stairs rose very abruptly from ground level; as reconfigured and lengthened in the early 1700s, the grade is reduced by half. Even with the reduced grade, a horse would have great difficulty maneuvering the extremely irregular surface of rough stones without injury; no sensible rider would have exposed his mount to such danger.

The latest publication of a prestigious architectural study group—a large, expensive tome written by authorities in the field—states in its discussion of our villa that the upper floor is divided into two suites, each approached by separate stairs. How did such a misconception arise? The floor plan upstairs is identical to the floor plan of the first floor, a single unified space. The authorities seem to have assumed that because La Malcontenta and several others have separate apartments upstairs, Villa Cornaro must also.

Numerous students from the universities of Venice, Padua, Udine, and once even Rome request our permission to study particular aspects of the villa for their theses: the interior brick stairs, the floor patterns, the capitals of the columns, the statues. We happily give permission, asking only that they furnish us a copy of the finished work, or at least the part relating to Villa Cornaro. We are almost uniformly disappointed in the ultimate theses because of the absence of primary research. Citation is usually centered on secondary sources of highly uneven quality, buttressed by a few desultory measurements and photographs. Meanwhile, thousands of cartons of documents rest unexamined in the archives of the Museo Correr and other archives of Venice, their difficult and challenging contents awaiting another Ivanoff or Lewis, someone with the imagination and diligence to challenge the authorities.

41

I Tatti

We step from our taxi at a broad iron gate barely off the narrow road and ring the bell of Villa I Tatti on the outskirts of Florence. Two housekeepers greet us in Italian and carry our bags through a graveled courtyard to the main door of the large square villa. Suffused light envelops us in a Tuscan palette of ochres and greens.

Reading an alumni journal last year, Carl learned that Walter Kaiser, his honors-program instructor at Harvard, is now director of I Tatti, Harvard's postdoctoral center for Italian Renaissance studies. Carl and I were still undergraduates when Bernard Berenson bequeathed his famous estate to Harvard. For years, long before the Harvard connection arose, I heard of I Tatti through my father, who considered Bernard Berenson one of the great geniuses of all time and who delighted in discussing B.B. (as my father called him, as if referring to a childhood pal) and the machinations he engaged in with Joseph Duveen, Nathan Wildenstein, and other fabled art dealers. Berenson, whom many (himself included) believed to be the greatest figure in Italian art history and connoisseurship since Vasari, moved to I Tatti in 1900 with his wife, Mary. Their home became a lodestar for famous aesthetes, art dealers, scholars, and collectors of his time.

Carl wrote to Walter—with whom he had not spoken in more than thirty years—to reintroduce himself and invite Walter to visit us at Villa Cornaro. Walter graciously reciprocated with an invitation to I Tatti. And so we have come. (We still await Walter's visit to Piombino Dese.) Upon our arrival we are shown upstairs to our suite, the same one Berenson's close friend Edith Wharton used when she visited I Tatti. The megadealer Duveen also stayed in the suite, though presumably not at the same time.

Walter Kaiser leads us back downstairs and out onto the terrace for coffee with several of the Fellows who have just arrived to begin a year of research at I Tatti: Clara, from Britain, who is working on a Carracci project while her husband—not a Fellow—ponders Kant; a Fellow from Germany researching medieval food and recipes, which he says are the key to a culture; a Fellow from Sweden with a new slant on Machiavelli; a visiting Englishwoman who is a friend of someone else and isn't studying anything other than this Edenic congregation of scholars. I am awed by the army of scholars about to be set loose upon the archives and monuments of Tuscany for the coming year. I say Tuscany because, although Harvard's I Tatti program is not formally limited in its scope, its location and the interests of its Fellows seem to dictate a weighting primarily toward Florence, Rome, and central Italy.

The throbbing heart of I Tatti is its research library. We're provided our own key to use during our stay, and I immediately lose Carl. He simply disappears into the stacks of the architecture section. I choose to wander among the 130,000 volumes, sampling a few, reading briefly in John Pope-Hennessy's book on Fra Angelico. I encounter not one soul. We are alone in this stupendous, sumptuous vault of books.

At 8:00 p.m. *aperitivi* are served for scholars and guests in the large living room, which is lined with beautiful and precious *oggetti d'arte*. Afterward, Walter hosts the two of us for a private dinner in the cozy French Library. Salmon mousse accompanies amiable conversation ranging from Italian literature to Sansovino and Palladio.

Amid such elegance, such refinement, such scholarship and art, why is Carl descending into such a funk? I am tempted to kick him under the table at dinner so that his glum look will at least be replaced by the animation of pain. Only a fear of kicking Walter by mistake restrains me. Back in our suite afterward, Carl vents the dour thought that has seized him.

"Why is it always Florence?" he exclaims. "Why doesn't Venice have something like this?"

"Carl," I explain patiently, "no one else anywhere has anything like this. This is one of a kind in the world."

Carl begins berating Vasari and Berenson in the same breath. "It's a matter of tastemakers," he says. "All the foreign scholars flock to Florence and Rome. Venice just doesn't get its fair share."

He is recycling the theory that the tilt to Florence started with Giorgio Vasari, the sixteenth-century Italian painter who practically invented the study of art history. Vasari was a Florentine himself and his principal patrons were the Florentine rulers, so in writing his *Lives of the Painters, Sculptors, and Architects,* he naturally directed most of his attention to his countrymen, flattering and reinforcing the taste of his patrons. Of course, Carl is overstating in order to make his case; Vasari's book was so successful because he really was a straight shooter. Nonetheless, anyone in Vasari's place would tend to emphasize the strengths of his own friends and countrymen.

Carl's point, not original with him, is that the qualitative judgments of Vasari, albeit culturally biased, shaped the taste of future generations, and that the popularizing influence of latter-day followers such as Berenson just solidified those judgments.

I tell Carl to take an aspirin and come to bed.

The following morning Carl returns to the library, but I remain in our room, sampling the books that surround me. I pick up S. J. Freedburg's classic *Painting in Italy, 1500–1600.* Freedburg discusses how the High Renaissance evolved in Italy through the lives of four men who each took giant strides forward: Leonardo da Vinci and Michelangelo in Florence, Raphael in Urbino, Giorgione in Venice. Freedburg has just died; Walter tells us he has been asked to give a eulogy at a memorial service planned for the near future.

With profound thanks to Walter, and a renewed invitation to visit us at Villa Cornaro, we leave by taxi to rejoin the real world in Florence, convinced that we have just spent a day and a half in the most ivoried tower the world has to offer.

Aboard our train back to the Veneto, I tell Carl about the Freedburg explication that I have spent the morning reading, and it returns us to our mental game of comparing Venice and Florence. Frankly, in the field of Renaissance art it would be a struggle for

Venice to ever claim more than a tie with Florence. Even that might be an ambitious comparison, though Venice has never been short on ambition.

Outside the field of art, on the other hand, it is medieval and Renaissance Venice, not Florence, that seems to have engendered the values that have grown and flowered in our modern culture. I pull out my notebook, as Carl and I begin to list some of them.

Republican government heads the parade. Venice managed to maintain a republican form of government for about a thousand years without ever falling into periods of dictatorship like Athens and Rome before it. Florentine governance had barely emerged from feudalism before falling under the rule of the Medicis, a regime punctuated by the religious despotism of Savonarola. Venice's oligarchic republic was certainly flawed, but it offered a serviceable model for the modern world to build upon.

Within the context of its time and geography, Venice also showed a plucky desire to keep a healthy distance from the Church Universal. The relative freedom that it offered to the press made Venice an early publishing center and repeatedly provoked rebukes from Rome; Florence, on the other hand, was closely aligned with the papacy. Venice nurtured scientific inquiry at the University of Padua, where cadavers were dissected for research despite the protests of the local bishop. Jews found greater tolerance in Venice than anywhere else in southern Europe, and it was the University of Padua that awarded the first university degree to a woman. These freedoms were not developed in Venice to a level that we would find acceptable today, but they reflect a concern with personal liberty that was perhaps unique in its time. Identifying the social and economic conditions, the leadership structures, the concept of the individual that fostered these early developments in Venice might hold important lessons for the modern world as it seeks to sow the seeds of democratic government in broader and sometimes less promising fields.

The Republic of Venice's relevance in the modern world is obscured by post-Napoleonic romanticism that has been captivated by visions of the Bridge of Sighs. And studying the factors that were shaping broad social views hundreds of years in the past is infinitely more difficult than investigating who influenced a single Renaissance painter.

Before our swift Eurostar train is even close to Mestre, Carl and I have agreed that the only sensible course of action is to move I Tatti to the Veneto—the research library, the dining room, the Edith Wharton suite, the artworks, everything. Walter will enjoy the view of the Alps.

42

Italian Drivers

"Heads up!" Carl exclaims. As we crest a gentle hill on the two-lane road to Vicenza, we confront two Mercedes sedans rushing toward us side by side. One spurts past the other and returns to the left lane just feet away from our fender.

"That's a seven-point-O," says Ashley from the back seat. Italian drivers, she has concluded, are engaged in a competition not disclosed to foreign drivers. The competition is judged on a point system similar to that used for springboard diving in the Olympics. Points awarded for a particular maneuver are based one-half on degree of difficulty and one-half on style. An example: A big Alfa Romeo passing a Fiat Uno is assigned a low degree of difficulty, but the passing car can earn "style points" by waiting until there is a curve over the crest of a hill in a no-passing zone with oncoming traffic. The presence of hapless bicyclers would add more points. Obviously, if a Fiat Uno were to pass an Alfa Romeo in those circumstances, the score would be off the charts. Carl and I agree that Ashley's explanation of Italian driving is better than any other we've heard.

Ashley has begun her third career. After two postcollege years as a paralegal, she attended law school and then practiced law for three years, first in Washington, D.C., then in Los Angeles. Now she has her dream job: television staff writer, albeit for the inaugural season of an unlikely new show entitled *Buffy the Vampire Slayer*. The program shows early signs of attracting the cultlike following of young adults and teens that sponsors cherish. When Carl is on a business trip to Los Angeles, Ashley takes him onto the set where *Buffy* is filming and introduces him to the cast.

"Buffy is a very healthy young woman," he tells me later.

Sometimes I think of the Italian peninsula as a Yellowstone Park of warm, bubbling springs. In an irregular rhythm, one and then another boils over in an outpouring of unprecedented creativity and innovation. In one period a Mantua moves to the cultural forefront, at another time a Ferrara or a Parma. In Urbino, for example, the eruption spanned a period of about two generations in the 1400s; for that brief moment the minuscule dukedom was one of the great cultural centers of Europe, the birthplace of famous artists such as Raphael and Bramante and a magnet for others. From time to time Carl and I escape Villa Cornaro for quick excursions to such towns.

On one such occasion we're headed homeward from Urbino, chatting about the treasures we've seen in the Ducal Palace and the Oratorio de San Giovanni and calculating the time it will take us to reach Piombino Dese. We don't realize that the harrowing part of our trip lies ahead. An hour of tedious autostrada driving brings us to a service-station/rest-stop for a brioche and coffee and a fill-up. Taking my turn at the wheel, I pull up to the pumps. *"Il pieno, per favore.* Fill 'er up," I tell the middle-aged attendant. What kind of fuel, *benzina* (gasoline) or *gasolio* (diesel)? he asks—to our surprise. We don't know how to answer him; this is our first fill-up since we rented the car and we're not familiar with the model, but the fuel type is usually specified on the little door to the fuel tank. Whatever it requires, we reply, lead-free or diesel. *"Ah, verde.*

Lead-free," he says. "*Il pieno, per favore,*" I repeat. He fills the tank; we pay him 92,000 lire and drive away, recalculating the time till we are home.

Forty miles or so down the road I feel the engine skip and I watch a mysterious dashboard light blink red. Alarmed and suddenly a bit queasy, I picture us stopping on the shoulder of the autostrada, the skinniest strip of pavement ever devoted to parking a car; I envision us smushed by a pasta truck, such as the mammoth Barilla lorry that crowded us earlier. What an ironic ending to our great Italian adventure! I alert Carl to help me watch for the next service station, adding cravenly that I hope we make it. If the motor dies, we'll have to pull onto the right-hand ribbon whether we want to or not.

After five miles more of motor-skipping, an Agip station's yellow logo shines before us like an emergency flare and I turn in. As we curve away from the autostrada, the motor conks out. I barely coast up to the island of pumps.

"Aha!" says the gray-haired attendant who awaits us. "What have we here?" He is wondering why I am out of the car and gesticulating dramatically before he can even ask how much fuel we want. I try to explain the enigma of a car that we know to be full of fuel but that is decidedly dead on its wheels. I am waving my hands ever more wildly and losing control of my Italian.

"Ahem," he interjects. "What kind of fuel did you put in?"

Carl and I respond in mini-chorus that we'd asked the last attendant to fill it with whatever it called for, and that he'd filled it with *verde.*

"Oh, but *signori,* it takes *gasolio,* not *benzina.* That is your problem." He walks away to service a car that has arrived at the adjoining pump.

He returns at last; we are not abandoned. The process of rectifying the wrong is extensive and little short of miraculous, but the attendant takes the matter in hand personally when he finishes his shift at the pumps twenty minutes later. His first ministrations are aborted: as he begins emptying the *benzina* from our tank with an electric pump, the station supervisor races over and in an unusually brief Italian dialogue tells him to stop before he blows up the station and everyone within two hundred meters. Our new friend begins again, this time with a slower, but safer, siphon. With the *benzina* removed and replaced with *gasolio*, he cleans the engine with arcane ablutions strange and wonderful to us, replaces filters, smiles beatifically, and assures us we have no further worries.

As we crank up and prepare to return to the road, he walks over to give us a final piece of advice. "Don't mention this to the car-rental company," he says.

43

Silvana, Film Star

One of the movie crew from Rome drives his small truck through the west *cancello* a few minutes after 9:00 a.m. The others, three men and two women, park their cars in Piazzetta Squizzato. Soon they carefully bring their equipment—large cameras, tripods, miles of heavy black electrical cable—up the front steps of the villa and into the entrance hall. Quickly and quietly, they assemble two camera stations, one in the kitchen and the other centered in the west doorway of the east salon with a sight line stretching into the kitchen. The cast will arrive at 1:00 p.m., the producer tells us.

Carl and I have rented the ground floor of Villa Cornaro to an Italian film studio for one day, in an effort to generate additional income for restoration. Only three scenes in the made-for-television movie *Morte di una ragazza per bene* (*Death of a Nice Young Woman*) will be filmed at the villa, one primarily in the kitchen, another in the grand salon, and a final one in the park. The producer faxes us a proposed contract ten days in advance; Carl studies it with his lawyer's eye. *Note to diary: If Carl can't answer a telephone in Italian, why is he undeterred by an Italian contract?*

"Actually, it's not a bad contract," Carl comments ruefully. Of course, that doesn't stop him from adding more negative clauses than a porcupine has quills. Some are specific: no rolling tripods or other gear, no direct lights on the frescos, etc. His favorite, however, is broad: If we feel at any time during the filming that some activity may cause harm to the villa, we can stop production on the spot. If the producer and director can fashion an agreeable alternative, filming may resume; otherwise the film company must leave and we will refund its payment.

"I can't foresee everything bad that might happen," Carl rationalizes, "but I'll know it when I see it."

The producer visits us one day before the filming in order to finalize the contract. To Carl's surprise, the producer accepts all Carl's changes, with just one minor clarification. In fact, he has a different worry in mind. The director of the film has just told him that an actress is needed to portray a cook in the kitchen scene. In reviewing the script, he has decided that the owner of such a grand house would not be cooking by herself; she would supervise a household cook instead. *Note to diary: Explain to Carl how life should follow art.*

"Can you suggest any local person for this role?" the producer asks.

The answer is obvious to both Carl and me: Silvana, your moment of fame has arrived! She requires some encouragement, but soon agrees.

When the crew members break for lunch on the day of filming to devour a huge basket of sandwiches and sweets ordered from Caffè Palladio, they invite us to join them on the front portico. We are left wondering whether the amount of wine consumed by the crew will be reflected in the final print—and whether for good or ill.

At precisely 1:00 p.m., a tall and svelte brunette enters the villa with an unassuming stride. She is followed by a second woman bearing a small, well-worn valise. The director introduces us to Virginia Castellano, the film's star. She disappears into our Moses room, still followed by her companion, who proves to be her dresser and makeup artist. Two men position themselves at the camera stations. Soon Signora Castellano emerges, wearing a large white paper collar to protect her clothing from her fresh makeup. She walks briskly to the kitchen, says "*Buon giorno*" to Silvana and the director, turns, and faces the camera.

"*Allora,*" she says—a word best translated in these circumstances as "Let's get this show on the road."

The scene has scant dialogue, all spoken by Signora Castellano, but the filming of it requires numerous trips to my refrigerator, as Silvana and the movie star concoct at least eight cakes in as many camera "takes." The director is not satisfied by the light, or the star's visibility behind the island, or the tilt of her chin, or where Silvana stands. A plane roars overhead during a perfect take, rattling the cameraman's concentration; a truck along Via Roma screeches during another shot. Finally, the kitchen scene is complete. Silvana's work is finished and she leaves, apologizing for using up all my eggs, milk, and flour.

It is the second cameraman's turn. As he stands in his appointed doorway, the tall actress tilts her head as if hearing a telephone ring, then walks quickly through the dining room and into the grand salon. She picks up the phone receiver from the central table and says "*Pronto.* Ready" (the Italian telephone greeting). Silence for two minutes. The director calls, "*Bene. Ancora una volta, per favore!* Good. One more time, please." Signora Castellano returns to the kitchen and repeats her walk. Five times she does this and we see no difference in her gait, in her facial expression or her hand movements. Later I learn that the character, upon picking up the phone in the grand salon, receives word of her daughter's death in an auto accident. During the two minutes of silence in the grand salon, the camera had recorded the grief transforming her face.

The third scene, in the park, is merely transitional. The company completes it in a heartbeat. That's it, they're finished. Everybody leaves, offering us thanks and a large check.

Silvana looks beautiful in her role.

44

Murano Magic

My first step into the swirl of gaudy tourists that always crowds Piazza di San Marco comes on a brilliant June day in 1984, three years before we first see Villa Cornaro. A long weekend in Venice caps our family's three-week sojourn at a tangerine-tinted farmhouse outside Florence. It is my first visit ever to Italy.

As we admire the vast, brilliantly colored playground of San Marco, a deeply tanned hawker plucks us abruptly from the crowd with an insistent "Glass? You want to see beautiful glass? We go to Murano! Free boat ride!"

The glass doesn't appeal but the *motoscafo* ride does, especially to sons Carl and Jim, whose scant years—they're fifteen and twelve—have not held enough boat rides to suit them. Soon the five of us clamber aboard our new friend's James Bond–like craft and roar off through teal-and-silver spume to Murano.

Seven minutes after boarding, we coast into the dock of a three-story warehouse and showroom on Murano. Murano, we learn, is the collective name for a group of five small islands in the lagoon north of Venice. There has been glassblowing in the lagoon since at least as early as 750, but in 1291 the Grand Council ordered all glassmakers to move their furnaces to Murano. The reason, they said, was to put an end to the destructive fires that the furnaces periodically unleashed upon the city, but a second reason may have been to isolate and thus protect the secret glassmaking technology that the artisans had amassed.

Our host leads us up long steps to the top floor of the warehouse. A brightly lighted salon explodes before us with shimmering objects in colored glass and *cristallo:* one room is a vast bestiary of dramatically posed animals; another is devoted to chandeliers and lamps. There is a room for tableware and one for human figures and flowers. Our children are entranced by shelf upon shelf of glass fish. The glass sparkles like an ocean aquarium teeming with mackerel and tarpon and salmon.

One special fourteen-inch-tall vase catches our eye. Its irregular oval shape begs to be caressed; its gray, white, and cerulean colors evoke a dark but placid sky.

"An exceptional piece," the salesclerk comments, when he sees where our eyes have settled. "It is designed by the master glassblower Seguso."

"Archimede Seguso!" I exclaim in wonder; he is the only glassblower I have heard of.

"Livio Seguso," the clerk says.

"They work together?" I ask hopefully.

"No, but they are related," he says apologetically, adding "All the Segusos are related." He watches my reaction. "Livio Seguso is very highly regarded, a great master."

Though we are not convinced that Livio Seguso is the Picasso of glassmaking, Carl and I cannot resist his vase. It has sat on our dining-room buffet in Atlanta ever since. Each year we admire its colors more. Occasionally when I pass it I offer a silent thank-you to the aggressive promoter who picked us from the mass of tourists that June day in Piazza di San Marco.

For the sake of argument, I'm willing to accept that there may be people who don't love Venetian glass. They may think its colors too garish, its shapes too wild, its surfaces too whimsical, its dragons and dolphins too fantastical. But they should realize that all this embodies the spirit of Venice itself. The spirit of excess in color and decoration, the conviction that no surface can be too rich, too gilded and bejeweled. It is the spirit celebrated in the mosaics and marbles of the Basilica di San Marco, in the rhythmic tracery of the Palazzo Ducale and the gold of Ca' d'Oro.

I'm pleased that my infatuation with Venetian glass began on Murano itself. It gives me a feeling of satisfaction each time I return to prowl the shops and revisit the historic old Murano Glass

Museum. The museum lays out the whole panoply of Murano glassmaking from its earliest history, with works by most of the contemporary masters as well. Napoleone Martinuzzi, Flavio Poli, Dino Martens, Carlo Scarpa—all the legendary designers are displayed in the large second-floor gallery. Added recently on the ground floor, flanking the entranceway with a certain pride of place, are two striking works. One is a creation by Dale Chihuly, the celebrated American glassmaker who once worked on Murano. The other—a geometric black-and-white tower rising like an op-art lighthouse—is by Livio Seguso.

One morning begins badly. Instead of catching the early train for an excursion into Venice, we are caught up in details and busywork at the villa.

The day begins with a long, depressing meeting with Angelo Marconato and his son Stefano. They explain why, when we arrived from Atlanta three days ago for our spring visit, we found the garden of the villa crisscrossed with a labyrinth of trenches that would have stumped Theseus. Connecting the villa to the regional water and sewer systems instead of continuing to rely on our own well and septic tank has proved more complicated than we anticipated when we authorized the project the previous fall. First, we learn that there was a second septic tank—unknown to us—on the side of the villa opposite the sewer connection. Second, an entirely separate system of drains is required for surface water.

"They didn't dig this much to excavate Pompeii!" Carl exclaims in frustration.

The rest of the morning slips away in shopping for the evening's dinner and planning for a *ricevimento* (reception) for performers, friends, and local officials to follow an upcoming concert at the villa. We need an exposure to the sensual feast of Venice to get us out of our grumpy mood, so we catch the 2:34 p.m. train, a jitney of just two cars, both covered in large-scale graffiti. Carl and I view this as vandalism, but an Italian friend offers a different perspective. "Perhaps the young people just need to express themselves," she says.

I shudder to think what I would do if a young person had an attack of creativity on the exterior walls of the villa.

We've just received an announcement of a new glass shop in Campo San Stefano specializing in Murano glass of the nineteenth century. At the Venice train station we catch the No. 82 vaporetto all the way to the Accademia. We cross the Accademia Bridge over the Grand Canal, jostling our way through the tourists, and walk quickly to our destination.

Like a child on his first visit to Toys "R" Us, we pause to marvel at the treasures displayed in the shopwindow. Bizarre glass dragons cling to the sides of pitchers in brilliant variegated pinks and limes; a broad round *cristallo* plate cradles a half dozen or so pieces of beguiling glass fruit; a large amber glass fish balances on its fins with its tail thrust high above and its mouth open as though singing.

The interior of the shop is small, perhaps two hundred square feet, and its shelves are suitably crowded with pieces as exotic as those in the window. Surely the motto of nineteenth-century Murano glassmakers must have been "Too much is not enough."

The shop manager—whose name, we later learn, is Puccio—is sitting behind a small desk when we enter, but promptly rises to greet us. We are to learn in the course of subsequent visits and research that Puccio is one of the great experts on early Murano glass. He discourses easily on the items that catch our eye, *lavadita* (finger bowls), *calici* (goblets), *brocche* (ewers). I am distracted, however, by what I see on the desk where he has been working: open sheets of musical staff paper. Several sheets are filled with handwritten musical notation.

"You must be a musician," I comment.

"Yes," he replies diffidently. "I'm a composer."

I explain that I am a church musician myself. He responds enthusiastically, "Would you like to hear something I've written?"

With our encouragement he produces a CD player from the shelf behind him and treats us to a ten-minute musical interlude. Puccio was one of several Venetian musicians commissioned to produce works for a recent musical gala, we learn. His contribution was the piano composition that we hear now. I admire the three-part work very much. Some of it is cantabile, like a Chopin nocturne; other sections are percussive and repetitive in a Stravinskian manner. I would like to hear it again, but Puccio immediately begins telling us about his current project, the manuscript that I spotted on his desk.

"An opera to be presented next winter," he says. He rapidly summarizes the plot—so rapidly, in fact, that the only thread of the story I retain is that the protagonist is the lover not only of both women in the story but of the priest as well.

"Would you like to hear some of it?" he asks. "It is somewhat like Bellini."

"Of course," Carl and I both reply, expecting another CD recording or perhaps an audiotape.

Puccio surprises us by opening a desk drawer, lifting an electronic keyboard to the desktop, and sitting down before it. Intrigued at the prospect of a piano presentation in the midst of a small Venetian glass shop, we sit in two chairs on the opposite side of the desk. Suddenly, after an opening measure, our host bursts into song—not in a modest voice, but full stage volume. He could fill La Fenice with that voice, which reverberates from the walls of the shop. Carl looks about nervously, as though he fears some of the glass objects might be in danger.

The multiple characters of the opera do not faze Puccio; he alternates easily between the tenor and contralto roles. At the end of one passage he pauses, asks our reaction, and then launches into the finale of the opera, which he says we will find especially suggestive of Bellini.

The whole experience is surreal. Why aren't curious crowds pressing through the doorway, I wonder, to hear Puccio's beautiful singing and fascinating music? Carl and I leave finally after abundant thank-yous for the performance. I turn to Carl as the door closes behind us.

"I love Venice!" I tell him.

45

The First of July

Years pass before I comprehend that the families of Piombino Dese are bound by a grim episode from the past, a shared community memory of a notorious day that seared the life of the town and shaped the way its residents—even those who were born afterward—view the world.

Why did it take me so long to appreciate the importance of the events of July 1, 1944? The infectious conviviality of the Piombinesi hides from newcomers any somber thoughts. Perhaps in the early years my Italian limited what I was hearing. Or maybe, as we have become closer friends, the Piombinesi have allowed their conversation to return more often to that July day.

I have decided that the major reason may be the oversimplified view that I brought with me as to the role of the Italians in World War II. In my early years in the Veneto I was amused by the recurring celebrations of the Alpini. The Alpini, I heard, were honored as the heroic Italian freedom fighters who fought as partisans to overthrow the yoke of oppression of the German invaders. This seemed to be dealing loosely with history, since I remembered that the Italians and Germans were allies in World War II and remained so until after the Allies had invaded Sicily in July 1943 and were poised to invade the Italian peninsula. On my first trip to Italy in 1984, Carl and I visited the American military cemetery outside Florence to find, amid the thousands of white crosses glistening on the hillside, the grave of my mother's only brother, who died in the bloody landing at Anzio in January 1944.

In time, however, I learn that my knowledge of Italy in the war was incomplete. The king of Italy forced Benito Mussolini's resignation as prime minister in July 1943 and put him in prison. The cabinet that succeeded Mussolini's surrendered Italy to the Allies, though the action was largely symbolic because the German army surged into Italy to continue the war. The Germans freed Mussolini from prison and set him up as the figurehead leader of a rival Fascist government based at Salò in the north, while the legitimate Italian government declared war on Germany and aligned itself with the Allies. It was in that late period from October 1943 to April 1945—with the front lines of the Germans and Allies mired at first below Rome and later north of Florence—that the Alpini emerged as true partisans in the Alpine region, not the opera buffa figures that I had envisioned.

Early on the morning of July 1, 1944, German soldiers who had been billeted in the *barchessa* of the villa and elsewhere in the surrounding area assembled in the center of Piombino Dese. With prepared lists in hand, they dispersed through the town and banged on the doors of families with young men who were thought to be less than fully committed to the Fascist cause.

The men were brought into the town square at gunpoint and then loaded onto decrepit German trucks bound for northern factories. A young woman with an enormous belly, obviously in the final weeks of pregnancy, burst from a doorway screaming. She ran to one of the trucks and struggled awkwardly to climb aboard. "You must take me, too!" she shrieked, grabbing one of the prisoners. "You can't take my husband alone; you must take me, too!" Madly screaming and crying, impervious to the shouts and imprecations of the German soldiers, she could not be pried from the man she clung to. Finally the German officer in charge threw them both off the truck and ordered the sorry cortege to depart without them.

Giuseppina tells me this story. The woman was her mother's sister-in-law.

"They took my father," Gastone tells me. "He was shipped to Germany for forced labor in the war plants."

"He returned after the war?" I ask.

"Yes, he walked back after the war. He was very, very thin, and he had a long black beard," he replies. "I'll never forget when I first saw him."

"Is he still living?"

"No, he died years ago. Would you like to see his picture?" Gastone reaches for his billfold and produces a small, worn photo of his long-dead father.

Young Epifanio Marulli, who later became custodian of Villa Cornaro for Dick Rush, happened to be at the parish church on the morning of July 1, helping the priests on some project. He was hiding in the campanile of the church when the Germans banged on the door of his home. They took three of his brothers away to Germany, but never found Epifanio.

"None of them came back," Epifanio says quietly. "Two died in an industrial accident in the factory where they were placed. The other died in a bombing raid on his factory, just ten days before the end of the war."

"Who did the bombing?"

"Americans, I think."

More than a score of boys and young men were taken from Piombino Dese that morning. The knocking came at front doors throughout the town and surrounding countryside.

Epifanio tells his tale of that July 1 with a kind of wonder in his voice. "My father worked for the *sindaco* of Piombino Dese during those years. He was a chauffeur and worked around the *sindaco*'s house. The *sindaco* knew everyone in town; he was the one who gave the Germans the list."

"Why? Why would he do that, especially to the family of his own employee?" I ask in amazement.

"*Un fascista*," he replies simply.

Epifanio is in his eighties now, living quietly with Elena in retirement in a modest home on the street that leads from the villa to the train station. Often I spot him and wave as I hurry to the station for a trip into Venice. I can see in his face that after all these decades since July 1, 1944, he still cannot fathom what hatred, cynicism, desperation, or depravity precipitated the events of that day.

The postwar years were cruel in the Veneto. "Find food for today" was the imperative of each morning. I think of Giacomo's story of his father desperately fishing for food when other resources failed, and of Ilario's emigration to Australia to relieve the strain on his family.

Now, in a strange reversal, the Veneto is the fastest-growing region in all of Europe. Prosperity abounds on all sides. Yet I am sure that the Piombinesi have their appreciation of the present anchored in their collective memory of the past. The Italian celebration of food is often noted. Surely a great part of it is grounded in the knowledge that today's food must be enjoyed because tomorrow's food is uncertain. In the same way, the overwhelming reliance on family ties must be influenced by experiences like July 1, 1944, when trust in the more extended circle of political leadership, community, and friendship failed.

46

Camillo Mariani

My father, a Scot by birth who lived most of his life in New Hampshire, always carried in his jacket pocket a wad of photographs of the primitive nineteenth-century New England paintings that he had collected—portraits mostly, a few landscapes, an occasional still life. The paintings crowded the walls of our Main Street house when I was growing up. Daddy eagerly displayed his photographs to everyone he met who showed even a slight interest in American portraiture. The subjects of the paintings looking down from the walls of our New England home—a sea captain and his wife from Bedford, a serious young girl from Concord named May Hill, and many others—became for him an extended family.

In this one way, the grand salon on the first floor of Villa Cornaro sometimes reminds me of my Littleton home. The portraits in the grand salon are not paintings, of course, but full-figure statues executed in *marmorino,* a type of stucco. Each of them measures eight feet tall and is set in its own niche in the wall. Palladio planned for the statues from the beginning; the niches are clearly shown on the floor plan in his *Four Books*. The Pisani family at Palladio's Villa Pisani at Montagnana elected to use the four similar niches there for statues representing the seasons of the year. The Cornaros took a different tack. After the original patron Giorgio Cornaro died, his son Girolamo in the early 1590s commissioned Camillo Mariani to create statues of illustrious Cornaros of the past.

It was a typical Cornaro gesture. The Cornaros loved paintings and busts of themselves. If their public offices did not generate enough portraiture, they were always ready to commission something on their own.

The two earliest figures among the statues at Villa Cornaro are

Statues in the grand salon, lower *piano nobile*,
with the villa's patron, Giorgio Cornaro, at left

of Marco Cornaro, who became doge of Venice in 1365, and his
grandson Giorgio, who died a hero of the Republic in 1434 after
being captured in battle and tortured in a Milan prison. There are
two of Giorgio's grandchildren. Giorgio's granddaughter Caterina
Cornaro, queen of Cyprus, is shown, of course, together with her
brother, who was also named Giorgio. This Giorgio was so influential in Venetian affairs that he was acclaimed as "father of his country" more than two hundred years before George Washington was
born. Giorgio's son Girolamo fills the next niche. The last holds the
third Giorgio, the one who commissioned Palladio to design and
build the villa.

The southern wall of the grand salon, opening onto the south
portico, fills the room with light and warmth from its huge doorway and eight windows, four below and four above. The other walls
each hold two of the niches and statues. Because of the four large
columns supporting the ceiling and upper floor, the six statues are
visible simultaneously from just one spot in the room, a position
about four feet into the room from the north. The effect on a visitor standing at that place in the early days must have been profound—to be confronted by six legendary heroes of the republic,
all larger than life, leaning outward from their niches with animated hand gestures and sharp gazes. Together they make up the
earliest full-figure portrait gallery of one family in western art.

Like Caravaggio on canvas, Mariani strove for lifelike portraiture. His Caterina seems poised to speak. His first Giorgio embodies patience and forbearance in features and stance. To arrive at the
likenesses, Mariani would have studied earlier commemorative
medallions and, when available, contemporary paintings.

Camillo Mariani was born in Vicenza in 1567, two years after
Michelanglo's death in Rome. He trained in Vicenza in the workshop of Agostino Rubini, but his talent was recognized early by the
architect Vincenzo Scamozzi and others, and he was entrusted with
important commissions. He was just twenty-one years old when he
sculpted three of the marble statues that look down on Piazza di
San Marco in Venice from atop the Marciana Library. Soon he had

his own workshop and was creating statues for Palladio's basilica and the church of San Pietro in Vicenza.

His six statues at Villa Cornaro can be viewed as a culmination of his work in the Veneto. First, the project marks his important role in the introduction to the Veneto of *marmorino* as a medium for sculpture. Second, it marks Mariani as a bridge from the Renaissance to the Baroque. In 1597, ready for a bigger stage, Mariani moved his workshop to Rome, where he was immediately accepted as a leading figure in its artistic world and tapped for works throughout the city. Pope Clement VIII commissioned him to execute several statues in *marmorino* for his chapel in Saint Peter's Basilica. Mariani's statues for the church of San Bernardo alle Terme and for Villa Cornaro are sometimes called his masterworks. Although Mariani died young, at age forty-four, he is viewed as an important influence on Gian Lorenzo Bernini, Italy's greatest sculptor of the seventeenth century, because Bernini's father and mentor, Pietro Bernini, trained in Mariani's workshop.

In quiet moments from time to time I sit in the grand salon studying the statues. Sometimes I feel as if I were at a Cornaro family reunion, with these famous Cornaros jabbering and socializing around me. At other times I focus on the short, brilliant career of Camillo Mariani and the treasures that Villa Cornaro is privileged to share with the historic churches and chapels of Rome.

47

Unstrung Pearls

At 2:00 a.m. the *squillo* (ring) of the telephone in Atlanta sounds more like a *strillo* (scream). Carl nudges me to answer the phone; it's on my side of the bed. My heart pounds with trepidation. What calamity is being announced? Where are the children?

"*Signora Gable,*" a distant voice says. "*Vorrebbero vedere la villa i vostri amici?* Would your friends like to see the villa?" What villa? What friends? My mind struggles to file these random questions.

My brain manages to construct an Italian response: "Excuse me, but who is this?"

"*Villa Valmarana, signora. Sono il proprietario!* I am the owner!" the voice explains. "You and your husband visited me last month. You said a friend in America was interested in buying a Palladian villa. I want to know if they are coming."

At last I'm beginning to make sense of everything—except why this call is coming at 2:00 a.m. During our last stay in the Veneto, Carl and I heard that Villa Valmarana was for sale; with a phone call ahead, we drive over for a visit. Friends of ours in Atlanta have expressed a vague interest in acquiring one of Palladio's villas, so we decide that a conversation with the owner and a careful new look at the villa is in order.

This is actually the second time we have visited Villa Valmarana, and we hope that the owner will not remember the circumstances of our first encounter. On that occasion we arrived unannounced and simply looked into the grounds from the street. Carl tried to photograph the villa from a corner of the property, but his view was obscured by the lower branches of a fruit tree about twenty-five feet away. A little guiltily—we would have frowned at anyone doing the same thing at our villa—he decided to climb atop a broken masonry fence post in order to get a clear shot. Suddenly he jumped down, grabbed my arm, and—amid my protests—began walking rapidly away. I wondered if we were being chased by wasps. Finally, I realized that Carl was struggling to keep from laughing. When we had turned the corner and were hidden from sight of the villa, he could contain himself no longer.

"The tree," he gasped. "The tree."

"What about it?" I asked in exasperation.

"There's someone sitting in the tree!"

I peered cautiously around the corner, trying to remain unseen. At last I perceived that there was indeed a man sitting in the tree like a latter-day Yossarian. I concluded that he must be pruning some of the upper limbs.

"I think that's the owner up the tree," Carl said. "I hope my photo comes out."

Our second visit to the villa is not humorous but sad.

Villa Valmarana is not pictured or described by Palladio in *Four Books*. The attribution to Palladio is based primarily on an early floor plan that scholars have uncovered among Palladio's original drawings, most of which are now in the collection of the Royal Institute of British Architects, known as RIBA. However, the villa's facade as built departs awkwardly from Palladio's rendering. One hypothesis is that the patrons—two brothers—encountered a spring on the site and, because they were unable to excavate a basement as planned, added an extra floor above in order to get the storage space they needed. Also, the interior has suffered extensive changes through the years. Carl and I discover during our inspection visit that the villa needs enormous restoration work to bring it to comfortable modern standards. The present owner, whose grandfather bought the villa in the late nineteenth century, supports it through farming and the hosting of wedding receptions in the grand salon. My mind visualizes how the villa might look if restored. The vast attic intrigues me. I can imagine an easy division of the space into at least four spacious bedrooms—perfect for a large family.

Not surprisingly, our Atlanta friends are not inclined to take on such a project.

The signore is disappointed when I tell him the news, but reacts with typical Italian resilience. "Well, perhaps you will have other friends who want to own a Palladian villa," he says in closing.

Slightly north of Villa Valmarana lies an abandoned gem of Palladio, Villa Forni. Forni is my favorite of the lesser-known villas; its petite, degraded face bears such a regal air that I can close my eyes and envision it in pristine, beloved condition.

I decide to show it to Ashley when she is visiting Piombino Dese this summer. Do I think she'll make a fortune as a television writer and want her own Palladian property in Italy? Do I imagine she will incorporate it into one of her scripts? Do I anticipate that she'll make a movie someday and use Villa Forni as a mysterious back-drop? Maybe all of the above. But I also know she will love it as I do—because of its architectural beauty and its need for affection.

We drive to Vicenza via Castelfranco and Cittadella and turn north toward Montecchio Precalcino. Heading north, we reach an abrupt left turn just before a bridge and wind along a country road, ultimately spotting our prize huddling between two farm build-ings. An ugly fourteen-foot-tall bully of a tree crowds the gently rising entrance steps, the front door hangs ajar, vines grasp at the *cantina* walls. Yet the arched opening to the portico embraced by two rectangular apertures (a "Serlian motif," architects would say), with sentient window-eyes above and crowned with a graceful ped-iment, begs us to enter. I can hear the villa whispering, Please come in, take care of me!

The front gate is locked. We can rouse neither neighbor to inquire about an entrance fee. So we walk along the dirt side road and spy a gaping hole in the ancient brick wall. Surely this is meant for us! I would not want walk-in tourists at Villa Cornaro, of course, but Villa Cornaro does not lie abandoned. We enter the *can-tina* door, fight back ivy tendrils, and wander upstairs. An enor-mous tree grows from the *cantina* out through a side window of the *piano nobile.*

Like Villa Valmarana, Villa Forni is absent from *Four Books;* its Palladian origin is deduced from a drawing at RIBA. Unlike Val-marana, however, Villa Forni does not suffer from deviations in its construction. Its coherent, rational floor plan makes clear that care-ful restoration would produce a Palladian jewel.

Carl and I develop a great curiosity to see the front facade of Villa Zen. Villa Zen is another of the Palladian villas that stand empty, although it would be unfair to say that it is abandoned. The villa, owned by a prominent family of Venice and Rome, sits on a large, actively managed farm property in a remote area far east of Treviso. On our first expedition to Villa Zen we were able to see the rear of the structure, which sits back from a narrow twisty highway, but we were frustrated by a large and securely locked gate in our effort to see the front.

Over time I've become quite brazen about phoning complete strangers to ask if Carl and I may come see their home. In this case, a member of the family responds graciously to my request and agrees to have someone meet us at the villa for a tour.

I drive while Carl navigates. We pass Marco Polo Airport and catch the A4 autostrada north, zipping up to the Cessalto exit. With a map in his lap, Carl unerringly directs me into the town and then back across the expressway, where we follow our noses to Villa Zen. Zen fronts on the Piovan Canal, though it has been separated from the canal for some time by an old eight-foot brick wall and a barrier of overgrown evergreens.

Our host, patiently awaiting us when we arrive, turns out to be a member of the owner's family. A slender man in his late thirties with thick, short silver hair and white, even teeth, he thoughtfully speaks Italian slowly for us. It is obvious that he understands English to some degree as well. He unlocks the gate and leads us around to the front of the villa. We push our way through knee-high weeds with a small, three-leaved plant peeping through. *Note to diary: Check for poison ivy rash tomorrow.*

Carl and I are exhilarated to see the front of Villa Zen at last. As we expected, the facade is articulated with the three-arch motif that characterizes most of Palladio's early work, but photographs have not prepared us for the height of the arches, which are dramatically taller than those we have seen elsewhere. Above the arches is a simple pediment punctuated by a small window, probably a later addition. The *intonaco* is in bad shape, with weeds encroaching on every surface. Uncontrolled vegetation and tall trees of numerous varieties guard the environs like undisciplined, ill-uniformed soldiers, frustrating our effort to discern the design of any garden lingering from the past.

We enter the villa through a small door opening into a dark, square room, one of seven rooms on the first level. Palladio would have wept. The floor is paved in concrete; crumbling walls and ugly doors, recently installed for security, mark the spaces. Our guide leads us up six short flights of stairs to the second floor, where we wander through the bleak spaces, dim light struggling to pierce the dilapidated shutters. A long, narrow central *salone* is flanked by six smaller rooms, three on either side. A blocked fireplace stands at one end of the large room, but does not look original. Wiring from early in the history of household electricity runs along the walls like bunting left from a party held long ago.

The others continue up into the attic via rickety stairs, while I wait in the gloom, imagining the spaces as they must have appeared in 1560. The Zen family never lived here, at least not longer than several months, and no other family ever assumed long-term residency, either. *Che peccato!* What a shame!

Villa Pisani at Bagnolo, a beautifully restored villa near Vicenza, was recently sold after centuries in the same family. Villa Chiericati, perhaps Palladio's earliest use of the Greek-temple-front motif—that is, with a single row of freestanding columns supporting a classical pediment—stands empty now like Forni and Zen, we read in the Padua edition of *Il Gazzettino*. Carl and I resolve that we will try to arrange a visit in the near future; we have seen only the exterior.

Contessa Emo visits me for tea one afternoon. She is the mother of the present Count Emo, owner of Villa Emo, one of the villas that Carl and I consider the Big Five. A tall, erect, handsome woman, the contessa is American-born, living now in Florence. She speaks of the maintenance expenses at Villa Emo and of her son's money-raising schemes, all of which she seems to disapprove.

The Count recently outfitted the east *barchessa* of Villa Emo as a restaurant, hiring an expensive chef away from a prominent hotel in Asolo and stocking impressive wines. He also spent *tanti soldi*—a lot of money—creating guest rooms on the estate, convinced he could turn Villa Emo into a country inn.

The restaurant was an exceptionally fine one, and Carl and I were regular customers. My favorite evening there was in the company of my friend Kathy from Atlanta—but we were the only guests. Now the restaurant is closed, the inn is closed, and Villa Emo is for sale.

Villa Emo has the unique distinction of having remained in the Emo family, descending in male lines, since it was built almost 450 years ago. The original patron of the villa expressed in his will a special request that the villa be retained in the family.

Where are the new Dick Rushes? What sense of art or history, what zest for challenge, what concern for posterity will stir them to step forward, gather these unstrung pearls, and return them to their natural glow? I cannot argue with the proposition that restoration does not always make economic sense. On the other hand, beauty offers one of our few escapes from the imperatives of economics and good sense.

48

A Good Mystery

Almost everyone enjoys a good mystery novel. For me they're a quick snack, like peanut butter and crackers. Late at night, when I'm tired but not ready for sleep, I'll retrieve a Josephine Tey or a Laurie King from the bookcase beside our bed. Like my father before me, I grade each book inside the front cover with an A, B, C, or D, and I don't mind rereading an "A." So my encounters with the real-life mysteries of Villa Cornaro are especially satisfying.

The first mystery is the purpose of the underground passages. Until the parish church acquired Villa Cornaro in 1951 for use as a kindergarten, there were two two-hundred-foot-long passageways running underground from the *cantina* to the bank of the lake south of the villa. One of them ran from the base of each of the villa's brick stairwells. The priest wisely bricked up the passageways at each end; otherwise he would have had an endless stream of kindergarten children cavorting through the tunnels at all hours.

"Secret passages!" The reaction of all three of our children is the same. "Let's open them and see what's there!"

Carl is unmoved. "Scorpions," he says. "That's what's in there. Scorpions and spiders."

Frankly, I would like to see what's in there myself. For now, I simply enjoy the mystery: Why are the tunnels there? Our friends in Piombino Dese suggest answers. Ilario proposes that the tunnels were for escape in case the villa was attacked by brigands. This seems unlikely to me, since the tunnels were not really long enough to carry one to safety from attackers. Ernesto Formentin plausibly suggests that the tunnels provided access to water for washing out wine casks in the *cantina.* My own conclusion is that the tunnels were designed primarily for air-conditioning. Carl thinks I have hit it on the head. Convection currents rising in the stairwells on warm days would draw cool air from the lake, bringing it through the tunnels and into the villa. Palladio does not mention such a cooling technique in *Four Books,* but the concept was definitely known and used in his period. I got the idea from visiting La Rocca, a villa designed by Vincenzo Scamozzi, but a somewhat similar device can be found at Jacopo Sansovino's Villa Garzoni at Pontecasale, which predates Villa Cornaro by five or ten years.

Several other mysteries crop up in the grand salon on the first floor of the villa. The first is the function of the twelve little shelves, or *mensole,* protruding at intervals along the walls. We ask everyone for suggestions as to what they might have held.

"Busts," says one. "Small busts of family ancestors." That would be a more compelling possibility if the room did not also have six giant statues of family ancestors.

"Family crests," suggests another.

"A place to display crossed swords and other military paraphernalia," offers a third.

Finally a visitor responds in a way that is totally convincing: "They were for lighting the room with oil lamps or candles. Remember, villas did not have central chandeliers in Palladio's time."

A more profound question about the grand salon concerns something that is not there: frescos.

Frescos—that is, paintings made directly on a plaster surface while the plaster is still wet—were ubiquitous among the Palladian villas. They were the wall coverings used practically everywhere. Their quality ranges from the splendor of Veronese's work at Villa Barbaro and Zelotti's at Villa Emo and La Rotonda to lesser examples at some other locations. Frescos were so sensible. Without them, a noble Venetian family traveling to its country estate in the spring would be forced to bring along its tapestries and oil paintings to decorate the walls; in the fall everything would have to be carried back. How much more practical to have Veronese stop by for a month or so and decorate the walls permanently!

Why then did Giorgio Cornaro leave his villa without frescos? The likely answer sounds paradoxical: Perhaps he did it to show how wealthy he was. After all, the frescos at Villa Barbaro, Villa Emo, La Malcontenta, Villa Poiana, and elsewhere all depict grand interior spaces centered on trompe l'oeil columns, niches, and statues. The grand salon at Villa Cornaro might lack the striking colors of those frescos, but the columns, niches, and statues are real, not trompe l'oeil.

Yes, there was cost and inconvenience in bringing tapestries and oil paintings all the way from the lagoon, but the Cornaros were the wealthiest family in Venice. What better way of flaunting it?

That, at least, is the explanation I like best. One scholar, how-ever, has suggested that perhaps Giorgio, with his wealth tied up in land and other illiquid assets, may have been a little short of cash and simply postponed the frescos for a later day.

That "later day" was December 10, 1716. That is the day Andrea Cornaro, the great-great-grandson of the original patron, commis-sioned Mattia Bortoloni, a twenty-one-year-old artist from Rovigo, to paint 104 fresco panels in the villa. On the first floor, the frescos cover the walls and ceilings of the six rooms surrounding the grand salon. Upstairs, two rooms are completely frescoed as well and five others—including the grand salon—have frescos above the doorways. The frescos are set into heavy stucco frames executed by another artist, Bortolo Cabianca. Cabianca also created three-dimensional putti and other motifs to surround the frescos on the ceilings and above the doors. (It was Cabianca's putti that the priest found to be too anatomically correct when the parish acquired the villa.) The work Andrea Cornaro commissioned in 1716 completely transformed the interior of the villa. Wandering through its rooms today, I cannot conjure up Villa Cornaro without the colors of Bortoloni's frescos and the animated Cabianca putti.

Painting style changed dramatically between the mid-sixteenth century and the early eighteenth. At Villa Emo or La Malcontenta, for example, Giovan Battista Zelotti's frescos depict disporting Greek gods and goddesses in bright Renaissance colors. The emphasis is on country pleasures. Bortoloni's frescos at Villa Cornaro, on the other hand, were created after artistic fashion had evolved from the Renaissance style through the baroque and awaited the saccharine rococo pastries soon to be produced by Bor-toloni's celebrated contemporary Giambattista Tiepolo. Zelotti's brightly colored mythological figures of 1560 give way to familiar biblical episodes rendered in an unusual soft, dusky palette of the early 1700s.

In *Frescoes from Venetian Villas,* Mercedes Precerutti Garberi comments on Bortoloni's work at Villa Cornaro.

The stories of Solomon and Moses, Noah, Abraham and Jacob come to life again in scenes large and small on the walls and ceiling, but the peculiar style, their slender, tortuous mannerism breathes into the holy text a breath of haunted legend. . . . Bortoloni's originality lies in crystallizing forms in haunting, metaphysical expressions, in a kind of new mannerism.

Here is the greatest mystery of Villa Cornaro: Why did Andrea Cornaro suddenly decide in 1716 to install frescos on the walls of his Palladian villa after four generations of Cornaros had been content with white walls embellished with paintings and tapestries?

Doug Lewis is the first person to ponder this question seriously. His answer, disclosed in his unpublished 1976 manuscript about the villa and later extracted for a 1988 article, is startling. The frescos, he argues, are Masonic, presenting themes of Freemasonry and incorporating strategically placed Masonic symbols, such as a draftsman's compass and a mason's square. As such, the fresco cycle constitutes the earliest Masonic art identified in Italy and one of the earliest examples anywhere.

Aside from the fact that George Washington, Simón Bolívar, and Giuseppe Garibaldi were all Masons, I know little about Freemasonry. My mental image of it is mostly formed by memories of Shriner parades down Main Street in Littleton. Carl's father and grandfather were Masons, but he knows nothing of the group. A look in the encyclopedia tells us that Masonry, also referred to as Freemasonry, is one of the largest fraternal orders in the world; by the early 1970s one in every sixteen adult American men was a Mason.

Carl is intrigued by the connection between our frescos and Freemasonry. So in order to learn more he begins buying books on the subject. He concludes that, despite its claims to origins as early as King Solomon or even Noah, Freemasonry can be traced to the second half of the seventeenth century, when it grew out of Rosi-

South wall of Tower of Babel room, with Mattia Bortoloni's
1717 frescos: *Abraham Receiving the Covenant of God* (left) and
Hagar and Ishmael in the Wilderness (right)

crucianism and other mystical movements of that era. Its primary
rituals and ceremonies, utilizing symbolically the terms of architecture and the masonry craft, were compiled about 1700. Freemasonry, according to its commentators, offers "a philosophy of the
spiritual life of man and a diagram of the process of regeneration."
That philosophy is traditionally described as "a system of morality
veiled in allegory and illustrated by symbols." Those symbols, W. L.
Wilmshurst explains in *The Meaning of Masonry*, center on the
terms of architecture because "they are ready to hand; because
they were in use among certain trade-guilds then in existence and,
lastly, because they are extremely effective and significant from the
symbolic point of view." Recasting certain themes from the group
of early mystical Hebrew texts known as Kabbalah, Freemasonry

posits a core system of scientific, religious, and moral wisdom and insights originating before the biblical Flood. According to this tradition, the system was preserved by Noah and communicated to his descendants; the system was largely lost when the building of the Tower of Babel precipitated the wrath of God and the dispersion of mankind; Abraham carried the system to Egypt; Moses acquired the system in Egypt and brought it back to Israel; Freemasonry was purified and organized by King Solomon and his builder Hiram Abif at the time of the construction and decoration of the first Temple at Jerusalem.

The fresco cycle at Villa Cornaro highlights those same biblical figures and episodes: Noah and the Flood, the Tower of Babel, Abraham and his sons and grandsons, Moses in Egypt and the Wilderness, King Solomon and the construction and decoration of the Temple with Hiram Abif.

Carl's research supports Doug Lewis's initial characterization of the frescos, but goes further. Carl concludes that the installation of the fresco cycle might have been just one part of an overall campaign by Andrea Cornaro to transform his Palladian country palace into a Masonic temple. For example, in the room with frescos featuring Solomon's Temple the original terra-cotta floor has been replaced by a wooden floor in which the boards are cut and laid out in a design of repetitive squares. Carl points out that this "checkerboard" motif is the pattern required by Masonic ritual for the floor of a Masonic lodge hall or meeting room. Bortoloni has incorporated the same pattern as a feature in several frescos in the room, including the one depicting the courtyard of Solomon's Temple.

As frequently noted by architectural historians, the exterior stairs leading to the south and north entrances of Villa Cornaro were reconfigured at some time in the past. Palladio in *Four Books* shows the treads rising in a direct, uninterrupted pattern, but the treads now are grouped in units of three, separated by sloping planes. Carl notes that the fresco representation of the stairway leading to Solomon's Temple shows the same pattern of treads and planes; on this basis he concludes that the reworking of the stairs

Temple Room—south wall

occurred as a part of Andrea Cornaro's Masonic program. He also speculates that two mysterious statues flanking the south entrance stairs and incorporating obelisks are Masonic as well. One of the statues incorporates the figure of a pilgrim to the holy shrine of Saint James at Santiago de Compostela; Carl has unearthed a historical incident linking Compostela with the Knights Templar, who in one widely accepted though presumably spurious account are said to be antecedents of Freemasonry.

Here is a mystery that will amuse us for years.

A preservationist in America once told me that the threshhold issue in any restoration project is "Restore to when?" Monticello offers an easy illustration of the problem. The meticulous restoration there has returned the famous home not to its original condition—when it had a double projecting portico based on Villa Cornaro—but rather to its remodeled state after Jefferson had enlarged it and reworked the exterior to incorporate the famous

dome inspired by Palladio's La Rotonda (by way of the Hôtel de
Salm in Paris). The decision not to return to the original structure
was easy for a variety of obvious reasons: the remodeling was done
by the original owner-architect within a decade of the original construction; the remodeled state is handsome, historically important,
and associated with Jefferson in the popular imagination; and a
return to the earlier model would have been structurally difficult
or impossible. Not to mention having to recall all those nickels!

The Miles Brewton House in Charleston, dating from about
1740, raises a more complicated issue. It was recently restored after
careful archival research, but no one suggested removing its double
projecting portico even though it was a later Federal period addition to a basically Georgian structure.

On the other hand, Ca' Cornaro Piscopia on the Grand Canal in
Venice (now known as Ca' Loredan) presents a different case. The
two amazingly beautiful and detailed lower floors, built around
1200, were topped in the 1500s by two utterly undistinguished
upper floors. In my opinion, a sensitive restoration of the building—unrestrained by budget limitations—would entirely remove
the two top floors even though they are almost five hundred years
old; the addition distorts and detracts from the harmony and unity
of the original facade without bringing any artistic value of its own.

That is the context for the bizarre suggestion that an official in
the office of the Soprintendente di Belle Arti once made to Dick
Rush in the early days of his work restoring Villa Cornaro. "You
should remove all these frescos from the villa," he said. "They are
not original."

"I was dumbfounded," Dick told us later. "I had to spend months
negotiating with him before he finally dropped the issue."

The suggestion reflected two misconceptions: first, the idea that
all architectural restoration should be to a structure's original condition; second, a trendy notion—now demolished by Doug Lewis
in his authoritative new book on Palladio's drawings—that Palladio
himself disliked frescos and that his villas should be viewed as spa-
tial forms without decoration or furniture. Fundamentally, the

suggestion failed to appreciate that two masterworks—in this case Palladio's villa and Bortoloni's fresco cycle—can exist in the same space and that, despite the 155 years that separate their creation, an intimate symbiotic bond can exist between them.

49

An Evening in Venice

Sally with Vittoria
on the south portico

Our Venetian friends Guido and Giovanna like bringing their daughters Vittoria and Antonia to Piombino Dese.

"They never see grass in Venice," Guido explains, watching them chase across our park. One of my favorite photos at Villa Cornaro shows me sitting on the south portico with Vittoria as a baby in my lap. Carl likes the picture so much he uses a slide of it in his Harvard Club speech to illustrate how Palladio's villas are happily alive today.

Guido and Giovanna own the third floor of Ca' Morosini, a fifteenth-century palace conveniently located just around the corner from busy Campo Santa Maria Formosa in the Castello section of Venice. On our first visit there, for dinner one evening, we learn to grasp the stair rail tightly because of the treads' distinct sag toward one side.

"You noticed how we're sinking toward the canal?" Guido asks cheerily as he greets us. "We'll soon fall in if we're not careful." He tells us the startling amount he and the other owners—including his parents on the floor below—have already paid to shore up the weakening foundations, and the infinitely larger sum needed for a longer-lasting resolution of the problem.

"You are so lucky that your villa is on solid ground," he adds. I learn over time that complaining about the perilous and costly infirmities of their homes is one of the major ties binding Venetian families. As mainlanders, Carl and I will never fully partake of the bracing spirit of pride and impending disaster that the old Venetian families share.

Giovanna seems suspiciously relaxed for a dinner party hostess, but she quickly explains her calm: Guido is the *cuoco*. "I love having guests," she says. "It's the only time Guido cooks."

At one point later in the evening I notice Carl discussing with another guest Venice's Fourth War with Genoa—in Italian. Carl's language ability is directly linked to subject matter. Fortunately for him, Venice is every Venetian's favorite subject.

50

This Old, Old House

Our fifteen minutes of fame comes up three minutes short.

Carl receives a phone call at his office one day from Hugh Howard, who introduces himself as a writer for Bob Vila. He explains that Vila, who began his television career with a PBS series on restoring and repairing old houses, also produces occasional specials for the Arts & Entertainment network under the general title *Bob Vila's Guide to Historic Homes*. His latest project is a three-part documentary to be entitled *In Search of Palladio*. The first two-hour segment will be "The Villas of the Veneto," to be followed by "Palladianism in England and Ireland" and "The Palladian Legacy in America." Can a visit to Villa Cornaro be included? Hugh asks.

Does Luciano Pavarotti sing opera? Within days, Carl has inundated Hugh with background material, copies of Doug Lewis's articles, magazine clippings. Well in advance, we schedule filming for a Friday in June.

On the preceding Sunday I receive a frantic call from the show's producer. Plans for filming the show's final three-minute summary in the garden at Villa Emo have gone awry because of a conflicting event there. Can they please film it in the garden at Villa Cornaro? On Tuesday?

We are still at breakfast when the technical crew arrives Tuesday morning. Their first task, to our surprise, is to lay what appears to be a small railroad track across the lawn of the park. Hugh Howard arrives to explain things.

"We need the track for a camera dolly, so the camera can follow Bob in a long smooth shot as he strolls across the lawn," he says.

Bob Vila himself arrives shortly after lunch in the company of his agent and his production assistant. Their goal is to complete filming during *riposo*, while Piombino Dese is at its quietest. The filming moves slowly. Bob's leisurely three-minute amble across the park, with Villa Cornaro looming majestically in the background, is chopped into small segments of two or three sentences, all repeated in countless retakes punctuated by changes in phrasing, lighting adjustments, and repositioning of the dolly track. In the summary Bob comments on Palladio's innovation, the stages of his development, his importance in western architecture. It's an effective discourse, and I'm convinced that I hear echoes of Carl's Harvard Club speech in it. Vila's delivery is as confident and relaxed on the sixth retake as on the first.

As the afternoon passes, it becomes clear that the time required has been seriously underestimated. *Riposo* comes to an end, and the normal noises of a small town return. A lawn mower barks to life in the town playground west of the *barchessa*. An Italian member of the Vila crew, whose job description apparently focuses on such challenges, is dispatched to reason with the mower operator. Everyone stands about in anticipation. Soon the racket shuts off and the "expediter" returns, followed by the mower operator, who has been invited to watch the filming. In less than ten minutes the cacophony of a jackhammer shatters the air. I remember seeing a work crew setting up on the Viale della Stazione this morning; apparently they are tearing up the asphalt to install a larger drain along the edge of the street. The expediter grimly strides toward the source of the hammering. Again the noise abates after a few minutes; a productive hour ensues. Then from the yard of the church youth center next door to the east arises the tap-tap-tap of a dribbling basketball; everyone turns to the expediter, who sets off again. In a few minutes the crowd of spectators has been augmented by a small group of basketball players. The rest of the work proceeds smoothly to a conclusion, with only minor pauses for airplanes overhead, screeching truck brakes, a barking dog, and a wailing baby. Three final minutes of videotape has consumed four hours.

We adjourn to the villa for a celebratory prosecco, amid praise for the expediter. He won't tell us his method for preserving the peace with the jackhammer, but I suspect he may have used a four-letter word: *lire.*

Looking ahead to Friday, when Bob and his crew will return to film the Villa Cornaro portion of the show, I begin to do some arithmetic in my head. If filming a three-minute segment took four hours, how many hours will it take to film a twelve-minute segment?

$$x = (4/3) \times 12$$
$$x = 16 \text{ hours}$$

"Friday will be a long day," I tell Carl as we drift off to sleep.

Friday brings other worries as well. We awaken to streaming sheets of rain. A low gray sky presses down on Piombino Dese. Will Bob and his crew even bother to show up under these conditions? In fact, everyone arrives exactly as scheduled. The villa will look as beautiful on film as if it had full sun, Bob assures me. The cameraman and lighting crew immediately set to work filming features throughout the villa. Bob and Hugh explain that the basic narrative of the Villa Cornaro segment will center on Carl and me greeting Bob on the south portico and leading him through the grand salon and the dining room, but other shots will be edited in to show particular details and elements from other rooms.

"We won't use a script," Bob says. "Just talk with me naturally as though I were a friend visiting your home." We take a preliminary walk through the villa with Bob and Hugh. Hugh has prepared an outline of subjects he thinks would be of interest, but he and Bob are open to suggestions from Carl and me. We agree that discussion of the graffiti on the portico and the Masonic symbolism of the frescos should be added. We don't rehearse specific questions and answers, however; Bob says we should just listen and respond naturally, as if in a friendly conversation.

Costumes: I decide to wear a bright sea-green pantsuit; Carl toys with the idea of a suit but settles on slacks and blazer. We join the group downstairs, where Bob's assistant hides a tiny microphone behind my lapel, connected to a wireless sending device hooked inside the waistband of my slacks. Carl is wired in similar fashion.

The camera begins rolling with Bob alone on the portico. Carl and I join him and are quickly caught up in conversation. Talking with Bob is easy because of his friendly, relaxed, and interested manner—and, of course, he's asking us questions about something we love! The greatest surprise is that we film each of the three scenes in a single uninterrupted take—except the very first scene, where I reflexively begin discussing one of the graffiti in Italian, rather than English. We pause after each scene while Bob, Hugh, and the others closet themselves in a dark room to review the tape carefully and see if a retake is needed; each time they return satisfied. Filming is complete within two hours. There must have been something wrong with that mathematical formula I was using.

The program does not appear on A&E until almost a year later. Our trepidation mounts throughout the wait. When we finally see the show, we're relieved that there seems little to embarrass us, although I wish I had not so enthusiastically responded "Absolutely!" to four different questions.

The week after the broadcast, Carl and I are in Concourse E at the Atlanta airport waiting to board for our trip back to Italy. Carl wanders away to the newsstand, but his progress is blocked by a middle-aged man.

"Didn't I see you on TV last week? On Bob Vila's show?" the man asks.

Carl hurries back to tell me the story. His grin is bigger than Texas.

51

Catastrophe

We should have read the clues. The signs were there, but we were blind to them.

For years we have observed a slight dip in the terrazzo floor on the south portico upstairs. We should have it leveled, we say to ourselves, so rainwater won't pool here. Standing water might seep down and damage some of the 450-year-old wooden beams supporting the pavement.

Two-thirds of the portico floor is covered in original *terrazzo veneziano;* the balance is patched in an ugly modern-day cement tinted red in an effort to be less obtrusive, but actually managing to suggest heavy rouge on the cheeks of an aging courtesan. The patch was the clue we overlooked. We should have asked ourselves two questions: Why was that patch put there? and Did it resolve the problem? Had we done so, we might have realized that the depression in the floor was merely a symptom of a problem that the cement patch had hidden but hadn't fixed.

"Sawdust, Sally," Carl tells me by telephone, anxiety clouding his voice. "Everything under the cement is completely rotten."

It is July and ordinarily we would both be in Atlanta. This year Carl, now newly retired, has flown to Venice to represent us at a special concert to be held at the villa. Usually we host concerts only during the spring and fall months when we are living there, but this program is sponsored by a regional organization, and the *comune* implored us to allow it. (The Miolos insist that we be present for any event, because otherwise their authority to enforce our rules for keeping trucks off the grass, maintaining locked gates, and the like is under constant assault.)

"Angelo and I opened up that cement patch upstairs. It's a disaster: the underflooring is completely rotted out, and the major beams under that are seriously rotted as well. We're lucky the whole floor hasn't collapsed on us while we're having prosecco on the portico downstairs," Carl continues.

Then his tale gets worse. "If the portico collapses, we lose lateral support and the back wall of the villa might go as well."

We discuss our next steps. Angelo Marconato, our faithful contractor, will install scaffolding right away to support the upstairs portico. Then he will remove more of the cement patch to see how widespread the problem is. Ernesto Formentin, our *geometra*, and his son Carlo, an engineer, will work with Angelo in evaluating the extent of the damage. Ernesto and Carlo will prepare an application to the Soprintendente di Belle Arti describing the proposed renovation and requesting approval for the work.

No one can even guess how much it will all cost.

Our return to Piombino Dese in the fall to see our ailing villa is joyously delayed for our younger son Jim's marriage to Juli Milnor in late September. Carl and I marvel once again at the good taste and good fortune of our sons in bringing such talented, attractive young wives into our family. Juli visited us at the villa with Jim two years earlier just as an American photographer was taking pictures for an article on Palladian villas in *Travel & Leisure* magazine. The photographer, upon meeting Juli, quickly decided that she—not Carl, Jim, or I—was the proper person to include in one of the photos.

The wedding day is glorious, a wonderful occasion made even happier by the presence of two special guests: Leonardo Miolo and his *fidanzata* Elisa. Leo is unquestionably the handsomest groomsman, while Elisa attracts her own admirers among the men in attendance. Carl and I spring a surprise at the rehearsal dinner the night before: as a memento we give each couple a ceramic tile hand-painted by Marina Rossetto, a wonderful Venetian artisan, with flowers, the names Jim and Juli, and the wedding date. (The tiles are such a success that we ask Marina to prepare some similar ones commemorating Carl and Lisa's wedding five years earlier.) Afterward, Jim and Juli fly off to Costa Rica on their honeymoon, Leonardo and Elisa travel to visit Dick and Julie Rush in Florida and then join Ashley for a brief stay in Los Angeles, and Carl and I board a plane for Italy.

In the dove-gray light of a late September morning we walk gingerly onto the upstairs south portico. Our beloved villa is masked in *impalcatura* (scaffolding) like an old lady swathed in bandages. I kneel to touch one of the old beams visible through the expanse where the cement patch has been removed; the wood disintegrates into dust between my fingers. I touch another spot and come away with another handful of powder.

Removing the cement patch has opened a fascinating window into the structure of the portico floor. Running north-south are twenty-four large structural beams. Atop them are two layers of thick planks, running at right angles to the beams on the upper level and then north-south again on the lower. The terrazzo pavement rests atop the planks. The bottom of the beams and the underside of the first layer of planks are visible from the downstairs portico twenty-four feet below, but it isn't possible to discern any details of their surface from that distance. The ends of the beams—the parts that engage niches in the wall and support the entire floor of the portico—seem to have disintegrated the most. Clearly, we have narrowly avoided a catastrophe.

Settling on a plan for restoration proves to be more contentious than I would ever have imagined. When a twelve-foot beam is rotten for half its length, it seems elementary to me that it should be replaced. In Italy, we learn, the matter is not so straightforward. Carlo Formentin tells us that if the middle half of the beam is still sound, that half should be retained, with new wood spliced and glued at each end! Angelo Marconato, practical as always, urges replacing the entire skeleton of rotten beams with new ones of specially aged Alpine timber. Carl's position is that we want to make the repair in a way that will last another 450 years. For us, the proper question is, What would Palladio do? The answer seems obvious: He would opt for new beams. Carlo insists that restoration of stubs of the old beams will produce a stable floor while pleasing the officials at the Belle Arti office. He has already had a preliminary meeting with them in Venice; the official to whom the application has been assigned will visit next week for a personal inspection. Our dilemma in the whole debate is this: We assume that the splicing and gluing will last beyond our own lifetime, but we feel a genuine obligation to posterity—an obligation to preserve this villa not just for the next generation or two but to the twenty-fifth century.

The inspector fails to appear; the press of "other work" prevents her visit, she tells Carlo later. Two subsequent visits are similarly scheduled and canceled.

So in mid-October, with the interior temperature of the villa falling by the day and forcing us into layers of sweaters, we leave for Atlanta with no work begun. We instruct Carlo and Angelo to proceed with utmost speed to secure permission and go ahead with the restoration. We want them to push for complete replacement of the beams and subflooring, but we are prepared to learn from the recommendations of the Belle Arti staff. Carlo says he will retain consultants to test all of the beams ultrasonically, especially the sixteen beams that are still covered by the original terrazzo. Angelo warns that he has no way to replace beams from below; the remaining terrazzo *must* be removed if the beams beneath it are rotten.

Through the winter I telephone Carlo Formentin at regular intervals. The news each time is the same: The inspector has not visited. Meanwhile the Miolos tell me with bewilderment that Carlo is taking hundreds of photos of the exposed areas. Carlo assures me he has prepared complete schematics showing how he proposes to resolve the problems. I stay in touch with Angelo as well; his rising impatience and blossoming disgust at the delay are manifest.

"Let's just go ahead," he pleads. "We must finish this work. You are paying daily for rental of the *impalcatura,* which I could be using on other jobs." Angelo suggests we have Carlo tell the Belle Arti office that we are going to begin emergency repairs on a specified date.

I stop sleeping well and begin drinking three cups of coffee a day. I shudder at the suffering of my villa each time I'm told of a new winter storm passing through the Veneto.

Finally, at the beginning of May, we arrive back in Piombino Dese. Nothing has been done to the portico; the south face of the villa is veiled in pipes, plastic, and a small construction elevator. Carl convokes an all-party meeting of our advisers within days of our arrival. We meet on the north portico of the villa amid a mass of blueprints, meticulous drawings, and engineering reports—and a sea of photographs. In addition to Carlo and Ernesto Formentin and Angelo Marconato, we are joined by a consulting architect from Venice whom we have retained to give us a fresh view of the situation. Midway through the meeting Silvana arrives with a round of coffee from the *caffè*.

A plan of action emerges, though there is no clear consensus. Carlo reluctantly agrees to write to the Belle Arti office stating that for the safety and preservation of the villa we must begin restoration of the portico in the middle of next week with or without a permit. The replacement of the beams will be determined on a beam-by-beam basis. Though the ultrasound inspection report indicates that sixteen beams will require complete replacement, six can be spliced and reinforced with steel and two will require only steel reinforcement. Angelo tells us that he will place the spliced beams in locations that seem to bear less lateral stress. The planks and terrazzo will be completely replaced.

I am not clear whether Carlo actually delivers our message to the Belle Arti office in the terms we directed. Nonetheless, on the day before we are scheduled to begin the repair, he advises us that the permit has been issued.

Angelo and his crew proceed expeditiously with the extraordinarily complex renovation. We watch anxiously as the terrazzo and planks are removed. The heavy beams are extracted and replaced in pairs so the lateral support is not compromised at any time. We feel relief only when all the subflooring planks have been installed and secured, leaving the portico ready for the installation of new terrazzo on top.

Ernesto identifies for us an artisan, Rodolfo De Monte, who has the skill to re-create *terrazzo veneziano* using the same techniques that Palladio's own workers used. Rodolfo inspects the old terrazzo carefully before Angelo removes it.

"Do you have any old bricks we can grind up, sixteenth-century bricks?" he asks.

"Yes," I reply. A few years ago, before my first encounter with

Villa Cornaro, I would have considered such an inquiry absurd, but in fact we have a tall stack of old bricks that Dick Rush acquired in an unfulfilled plan to built a period wall along one side of the property.

"*Eccellente!*" Rodolfo nods. "That will save money." In addition to ground bricks, the terrazzo will have fragments of local stone in several colors, all set in a cementitious paste and then ground down to a smooth, shining surface.

Palladio gives some practical advice on terrazzo in *Four Books.*

Those terrazzi *are excellent which are of pounded bricks, and small gravel, and lime of river pebbles, or the* paduan, *well pounded.* [Elsewhere he defines *paduan* as "a scaly rugged stone, taken from the hills of Padua."]

Palladio omits the fact—which he must have known—that workers in his time tended to dump into the terrazzo not just "pounded bricks," gravel, and river pebbles, but almost anything else they found around the job site. The original terrazzo in one of Villa Cornaro's upstairs bedrooms includes a smoothed and polished peach pit, as well as part of an old handmade nail. Contessa Emo told me that the original terrazzo at Villa Barbaro has a fragment of a blue-and-white plate.

Rodolfo's disappointing news is that he cannot begin his work until the fall; cool weather is required for mixing and applying the terrazzo.

The centuries-old process that Rodolfo and his crew commence in the fall is fascinating. If the elevator for bringing the materials up from the ground were not there to spoil the effect, I could imagine Elena Cornaro standing in my stead, watching as the original pavement is installed. Rodolfo begins by having his men spread a four-inch layer of a wet pewter-gray cementlike material. While the mixture is still a viscous liquid, he personally sprinkles the brick shards and two types of colored stone onto the surface, pulling large handfuls from big gray cloth sacks slung over his shoulders. The key to the final look is the density and mix of the stones he is scattering with a deliberate, repetitive motion. The fragments are pressed down into the matrix with large flat boards. Like all true artisans, Rodolfo uses no guide except his own lifetime of experience and his memory of the original terrazzo pattern, which he has studied carefully. He is the third generation of pavement artisans in his family; he confides to me with a sigh that he has no sons, and his daughters cannot be expected to continue the strenuous family tradition.

When the last of the scaffolding has been dismantled and carted away, the last worker has left, and Carl and I stand alone on the portico with the fields stretching away from us to the south, it is easier to admire the glistening new surface—a perfect re-creation of the sample we have retained of the old pavement—than it is to recall all the exasperated transatlantic phone calls and frustrating meetings that were required to bring it about. And, though the process still rankles, we are comforted by our assurance that the work meets the ultimate test that we apply to everything we do at Villa Cornaro: Palladio would be pleased.

52

Natives

"*Che bella!*" Giacomo exclaims as we emerge from the *stazione* and pause at the top of the steps leading down to the streaming life of the Grand Canal. Fractals of sunlight dance on the water. Vaporetti stream back and forth on the busy waterway, ferrying commuting workers from Piazzale Roma to their offices and shops, students to their schools, and tourists to their first monument of the day. On the opposite shore the oddly proportioned dome of the church of San Simeone Piccolo sits atop the skyline like a green overcooked egg. A liquid ochre light suffuses the morning air.

Silvana joins Giacomo in admiring the fairyland scene. Silvana has accompanied me on several previous excursions into Venice, but this is only Giacomo's fourth visit to Venice in his entire life—and the first in more than twenty years—despite his living just twenty miles away.

Silvana surprised Carl and me two weeks ago by asking whether on some future Monday—"closed" day at Caffè Palladio—we would lead them on a tour of Venice. For years Giacomo has watched as Carl and I troop off to Venice, sometimes several mornings a week. At last his curiosity about Venice's attraction for us has overcome his reluctance to leave his familiar world of Piombino Dese. We are quick to comply, happy for two reasons: first, because they feel comfortable asking us and, second, because they would trust so much of their limited free time to our guidance.

Carl is careful to put a Venice street map in his back pocket for the excursion, even though we seldom use one anymore. "I couldn't stand the embarrassment if we got lost with the Miolos in tow," he says sheepishly.

From the train station we set off on foot. Silvana has quietly reminded us that Giacomo is timorous around water, so we forgo a vaporetto ride. Our first stop is a quick peek into the church of San Simeone Grande. Confusingly, the church of San Simeone *Grande* (large) is quite small—much smaller than the nearby church of San Simeone *Piccolo* (small). Originally, each of the islands that make up Venice was a separate parish with its own parish church. Most of those parish churches remain active today, avoiding the merger and conglomeration that assail most other aspects of modern life.

We want the Miolos to see San Simeone Grande because it typifies so much of the charm and constant freshness of Venice. Its exterior is as nondescript as the small *campo* on which it sits; it appears in no guidebook itinerary of suggested tourist stops. Yet, when we step into the cool, calm interior, we point Giacomo and Silvana to a magnificent painting hanging on the north wall, *The Last Supper*, by the late-Renaissance master Tintoretto. The impact of the painting itself is heightened by the zest of discovery.

Standing before it, we are suddenly washed by streams of Buxtehude's Prelude in C tumbling from a small tracker organ high above the main entrance. No Mass is under way, so we are free to wander about, but we stand immobile, deeply moved by the music filling the nave. The organist concludes his performance with the final prolonged chords, then breaks the spell cast upon us by beginning to practice separate passages of the work. Giacomo wants to tarry, but we pull him away. Carl and I call the constant drive to see as many sites as possible the "tourist imperative," but I don't know how to say that in Italian.

"This is just an antipasto," I tell him instead. "The feast is still ahead."

We're headed for the church of the Frari, but we pause en route at Scuola Grande di San Giovanni Evangelista to admire Pietro Lombardo's stately marble entranceway, from about 1480. Inside is Codussi's masterful early-Renaissance stairway, but we don't have time this morning to talk our way past the obdurate receptionist who usually blocks access to it.

The Frari looms over its San Polo neighborhood, not far from the geographical center of Venice. The church, begun by the Franciscan monks in the late thirteenth century, is one of the two great mendicant-friar churches of Venice. (The other is the Dominicans' church of Santi Giovanni e Paolo.) Much grander than parish churches, both are towering testimony to the appeal of the mendicant orders in early Venice. Today they are potent reminders of the contemporary burden of the Church in maintaining the thousands of religious and artistic treasures throughout Venice and the rest of Italy.

The Frari has been a particular favorite of ours, I tell the Miolos, since we attended an organ concert there during our first spring at Piombino Dese. The monastic church is home to two magnificent period organs; both date from the 1700s, but one is from early in the century and the other late. The concert was carefully planned to show the evolution of organs in that period. With the audience seated on folding chairs placed temporarily in the choir, facing Titian's luminous *Assumption of the Virgin* over the central altar, the recitalist played the first half of the program on the 1732 organ, perched high over the north choir stalls, creating a simple, sweet singing tone. For the second half of the program he crossed to the 1794 organ, whose flute and reed stops produced a much more complex and colorful—though no more beautiful—sound.

Carl leads Giacomo and Silvana into the Frari's Cornaro Piscopia Chapel, added at the north end of the main altar in about 1420 by Giovanni Cornaro of the family's Piscopia branch. Although ostensibly created to honor Saint Mark, the patron saint of Venice, the chapel has as its highlight a statuary monument depicting an angel with a scroll eulogizing the patron's father. One writer calls it "one of the most beautiful monuments of the Venetian Renaissance." Nonetheless, many guidebooks mention it only in passing, if at all.

Next we shuttle the Miolos to the sacristy on the opposite side of the church. The wall facing the entrance features an elaborate marble installation deeply carved in dramatic late-baroque figures by Francesco Cabianca, whose brother Bortolo in 1716 created the putti and other stucco decorations at our own Villa Cornaro. For Giacomo, however, the highlight of the Frari—his favorite sight of the whole day—is the *Madonna and Child* of Giovanni Bellini above the altar of the refectory. The enthroned Madonna is serene, mysterious, oblivious to the cherub musicians playing at her feet.

"*Una meraviglia, una meraviglia.* A miracle," Giacomo murmurs over and over.

On our way toward the Rialto Bridge we stop for an espresso and brioche. I watch with amusement as Giacomo discreetly studies the small *caffè,* evaluating it with the trained eye of a competitor. He solemnly agrees with us that Caffè Palladio is handsomer—and has better prices to boot.

We proceed like chickens: three steps forward, then a pause. Giacomo finds a constant stream of new things to stop and inspect: a Gothic building facade, a strangely shaped chimney, an old religious plaque mounted high on a wall. At the church of San Salvatore we point out the tomb of Queen Caterina Cornaro and her

funeral monument carved by Bernardino Contino in the early
1580s—less than ten years before our own statue of her at Villa
Cornaro was created by Camillo Mariani.

From San Salvatore we detour to show Giacomo and Silvana the
lugubrious face carved at the base of the campanile of the church of
Santa Maria Formosa. With his usual hyperbole, Ruskin describes
it as "huge, inhuman, and monstrous,—leering in bestial degrada-
tion, too foul to be either pictured or described, or to be beheld for
more than an instant." Giacomo laughs at its grotesqueness, and
we all wonder what inspired such a decoration.

We finish the tour with visits to the church of Santi Giovanni e
Paolo to see the grave and funeral monument of Doge Marco
Cornaro, and to the church of the Holy Apostles, where Giorgio
Cornaro—the brother of Queen Caterina Cornaro—is buried in a
richly detailed chapel in which both Mauro Codussi and Tullio
Lombardo had a hand.

By this time we are all dragging a bit, and Carl and I are concerned that we have worn out our tourists by trying to see too
much. We have a late lunch at a small hotel near the train station—
a meal distinguished more by the company than the food—and
rest our legs on the train ride back to Piombino Dese.

The next morning, when Silvana arrives to open the shutters at
the villa, she brings along a street map of Venice. Will we please
trace our itinerary on it? she asks. She and Giacomo want to keep it
as a reminder of the day. Carl and I retain our own memories of the
day as well; we felt that we were a part of the fabric of the city, like
natives showing our home.

A pleasant group of about twenty visitors from Houston has just
finished its tour through the ground floor of the villa. On the south
portico I've explained and translated the graffiti and sent them off
into the park, recommending that they walk to the seven-arch
bridge for the view back at the villa's south facade. I also ask that
they exit the grounds by walking around the side of the villa to the
front gate, instead of tracking grass clippings and morning dew

back through the grand salon. One woman tarries to speak with me.

"How fortunate that you and your husband are both passionate about the same thing!" she says.

Her remark startles me. I have never considered the possibility that Carl might have fallen in love with the villa but not I. Or that I might have been enamored by these bricks and *intonaco,* but Carl not.

Yet it could have happened that way. How fortuitous, how unlikely, that we both find in our villa, in Venice, in Italy a source of such infinite fascination.

Villa Cornaro has been the cornerstone of it all. Like a great athletic coach, the villa is at once a disciplinarian, a trainer, and a motivator.

You can step onto new stages and play new roles, the villa whispers. Find your hidden pools of strength, open yourself to see art with fresh and wider-ranging eyes, examine whole new palettes of color in your everyday life, vault past barriers of language, culture, and habit.

All to better care for me, my villa tells me.

53

Groundhog Day

Often in Italy I feel like Bill Murray in the film *Groundhog Day.* The same day is repeated over and over. Each evening I sit on the south portico, mesmerized by the swallows in their timeless gyres. I watch the Cagnins at work in their field across the bridge, or hear their tractor's struggling chug when they pass out of sight. Ilario Mariotto and his brother Silvano work their own fields to the west. Sometimes the crop is corn, sometimes oats or barley; sometimes the field lies fallow for a season. But the same cycle is forever repeated, summer and winter. This portico where I'm sitting has overlooked these fields for 450 years. The Cagnins' complaining tractor has replaced a team of oxen that were probably equally plaintive; the Cagnins own the field instead of sharecropping for the Cornaros, but the pattern of everyday life is unchanging.

The national scene gives me the same impression as I puzzle my way through the newspaper account of each day's meaningless changes. The fall of governments follows the fall of governments, bribery scandals succeed bribery scandals, soaring budget deficits surpass soaring budget deficits, *scioperi* (labor strikes) follow more *scioperi*.

Rome is the Eternal City, I think to myself, not because it's ancient but because absolutely nothing ever really changes.

But then I am awakened by a remark from Silvana at a dinner party for some friends—the Miolos, the Battistons, the Bighins, the Cechettos. Silvana is speaking to Lino Cechetto, but I overhear her.

"The Mariottos are the last real *contadini*," she says, using a word that once denoted peasant farmers and now applies to landowning small-scale farmers as well. Silvana is actually focusing on that peasant tradition. "Ilario farms in all the old ways, uses no fertilizers or insect sprays, shares his home with his cows, makes his own wine from the grapes that he grows, has his own fruit and vegetable garden behind his house," she continues.

Silvana leaves me wondering if my original perception has been essentially flawed. These traditions that I see every day, repeating the daily life of centuries, may be in their last generation. Then the *contadini*—and the way of life they epitomize—will disappear.

The same may be true on the national level. While nothing seems changed on a daily basis, the contrasts in Italy's political life over time are startling. Rome's government-by-splinter-party has lurched suddenly toward a two-party system. At least the parties have begun to organize themselves into alliances of the center-left and center-right for major elections.

I'm led to ponder Villa Cornaro itself. Is it the solid and immutable rock that I have always envisioned? Or will it, too, be changed by the transformations that surround it?

When I first came to Piombino Dese, bicycles filled the racks at the Battistons' *supermercato*. Women would purchase only as many groceries as they could carry in two or three plastic bags on their handlebars; they bicycled home through the Via Roma gauntlet of trucks and autos. Now cars crowd the recently expanded parking lot. Women are still the predominant shoppers, but most drive their own cars.

Many more women work outside the home today than when I first arrived. They drive to dozens of small *fabbriche* dotting the outskirts of Piombino Dese, or they drive to work at shops in nearby towns. Last Saturday evening Nazzareno joked—but with nostalgia—about Italian women turning into American women, driving their own cars, spending their own money, tending less to homemaking and cooking. *Nidi*—literally "nests," but signifying child-care centers—have sprung up in town, both church-sponsored and private, to care for the small children of working mothers. Some working mothers rely on a network of babysitters and their own mothers, but often the grandmothers are working themselves and other would-be babysitters want full-time employment with better wages and pension benefits.

A take-out pizza parlor appeared last year on Via della Vittoria; it even delivers if you telephone your order. Efficiency is breaking out in state-owned enterprises: staffing in the Piombino Dese train station has shrunk from three workers per shift to just one, as preprinted tickets have replaced the handwritten ones that prevailed earlier.

Creeping multinationalism invades the school curriculum. English, once a specialized elective, is taught in elementary school in Piombino Dese, with children as young as six receiving three hours of instruction a week. When we first arrived in Piombino Dese I had to speak Italian in order to communicate even the simplest observation or need; abstruse terms—*rubinetto* (faucet), *scaldabagno* (water heater), *fognatura* (sewage), and *fossa* (ditch)—salted my new vocabulary. Now many young people speak English well, including Riccardo Miolo and Elisa, Leonardo's *fidanzata*.

We can debate whether take-out pizza and English fluency are positive developments or negative, but some of the changes taking place are undeniably for the worse. Michela Scquizzato tells me that her *telefonino* (cell phone) was lifted while she was shopping at Battiston's. For the last several years, upon leaving the autostrada at the Padova Ovest exit near Limena, we have come to expect a clutch of prostitutes standing beside the road, not just at night but throughout the afternoon. Pulling out from the parking lot of Barbesin, a favorite restaurant near Castelfranco, we are puzzled by the erratic driving of the car ahead of us. Finally we realize that the driver is slowing to inspect the prostitutes strung like gaudy beads along the roadside. Albanians, the newspaper accounts say. The warfare and unrest in the Balkans since the fall of Communism bring boatloads of illegal immigrants across the narrow Adriatic Sea every night. Once in Italy, the immigrants must find an employer willing to hire them without work permits or else drift into burglary, prostitution, or other crime. Albanian gangs are said to be providing competition for the Italian *mafiosi*. Our Italian friends are as shocked as we to learn one May morning that two young Piombino Dese boys have discovered the body of a murdered Albanian prostitute in the industrial district of town; we find only minimum comfort in the police theory that the body was merely dumped in Piombino Dese after the murder occurred elsewhere. In the same month, burglars attempt to explode their way into the ATM machine at the branch of Banca Ambrosiana just down Via Roma, and nighttime vandals try to burn the mammoth wooden doors of the parish church by setting fire to oil-soaked rags they have tacked onto them.

Italy seems certain to survive it all. In his last year in office, Prime Minister Giuliano Amato exhorted his countrymen to respect the tax laws. "Of course we expect a businessman to buy a fur coat for his mistress," he said understandingly, "but he should not deduct it on his taxes as a business expense."

When Silvio Berlusconi, Amato's successor, complained about having to move into Palazzo Chigi, the official government residence, because "the food is horrible," Italians *understood*. Good food binds Italians in a way that will, I'm sure, survive government efficiency, English fluency, and the euro, just as market day will survive e-commerce.

And Villa Cornaro? Is it fated to change, to modernize and homogenize? I want to avoid being a Pollyanna; the ability of an ancient structure to survive in the modern world cannot be assumed. One thing I have learned: Villa Cornaro is a part of its community. Villa Cornaro will prosper as long as it retains the respect, love, and protection of its people. The modern world needs Villa Cornaro as a token of a civilized past and as a vibrant part of the present; posterity can take the preservation of it in our time as a token of our own civilization.

Coda

We are in Piombino Dese on September 11, 2001. Italian television starts following the horrific events in New York and Washington, D.C., within minutes of their onset, so we are apprised of developments as they unfold. Sympathetic phone calls from local friends begin immediately, offering condolences and *solidarietà*. Francesca arrives at the gate to give me a hug; Bianca embraces me when I enter the *supermercato*. Silvana weeps when she arrives in the evening to close the *balcone,* expressing her bewilderment at the madmen of the world. One friend appears at the front gate the next day with a plate of food, as though we have had a death in the family and need something to comfort us.

Hurrying along Via Roma the following week, I am hailed from behind by the elderly local pharmacist. His daughter usually staffs the counter in his shop, and he and I have never shared more than a *buon giorno.* He expresses in traditional terms his sorrow at the recent tragedy, but asks me to wait until he shows me something.

"Un attimo, un attimo, signora. One moment," he says as he pulls out his wallet and searches through it. He finds the item he is seeking and holds it out for me to take: a recent newspaper clipping. I unfold it to discover an Italian translation of "God Bless America." He waits for me to read the verses, then retrieves the clipping, refolds it, and returns it to his wallet.

I stand and watch as he walks away and disappears among my neighbors.

Appendix 1

Si Mangia Bene in Italia

Living in Italy inspires even the most creativity-deficient gene to mutate. Long ago I accepted that I must be an energetic admirer of creative endeavor because of the absence of any personal aptitude for it.

But Italy! Italy has taught me to reconsider. Italy celebrates daily every cook's good food, every woman's flower display, every woman's bold scarf arrangement. Every community promotes art shows for local artists, exhibitions for workers in decorative iron. To encourage its lamp industry, Piombino Dese sponsors a local competition in lamp design. Italy *expects* artistic enterprise from everyone.

So I join in where I can, drawn to experimentation in the kitchen, artful presentation of food in the dining room. But first, I copy: my Italian diaries are laced with local recipes and notes on Venetan food and the way the Venetans serve it. The recipes are simple, the dishes are presented with great fantasy, and the food is delicious.

I tease Francesca and Wilma, telling them I want to prepare a cookbook of their recipes and will follow them around for a week, Naomi-like, to jot down the recipe for every dish they prepare. They laugh and say such a book will never sell; their food is too simple. I think the simplicity is what makes it special.

Here are two simple vegetable recipes from Wilma.

WILMA'S EASY PEPERONI

2 sweet red peppers
2 yellow peppers
2 tablespoons olive oil
1 clove garlic, crushed
Salt and pepper

Cut up the red peppers and yellow peppers into large squares, being sure to remove any membrane. Place in a frying pan with the olive oil. Cover and cook over high heat until the peppers are sizzling, then reduce the heat and simmer, covered, for 20 to 25 minutes until they are softened but still firm. Turn off the heat and let sit for 20 minutes.

Transfer the peppers and oil to a small bowl. Add the crushed garlic, and salt and pepper to taste. Cover with plastic wrap. Let sit several hours before serving.

A variation is to include several anchovy fillets with the peppers.

WILMA'S PLUM TOMATOES

8 to 12 fresh plum tomatoes
½ cup dry white wine
Bread crumbs
Salt and pepper
Fresh basil, chopped
Olive oil

Preheat the oven to 375°F. Cut the plum tomatoes in half lengthwise. Arrange the halves in a baking pan, cut side up. Pour the white wine around them. Lightly cover each tomato half with bread crumbs; then drizzle with olive oil. Sprinkle with salt and pepper and chopped fresh basil. Bake for 25 minutes. (This can be prepared early in the day; just reheat under a low-heat broiler for 5 to 8 minutes before serving.)

Serve as a first course with *burrata* mozzarella and thinly sliced firm bread.

Every woman in the Veneto prides herself on her culinary skills. Carl and I regularly begin our sojourns in Piombino Dese with several small dinner parties, inviting six or eight friends each evening. Our object is to greet friends, learn local gossip, and awaken our hibernating Italian tongues. The evenings also produce something much more valuable than mere news. They spur a food contest to rival *The Iron Chef.* Each wife invites us to dinner in the ensuing three or four weeks, plotting her meal as she would a military campaign.

Last night, for example, Silvana—who opens Caffè Palladio every morning at five and spends her Monday "day off" cleaning the premises—reciprocated our dinner of three weeks ago with a banquet for twelve. Her first sortie consisted of prosecco with antipasti: small soft balls of white mozzarella, sweet chunks of orange cantaloupe, tangy strips of red-brown sun-dried tomatoes, smooth black Sicilian olives. This course was served on their patio; Giacomo's forty rosebushes and thirty caged songbirds provided the backdrop. On Silvana's request, we moved inside to their long, narrow table for the *primo piatto,* served in two handsome tureens:

SILVANA'S PEA SOUP

2 pounds fresh peas
1 quart chicken broth
1 small yellow onion, chopped
Parsley
2 cups béchamel
½ cup grated Parmesan cheese

Shell the peas. Simmer them for 1 hour with ½ cup of the broth, the chopped onion, and several sprigs of parsley. Puree, then add to the rest of the broth. Heat to a simmer.

Prepare separately a béchamel made with 4 tablespoons butter, 3 tablespoons flour, 2 cups milk. Blend it into the broth, along with the grated Parmesan, stirring constantly. When the soup is blended and hot, serve with a good crusty bread.

Next at Silvana's party came whisper-thin slices of roast beef accompanied by a colorful palette of fresh vegetables, simmered *en brodo,* and a salad with as many colors as Joseph's coat.

A truncheon of cheeses—Parmesan, *mezzano, Montasio*—followed, then large bowls of chilled, almost black cherries and plump green grapes. Then fruit tortes, followed by *fior di latte* (a flavor similar to vanilla) *gelato* crowned with fresh sweet strawberries that had been soaked in *limoncello* liqueur. Giacomo was the wine sergeant throughout, refilling glasses and then consummating the campaign with liqueurs of dizzying variety. Conversation flowed as rapidly and amiably as the wine.

Nazzareno Mason greets our arrival one spring with a large bunch of white asparagus. One stalk is as thick as the handle of our hammer, but Nazzareno assures me this will be the tenderest of all. The asparagus was pulled from his cousin's garden just thirty minutes earlier. He tells me how to cook it:

NAZZARENO'S WHITE ASPARAGUS

First, buy only asparagus with a credible claim to being very fresh. Peel each stalk, not with a knife (which would remove too much pulp) but with a vegetable peeler. Tie the bundle securely with string and place it upright in a narrow but deep pot, with water covering only the bottom two inches of the stalks. (Best: buy an asparagus steamer, which holds the stalks upright off the pan bottom.) Steam for 20 to 40 minutes, depending on the size of the stalks and their age. Test the stalks with a knife. When they are tender but not mushy, pull them from the water.

Memi Scquizzato taught us how to eat white asparagus our first spring in Piombino Dese. You place several tender stalks on your plate beside two halves of hard-boiled egg. Dress with a drizzle of deep green olive oil, a drop or two of balsamic vinegar, and lots of salt and pepper. Mash the eggs finely with a fork, then munch with bites of asparagus.

Surely the Olympian gods dined on this vegetable regularly!

Ham, glorious ham! One of our favorite treats in Italy is prosciutto—preferably the San Daniele variety. I learned several years ago from an Acquarello tape that there are three kinds of prosciutto, each from a different area of northern Italy and each with a somewhat different curing process. Parma prosciutto is known for its tangy bite, its piquancy; San Daniele prosciutto is sweeter—and is my favorite accompaniment for chilled melon slices or luscious split figs. The third type, Veneto prosciutto, combines the intense savoriness of Parma and the sweetness of San Daniele, but much less of it is produced. In the production process, the raw hams are packed in sea salt for a week, then exposed to mountain air for a twelve-to-twenty-month curing period. No wonder prosciutto is so expensive!

In May the Veneto imports from Sicily pale green melons the size of large softballs. The melons have luscious red-orange flesh and we devour one every day until Battiston's supply runs out. We often combine them with bright slices of San Daniele prosciutto. Cristiano, a regular behind the Battistons' meat counter, always prepares a perfect bed of slices, lean but with fat enough for flavor, thin but not torn.

In September we eat the prosciutto with our own fat purple figs from the two trees on either side of our south portico. I like the figs peeled and halved, set atop the bed of prosciutto like "Sweet Nothings" miniature roses. Fresh, thinly sliced white pears are another good accompaniment for prosciutto and can be assembled into a flower design for the prosciutto platter.

I have not passed a single day in Italy without learning of a new type of food, a new way of cooking food, or a new way to enjoy food. Last week, at a dinner at the Zambons'—they live across the street and have unquestionably the finest view of the villa from their balcony—Lucianna placed on the table a large wheel of a platter bearing a brilliant garden of baked stuffed vegetables. Her mother's recipe, she said. It was both beautiful and delicious.

LUCIANNA'S STUFFED VEGETABLES

5 sweet peppers (medium-size, not huge)
4 ripe round tomatoes
4 long eggplants
4 zucchini
1 pound lean beef and 1 pound lean pork, ground together twice
Parsley, chopped fine
1 clove garlic, chopped fine
2 eggs, beaten
$\frac{3}{4}$ cup grated Parmesan cheese
$1\frac{1}{2}$ cups milk
3 slices American-type commercial bread, cut in cubes, then soaked
    in the milk (above)
Salt and pepper
Ground nutmeg
Vegetable oil (not olive oil)
Bouillon powder

Preheat the oven to 300°F.
Wash and core the peppers and tomatoes, leaving the bottoms unpierced. Cut the eggplants and the zucchini in half; remove the pulp from each piece with a teaspoon. Set aside.
To make the stuffing, combine the ground meat, parsley, garlic, eggs, Parmesan, milk-soaked bread cubes, salt and pepper, and a pinch of nutmeg. Mix well.
Stuff the vegetables loosely with the meat mixture. Drizzle them with oil and dust lightly with bouillon powder.

Bake for 1½ to 2 hours, turning regularly. The vegetables are done when the shells are soft but not mushy. Halve or quarter the vegetables, then arrange them attractively on a large platter.

When I prepared this recipe for the first time, I discussed with Stefano, the butcher, what I was making and the need for him to grind the meats together. A woman waiting at the door shot up to the counter and said, "Oh yes, this is one of my own recipes! You must grind the meat together twice and then be sure that you don't pack the vegetables too firmly."

That afternoon this same woman was bicycling south on Via Roma in front of the villa and pulled to a stop when she saw me standing on the curb to cross the street.

"*Ah, signora,*" she said. "You will make delicious vegetables if you just follow my advice. I am known throughout the town as an excellent cook!" And she sped off.

My favorite of all Venetan meats is veal served with a tuna sauce. It may sound difficult, but it's not. The recipe, however, has one challenge: the veal must be sliced very, very thin so that it absorbs the tuna flavor; this requires slicing it when it is cold, preferably using a commercial meat slicer, which most of my Italian friends count among their kitchen appliances.

The butcher at the Battistons' *supermercato* provides me with a lean four-pound veal roast, more than enough for our party for twelve tomorrow. He's tied it securely, and I've bought a special oblong cooking pot that the roast barely fits into so that it won't swim in liquid. Now I'm ready to try Gabriella's recipe.

GABRIELLA'S VITELLO TONNATO

1 carrot
1 celery stalk
1 onion
1 vegetable bouillon cube
1 lean veal roast (3 to 4 pounds)
10 anchovy fillets
⅓ cup fresh lemon juice
⅓ cup small capers
2 6-ounce cans tuna (preferably Italian) in oil
1½ cups olive oil
2 cups Hellmann's mayonnaise

Bring to a boil in a large, heavy pot about 1½ quarts of water with the carrot, celery stalk, onion, and boullion cube. Add the roast, taking care that the water comes up to the top of the roast (if not, add boiling water). Bring back to a boil and simmer gently for several hours, until the veal is tender to the prick of a knife. (I simmered my 4-pound roast for 2½ hours.)

Take the pot off the heat and let cool for at least four hours before removing the roast from the liquid. Then chill the roast for several hours or overnight, for easier slicing.

The tuna sauce is quick and easy. Blend well in the food processor: the anchovy fillets, lemon juice, capers, tuna fish, and olive oil. When the mixture is smooth, add the mayonnaise (Gabriella makes her own mayonnaise, but I carry Hellmann's from Atlanta) and blend in well.

Slice the veal as thin as possible without shredding the meat. (I use my bread-slicing knife.) Spread some tuna sauce on the bottom of a long, deep dish or platter, then arrange slices of veal on top; repeat until the veal and sauce are all layered, ending with a sauce layer. Cover tightly with plastic wrap (after placing toothpicks at even intervals across the meat in order to keep the plastic away from the surface) and refrigerate at least overnight.

Serve within the next week.

I love this dish, so I always hope there are leftovers from a party!

Carl's favorite vegetables are those I roast in the oven, following a recipe given me years ago by an Italian-American friend of our daughter Ashley. *Molto semplice!*

CHRISTINA'S ROAST VEGETABLES

3 potatoes
3 zucchini
2 large sweet peppers, red or yellow
3 onions
1 fennel bulb
⅓ cup extra-virgin olive oil
Salt and pepper

Preheat the oven to 400°F. Wash and peel the potatoes and cut them crosswise into ½-inch slices. Scrub the zucchini and slice them lengthwise in quarters, then halve these. Cut the peppers into 1-inch strips, then halve the strips. Quarter the onions. Remove the top and base from the fennel bulb, then cut the bulb vertically to make slices about $\frac{1}{2}$ inch thick. Place all the vegetables on a towel for five to ten minutes to remove excess water.

Place the vegetables in a large bowl and dribble with the olive oil, mixing thoroughly to coat. Spread the vegetables evenly on a single large, shallow baking pan or two smaller ones; don't let your pieces overlap. Season with salt and pepper.

Pop the pan into the oven and bake for 25 to 30 minutes, turning every 8 to 10 minutes. If the vegetables brown too quickly, turn down the heat.

Supper at Wilma and Paolo's apartment is, as always, a feast for the eyes as well as for the stomach, as the pastor's wife said to Anne in one of my favorite passages from *Anne of Green Gables*. White plates on a pale blue cloth. Yellow chrysanthemums on pale blue paper napkins. Medium-blue glasses to hold our Gavi wine. The first course is so simple the recipe might seem hardly worth jotting down. But several times it has saved me when we have unexpected guests on a Wednesday afternoon and all the stores including the Battistons' are *chiusi*—closed.

WILMA'S SIMPLE TOMATO SAUCE

1 yellow onion, chopped
Olive oil
4 or 5 fresh tomatoes (or 1 can good plum tomatoes), chopped
Salt and pepper
Pasta
Smoked cheese, such as ricotta *affumicata*

Sauté the chopped onion in olive oil until soft. Add the chopped fresh tomatoes and simmer for 20 minutes. (If using canned tomatoes, drain them and chop them, then simmer for 10 minutes.) Blend lightly in a food processor. Season with salt and pepper to taste.

Serve on a bed of interesting pasta such as *orecchiette* (little ears) or *farfalle* (butterflies) cooked al dente. Top with the grated smoked cheese.

Last Sunday Francesca introduced me to her fried zucchini blossoms.

FRANCESCA'S DELICATE FRY

8 fresh zucchini blossoms
24 fresh sage leaves
1 egg
$\frac{1}{4}$ cup beer (preferably flat)
$\frac{1}{4}$ cup flour
$\frac{1}{2}$ teaspoon salt
Peanut oil

Rinse the zucchini blossoms. Cut each blossom along one side and spread it out flat on a paper towel to dry. Rinse the sage leaves and dry them on paper towels.

Beat the egg with $\frac{1}{4}$ cup water, the beer, the flour, and the salt.

Heat oil over medium-high heat. Dip the zucchini blossoms and sage leaves in the batter, then fry in hot—not smoking—peanut oil (about $\frac{1}{2}$ inch deep) for two to three minutes, turning once. Dry on paper towels and serve as an antipasto, with crackers and a soft cheese such as Robiolo.

As I draw these favorite recipes from several years of notes, it seems that I am eating at Francesca's or Wilma's every evening. Although I try to reciprocate with equal taste and fantasy, my efforts seldom reach their standards. But I keep trying and, right now, *tocca a me.* It's my turn.

Appendix 2

A Sixty-Second Guide to Venice

All of Venice is a museum! You only need to wander the streets, without going in anywhere, to experience some of the world's great Gothic and Renaissance treasures. And if you choose to step into some church that you are passing—almost any church—you'll stumble upon some painting or sculpture by a famous Renaissance artist. In other words, you don't really need a guidebook to tell you where to go.

Buy a guidebook anyway! (It will tell you where you are when you get there.) And, of course, a street map. (The ones in the guidebooks are helpful, but frequently not detailed enough.) Here are our favorites:

- Sheila Hale, *The American Express Pocket Travel Guide: Venice.*
- Hugh Honour, *The Companion Guide to Venice.*

SOME KEY SIGHTS

1. *Piazza di San Marco.* There's a good reason why St. Mark's Plaza is the most touristy, crowded place in Venice: It's filled with incredible monuments!

Basilica di San Marco. Is it "a treasure heap . . . hollowed beneath five great vaulted porches" (Ruskin) or "like a vast and warty bug taking a meditative walk" (Twain)? Be sure to go inside. Don't miss the Pala d'Oro-golden altar screen—and the museum up the stairs near the front entrance. Small admissions for each.

Doge's Palace. An architectural masterpiece steeped in the history of Venice, which was an independent and powerful empire for more than a thousand years, ending with the surrender to Napoléon in 1797. Everything is here: council rooms, art treasures, dungeons. Allocate an hour minimum.

Campanile (Bell Tower) and the Loggetta at its base. Wonderful view of Venice from the top of the Campanile, if you have the time.

View (across the basin of the Grand Canal). That's Palladio's spectacular church of San Giorgio Maggiore sitting on the island across the way.

Everything else in sight.

2. *Rialto Bridge.* Hustling, bustling shops, souvenirs, view of the Grand Canal in two directions. Prices here are generally better than at Piazza di San Marco.

3. *Grand Canal,* via vaporetto or gondola. The No. 1 vaporetto (boat bus) gives a slow and majestic (sometimes crowded and hot) ride along the whole length of the Grand Canal, allowing you to view all the palaces from the water, which is their principal facade. (Many vaporetti go two ways; be sure you get the one going in the direction you want!) Or for an infinitely more romantic (and pricey) view of the Grand Canal and other, smaller canals, spring for an hour (i.e., 45–50 minutes in gondolier time) on a gondola one evening near sunset.

4. *Accademia.* Venice's major museum for paintings. The number of visitors allowed inside at one time is restricted; this policy can result in a long waiting line outside during busy times of day.

5. *Church of San Zaccaria.* A somewhat arbitrary selection from the many incredible churches. The facade shows Gothic styling on the ground level (architect: Gambello) shifting to Renaissance motifs on the floors above (architect: Codussi). Inside, look (left aisle) for Giovanni Bellini's masterwork, *Sacred Conversation.* Don't miss the sacristy and crypt (small admission fee).

6. *Church of the Frari* and *School of San Rocco* (beside each other). The Frari is filled with treasures, including Titian's famous *Assumption of the Virgin* over the central altar. San Rocco's walls are covered with all the Tintoretto paintings you could possibly want to see, plus two or three.

Acknowledgments

The story of our years in Piombino Dese should make clear the support and encouragement we have received from all directions. Nonetheless, we feel a need to acknowledge specially a few individuals for the friendship and tireless assistance they have bestowed on us personally, and the protection and interest they have extended to Villa Cornaro.

Giacomo and Silvana Miolo and their sons, Leonardo and Riccardo, together with Ilario and Giovannina Mariotto, have been the linchpins of our Italian experience, loving and defending Villa Cornaro as fiercely as we do ourselves.

We are grateful to Monsignor Aldo Roma and to Mayor Luciano Cagnin and his predecessors for responding to every call that we have made for their advice and assistance. We have benefited as well from the care and protection that the office of the Superintendent of Fine Arts in Venice extends to Villa Cornaro and all the other great treasures the Veneto shares with the world.

Others who have been critical to our experience include Richard and Julia Rush for entrusting Villa Cornaro to our care, Douglas Lewis for his extraordinary pioneering research that opened our eyes to the fascinating history of our villa and the Cornaro family, and Lola Butler for her tenacity and good humor in teaching us Italian.

Our children love Villa Cornaro as much as we do, and each assisted in bringing this book about. Ashley inspired our efforts with her own writing career and offered valuable comments on an early draft, Carl assisted us in assembling photos, and Jim consistently encouraged us.

Ogden Robertson, Blaine Wiley, and Jean-François Jaussaud have taken beautiful photographs of the villa and generously allowed us to use them here. The enthusiasm and assistance of our editor, Ann Close, and our literary agent, Kitty Benedict, deserve special mention, as does the foresight of Lydia Somerville in bringing us together. Branko Mitrovic graciously reviewed several technical sections of the text for us. We thank them all.

Sally and Carl Gable
May 2005

Photographic Credits

Grateful acknowledgment is made to the following for use of illustrations appearing on the pages indicated:

Jean-François Jaussaud, pages 11, 133, 228
Wiley-Robertson Photography, pages ii–iii, 77, 78, 129, 213, 226
Local Piombino Dese collections, pages 97, 98

All other illustrations are from the authors' collection.

A TUSCAN CHILDHOOD

by Kinta Beevor

In 1916, when Kinta Beevor was five, her father, the painter Aubrey Waterfield, purchased the sixteenth-century Fortezza della Brunella in the Tuscan village of Aulla. There he and his writer wife lived at the heart of a vibrant artistic community that included Aldous Huxley, Bernard Berenson, and D. H. Lawrence, while Kinta and her brother explored the glorious countryside and came to love the tough, resourceful Italians. With the coming of World War II the family had to leave Aulla; years later, though, Kinta would return to witness the courage and skill of the Tuscan people as they rebuilt their shattered world.

Travel/Memoir/0-375-70426-4

AN ITALIAN AFFAIR

by Laura Fraser

When Laura Fraser's husband leaves her, she takes off for Italy, hoping to leave some of her sadness behind. There she meets M., a professor from Paris with an oversized love of life. What they both assume will be a vacation tryst turns into a passionate, transatlantic love affair, as they rendezvous in London, Marrakesh, Milan, the Aeolian Islands, and San Francisco. And with each experience, Laura brings home not only a lasting sense of pleasure, but a more fully recovered sense of her emotional and sexual self.

Memoir/Travel/0-375-72485-0

ON PERSEPHONE'S ISLAND

A Sicilian Journal

by Mary Taylor Simeti

When Mary Taylor Simeti first came to Sicily, she intended to make a short visit. Instead, she stayed for twenty years. She chronicles a year in the place she calls Persephone's Island, after the goddess who once made Sicily her home. Simeti navigates through Sicily's history of Greek, Arab, Norman, and Spanish conquests. She savors the fruits of its harvests. *On Persephone's Island* is an absorbing account of a woman's love affair with a place that beckons with sounds, tastes, colors, and myth.

Travel/Memoir/0-679-76414-3

A HISTORY OF VENICE
by John Julius Norwich

A History of Venice traces the rise of the empire of this city from its fifth-century beginnings all the way through 1797, when Napoleon put an end to the thousand-year-old Republic. At once the most comprehensive and the most engaging history of Venice available in English, this book will be treasured by all those who share the author's fascination with "the most beautiful and magical of cities."

History/0-679-72197-5

A VENETIAN AFFAIR
A True Tale of Forbidden Love in the Eighteenth Century
by Andrea di Robilant

In the waning days of Venice's glory in the mid-1700s, Andrea Memmo was scion to one of the city's oldest patrician families. At the age of twenty-four he fell passionately in love with sixteen-year-old Giustiniana Wynne, the beautiful, illegitimate daughter of a Venetian mother and British father. Because of their dramatically different positions in society, they could not marry. And Giustiniana's mother, afraid that an affair would ruin her daughter's chances to form a more suitable union, forbade them to see each other. Her prohibition only fueled their desire and so began their torrid, secret, seven-year affair.

Biography/0-375-72617-9

SPREZZATURA
Fifty Ways Italian Genius Shaped the World
by Peter D'Epiro and Mary Desmond Pinkowish

No one has demonstrated *sprezzatura*, or the art of effortless mastery, quite like the Italians. From the rise of the Roman calendar and the birth of the first university to the development of modern political science by Niccolò Machiavelli and the creation of the modern orchestra by Claudio Monteverdi, *Sprezzatura* chronicles fifty great Italian cultural achievements in a series of witty, erudite, and information-packed essays.

History/0-385-72019-X

ITALY IN MIND

An Anthology

Edited and with an Introduction by Alice Leccese Powers

Lord Byron came to contemplate ruins and fell "damnably in love" with a young married countess. Barbara Grizzuti Harrison marveled at Sicilian confections. Henry James's Isabel Archer was fatally seduced by the antiquities of Florence, while Mary McCarthy reveled in Venice's dignity and wit. These are just a few of the forty-one writers who celebrate, puzzle over, occasionally bemoan, and always shrewdly observe Italy in this vital and lusciously atmospheric volume.

Travel/Literature/0-679-77023-2

THE ART OF TRAVEL

by Alain de Botton

Any Baedeker will tell us where we ought to travel, but only Alain de Botton will tell us how and why. With intelligence and insouciant charm, de Botton considers the pleasures of anticipation, the allure of the exotic, and the value of noticing everything from a seascape in Barbados to the takeoffs at Heathrow. Even as de Botton takes the reader along on his own peregrinations, he also cites such distinguished fellow-travelers as Baudelaire, Wordsworth, van Gogh, the biologist Alexander von Humboldt, and the eighteenth-century eccentric Xavier de Maistre, who catalogued the wonders of his bedroom.

Travel/Essays/0-375-72534-2

VINTAGE AND ANCHOR BOOKS
Available at your local bookstore, or call toll-free to order:
1-800-793-2665 (credit cards only).